1981

CHILD ABUSE

CHILD ABUSE
An Agenda for Action

Edited by

George Gerbner
UNIVERSITY OF PENNSYLVANIA

Catherine J. Ross
YALE UNIVERSITY

and

Edward Zigler
YALE UNIVERSITY

New York   Oxford
OXFORD UNIVERSITY PRESS
1980

Library of Congress Cataloging in Publication Data
Main entry under title: Child abuse
    "Developed from a national conference, 'Child
abuse: cultural roots and policy options,' held in Philadelphia on November 20–21, 1978."
    Bibliography: p.   Includes index.
    1. Child abuse—United States—Addresses, essays,
lectures.   2. Child welfare—United States—Addresses,
essays, lectures.   I.   Gerbner, George   II.   Ross,
Catherine J., 1949–   III.   Zigler, Edward Frank,
1930–
HV741.C465   362.7'1   79–23617
ISBN 0–19–502720–5
ISBN 0–19–502721–3 pbk.

Printed in the United States of America

This book is dedicated to
John Brademas and Walter Mondale,
who have done so much for our nation's children,
in recognition of their special role
in the effort to combat child abuse.

Preface

Each year mounting reports of suspected child abuse reach protective service workers in the United States; the panorama of a prison corridor interrupts evening television viewing as the announcer explains that almost all criminals suffered abuse as children; and the term "child abuse" calls forth for the average American the image of a battered and bruised child who fell victim to inexplicable psychopathic rage. Myth and the mystique that child abuse stems from a disordered personality have dominated the field of child abuse in the United States which, alone among Western nations, has separated child abuse from the range of social problems facing children and families.

The collaboration between an expert in communications, an historian, and a psychologist that resulted in this volume reflects our conviction that studies of child abuse and policies for curbing it have been isolated from the mainstream of scholarship and social policy. We asked authorities from a variety of fields related to child abuse to apply their special knowledge to this social problem in order to examine the causes of abuse, define it more usefully, and reevaluate what the United States should be doing to prevent abuse. The editors shared in developing the idea for the book. George Gerbner bore responsibility for the section on the media. Catherine J. Ross and Edward Zigler shared responsibility for the rest of the volume.

This collection of original essays opens with an overview in which Edward Zigler assesses the current state of knowledge about child abuse. He examines what child abuse is, its incidence, and what our society might do about it.

Turning to "The Psychological Context" of abuse, leading experts on maternal attachment and theories of aggression explore how those two phenomena affect abusive responses to children. Four authors then place abuse in its "Social Context." An historian explores how attitudes toward children, child abuse, and intervention in families have evolved over the centuries. A sociologist reports on what the results of the first national survey of domestic violence reveal about the incidence of child abuse in different kinds of families. An expert on primary prevention challenges responses after the fact, and examines social factors that contribute to abuse. And authorities on the cross-cultural study of social welfare systems compare the approach of the United States to child abuse with that of other Western industrialized nations.

Although this collection does not focus directly on the problems clinical workers face in confronting abuse, it does explore both the legal context in which decisions about children who may have suffered abuse are made, and ways in which social institutions sanction abuse of children. In the section on the "Legal Context" of abuse, a psychiatrist, a lawyer, and a policy analyst examine when the state should intervene on behalf of children, what the family's rights are when the state does intervene, and what is likely to happen to children once the state becomes involved. Scholars then consider two specific examples of "Socially Sanctioned Abuse" of children: corporal punishment in the schools, and institutionalization as exemplified by the care of the mentally retarded.

Because the communications industry contributes to the public image of abuse, we asked some leaders of that industry to place child abuse in its "Cultural Context" by commenting on the constraints that apply to their coverage of provocative topics such as child abuse. Their responses are placed in perspective by statistical studies of how television and magazines portray children and child abuse.

The volume closes by placing child abuse in the broader context of developing a social policy in the United States. A psychologist with a background in government service proposes a model for exchange between scholars and those who design and carry out policies. Two health professionals currently in government integrate abuse with national health policies. Finally, two of the editors draw on the essays that make up this collection to propose a realistic "Agenda for Action." That agenda assigns responsibility to private and public organizations and to every reader who cares about America's children.

New Haven   George Gerbner
July 1979   Catherine J. Ross
                                                                     Edward Zigler

Acknowledgments

This book developed from a national conference, "Child Abuse: Cultural Roots and Policy Options," held in Philadelphia on November 20–21, 1978. Nearly 400 invited representatives of state and national government, the service delivery and research communities, and the communications professions attended that meeting. Financial support for the conference was provided by the Annenberg School of Communications at the University of Pennsylvania, and by the Bush Foundation through the Bush Center in Child Development and Social Policy at Yale University. We are grateful to the staff of the Bush Foundation for the personal interest they took in this project, and to the Foundation for its support during the preparation of this volume. Special thanks are extended to Ambassador and Mrs. Walter H. Annenberg, who have demonstrated deep concern over the problem of abused children, for their personal interest and encouragement.

The original conference staff helped in many ways. We are grateful to members of the Annenberg School staff, including Elvira Lankford, who managed conference arrangements, Nancy Signorielli, who coordinated research, and Mary McNamee, who served as conference secretary, for the expertise that contributed to a successful meeting. That success, in turn, gave our authors an enthusiasm for continuing the work. Jane Wilson, also of the Annenberg School, handled public relations for the conference and edited Section Five of this volume jointly with George Gerbner.

Karen Nelson at Yale, as assistant to the program director, contributed to our work from the early planning stages through the completion of this manuscript. Her attention to detail, her intelligence, and her energy are much appreciated.

Phyllis Lafarge brought a wide knowledge of children's issues to the careful copyediting she performed on the entire manuscript. Jonathan Rieder offered intelligent criticism on numerous chapters. Many members of the Bush Center staff contributed to the completion of this volume. Karen Anderson's assistance proved invaluable. Deborah Reumann, who helped with the conference planning and follow-up, was joined by Audrey Meusel and Margot Sheehan in preparing early drafts and final manuscript. Greg Bialecki, Cynthia Klein, and Kitty Simons offered many kinds of assistance. Kirby A. Heller helped review portions of the manuscript. Helena Mullett and Teri Bennett shouldered additional administrative responsibilities in the course of this project.

We are also grateful to Marcus Boggs, Jr., of Oxford University Press, for his enthusiasm during the early stages in the preparation of this book. Above all, we thank the many authors who gave generously of their time and knowledge to make this collection possible.

Contents

CONTENTS

I

AN OVERVIEW

1

Controlling Child Abuse: Do We Have the Knowledge and/or the Will?

Edward Zigler

Child abuse has captured the attention of an ever increasing number of scholars, professionals, government officials, and laymen across the United States. Using the knowledge, experience, and expertise of each of those diverse interest groups in the design of programs and policies to reduce the incidence of child abuse will enhance their effectiveness immeasurably. Scholars can play a crucial role in that effort in a number of ways. They can both consolidate and evaluate past research about when and why parents abuse their children and highlight the kinds of programs that research has already shown are effective in curbing the problem.

People have great difficulty approaching child abuse objectively and analytically. The phenomenon almost always arouses intense emotions and moral outrage, and the magnitude of people's reactions to it reveals its associations with a number of poorly understood prejudices and anxieties. There are three main reasons why child abuse elicits revulsion. First, the knowledge that parents can and do act violently toward their children probably touches on everyone's deep-seated dependency needs. People are very threatened by the thought of a small, helpless child not receiving proper care and concern. Second, the physical battering of children seems monstrously perverse to adults who cherish and receive great satisfaction from loving relationships with their children. Some laymen and professionals have resurrected an outmoded and misguided approach to human behavior that leads them to conclude that abusive behavior runs contrary to the

I wish to thank Karen Nelson for her valuable assistance in researching and revising this paper.

3

basic instincts of the human species. The notion that child abusers lack maternal instinct has reinforced the anger and revulsion associated with abuse.

Child abuse, like many other social problems affecting children, cannot be eliminated overnight. Researchers must pinpoint the underlying roots of the problem and then the federal government must commit itself both politically and financially to implementing policies that will address the conditions that perpetuate abuse. Given the limited quantity and quality of current child abuse research and the historical reluctance of the United States government to assign high priority to children's issues, the title of this article reflects a pessimistic outlook concerning this nation's capacity or willingness to eliminate the problem. Despite the pessimism of the title, research has uncovered information that offers some promising directions for policymakers to pursue in their efforts to curb the incidence of child abuse in America.

Is There a Child Abuse Problem?

The apparent surge in public concern for the victims of abuse is not unanimous, and controversy still surrounds the question of whether the problem deserves so much attention (Bourne & Newberger, 1979; Divoky, 1976). Need this country devote so much attention, money, and energy to eradicating abuse or has the issue become a false rallying point for child advocates? Many people react to child abuse with the psychological mechanism of denial and do not believe that parents could ever be violent with children. Others believe that it occurs too rarely to be considered a national problem. The popular reluctance to acknowledge the problem of abuse was dramatized by the fact that radiologists rather than social service workers or private citizens first drew attention to abuse in the early 1960s. Only sensationalized exposés and photographs of bruised and battered children finally convinced the public that parents can and do intentionally injure their children.

The public's general tendency to compare issues on the basis of absolute numbers further made the public all the more reluctant to acknowledge the pervasiveness of child abuse and the need for action. For example, Furrow, Gruendel, and Zigler estimated that 28 million accidental injuries occurred annually among children 16 years old or younger. They found that accidents constitute the single major cause of death among children in that age range (Furrow et al., 1979). Using even a generous estimate of the annual incidence of child abuse, or four million (Gil, 1970, p. 59), as the basis for comparison, childhood accidents harm more children than do child abusers. Children suffer from a variety of health problems (including childhood diseases and congenital defects) and using absolute numbers, many of those probably occur more frequently than does child abuse. Using the comparative approach to designate emphasis to social problems, however, is dangerous. Taken to its extreme, that approach could lead child advocates, many of whom are already working in a variety of ways to improve children's status, to abandon their activities until they had all agreed which social problem affecting children was *most* serious. The issue is not whether child abuse is a problem more serious than others but whether its magnitude is extensive enough to merit public concern and intervention.

Even leading researchers in the area of child abuse question whether the issue is statistically a major social problem. For instance, David Gil wrote that "the 'battered child syndrome' is a relatively infrequent occurrence. Even if allowance is made for the gross under-reporting of fatalities, physical abuse cannot be considered a major killer and maimer of children" (1969, p. 862). Gil made that assertion despite his own suggestion that between 2.5 million and 4 million American adults polled in a single year each had personal knowledge of a separate case of child abuse (1970, p. 59). Gil admits that his statistics are unreliable and that they seem to overestimate the number of child abuse cases that occur. Nevertheless, his assertion that 79 percent of the adult population of the United States had knowledge of a case of abuse indicates that violent acts between parents and children that range from spanking to severe beating are not uncommon. Public concern about intra-family violence has intensified over the last decade and people's perceptions of the pervasiveness of child abuse vary according to the definition of abuse that they use. Questions that remain unanswered include whether spanking is as harmful to a child as beating; what kind of parent-child violence this society should commit itself to eliminating; and how child abuse should be defined.

THE DEFINITIONAL DILEMMA

No standardized definition of child abuse has yet been developed or accepted by all of the professionals and social service personnel who work in the field (Bourne & Newberger, 1979; Lauderdale, Anderson, & Cramer, 1978; National Center on Child Abuse and Neglect, 1978a; Parke & Collmer, 1975). That lack of consensus about a definition reveals the primitive theoretical level of child abuse research. Without a standardized definition, research findings and data are misleading because identical labels are used to describe different phenomena. As a result, policymakers find themselves faced with the impossible task of solving a problem whose magnitude, roots, and solutions remain undefined. The lack of a practical definition is particularly serious in the child abuse field because the definition actually determines which families are eligible for services. Employing a narrow and precise definition of abuse, for instance, means that a limited number of parents and children will qualify for aid. The commonly accepted definitions of abuse have changed over the past two decades. A brief look at how the definition of abuse has evolved offers a valuable perspective in developing a standardized definition of abuse.

Child abuse is not a phenomenon unique to twentieth century America, although radiologists essentially "re-discovered" it in the early 1960s when they coined the term "the battered child syndrome" to explain repeated fractures revealed on children's X rays (Kempe, Silverman, Steele, Droegemueller, & Silver, 1962). The medical model of abuse that grew out of that phrase emphasized the pathology of abusers and implied that by "curing" parents of their abusive tendencies, the problem would disappear. For the first few years after the "re-discovery" of abuse, the media focused on the most extreme cases of battery in which children were beaten, burned, and tortured by their caretakers. The sensationalism of those reports drew public attention to the problem. The emphasis on cases of extreme physical abuse, however, limited the usefulness of that perspective because it excluded less extreme cases of assault and neglect.

Recognition of the limitations of the narrow "disease model" definition of abuse forced scholars and policymakers to reconceptualize abuse and to consider a variety of abusive and neglectful parental behaviors that could hinder a child's optimal development. The inclusion of neglect as a form of violence toward children marked a critical conceptual change in the evolution of a definition of abuse. The broader definition of abuse forced people to recognize the roots of the problem in the structure of the society and the pervasiveness of socially sanctioned forms of abuse. Corporal punishment in schools and children's institutions is an isolated example of the way that children are subjected to violent disciplinary treatment outside of their homes. The inclusion of neglect in the definition dramatized the wide range of behaviors potentially harmful to children. The two-category system that discriminated between parents who abused their children and those who did not was inadequate because it failed to describe realistically the relationship between parents and children. The broader definition implied that the label "abuser" did not apply solely to parents who maim or kill their children. Broadly defined, the labels "abusive" and "neglectful" are applicable to all parents who use any form of physical discipline as well as to a host of socially sanctioned practices (like behavior modification techniques) that often hinder a child's development.

The definitional dilemma remains unresolved. In developing a new definition of abuse, workers need to consider blending ideas from both the broad and the narrow perspectives of abuse. A definition must be broad enough to take into account forms of abuse less obvious than cigarette burns and torture but not so broad as to make it impossible to distinguish abusive behavior from "normal" adult behavior. The problems inherent in defining the limits of all kinds of "normal" social behavior plague researchers in a variety of disciplines. Thus, for instance, in defining suicide, A. Haim observed how "uncertain the delimitation of the suicide field can be." He concluded that:

> The choice of definition of suicide is very difficult and demands the utmost care. . . . The definition that we finally adopt must be sufficiently flexible, and must go beyond the bounds of excessive objectivity . . . but it must not include innumerable modes of human behavior that would dilute the concept. (1974, p. 24)

A number of interrelated issues need to be resolved in order to develop a sound and useful definition of child abuse. Scholars have proposed a variety of definitions of abuse and each definition reflects a different conceptualization of the problem. Definitions range in scope from an emphasis on serious physical abuse (Kempe et al., 1962) to a somewhat broader emphasis on maltreatment (Fontana, 1970) to the broad focus on the failure of the environment to meet a child's developmental needs (Alvy, 1975). The American Bar Association recently proposed a legal definition of abuse to limit court intervention into families to those cases where a child has suffered serious nonaccidental physical injury (IJA/ABA, 1977). The scope of the solutions proposed to eliminate abuse will depend, in part, on how broadly the limits of abusive behavior are defined. A narrow definition implies a commitment to eliminate severe cases of physical abuse while a broad definition implies a commitment to improve the lives of all children in the society. The two extremes differ in that one places an emphasis on individual solutions to abuse while the other places an emphasis on structural social solutions to the problem. The broad definition threatens the society because it infers that until social sanctions for violence toward children are eliminated, everyone is guilty of abuse.

One of the most perplexing issues in the definitional dilemma is determining the point on the punishment continuum at which discipline becomes abusive (Alvy, 1975; Hurt, 1975; Maurer, 1974). That question has posed sticky problems for federal and state policymakers who must define standards for intrusive intervention into families. As Gil points out:

> Excessive use of physical force against children is considered abusive and is usually rejected in American tradition, practice, and law. [However there are] no clearcut criteria . . . concerning the specific point beyond which the quantity and quality of physical force used against children is to be considered excessive. (1970, pp. 134–35)

Some scholars argue that the definition should be very explicit about the kinds of injury that constitute abuse in order to protect the privacy and integrity of the family unit (Uviller, this volume; Wald, 1975). Others, however, maintain that it must be general enough to focus public attention on the roots of abuse because individual cases are only symptomatic of a deeper problem. The definitional dilemma stems in part from the fact that some groups, including lawyers and government officials, use the definition to determine standards for intervention into families while other groups, including scholars and social service workers, use it to focus attention and funding on families in need of assistance.

The nature of the problem demands a highly differentiated and conceptually based classificatory system that allows people to distinguish between the severity of different acts of abuse. Eli Newberger and his colleagues, for instance, made an interesting effort to reconceptualize child abuse by including it in a broader classificatory system involving pediatric social illness (Newberger, Reed, Daniel, Hyde, & Kotelchuck, 1975). They recognized the limitations of old classificatory systems that fit child abuse into a simple two-class typology that discriminated between adults who abused their children and those who did not. Traditional classificatory systems often relied on over-simplified distinctions between abusers and non-abusers and placed too much emphasis on the actual behavior emitted by parents toward their children. While that emphasis has certain value for the formation of operational definitions, it is purchased at a high conceptual price. Classificatory systems rarely took into account adults' intentions and, as a result, they often ignored the less obvious ways that parental behavior hinders a child's development. As Piaget pointed out in his writings on moral development, children's moral perceptions change during their early development so that they are often more aware of the intentions rather than the consequences of their parents' behavior (Zigler & Child, 1973). Child abuse classificatory systems rarely reflect that shift in moral judgment so they are unable to account for the fact that children may suffer more serious long-term damage from repeated emotional rejection than they would from isolated instances of physical abuse.

In developing a new classificatory system to explain child abuse, the phenomenon might best be reconceptualized as a continuum of behaviors that includes all of the possible ways that parents can relate to their children (Burgess, 1978). The continuum would range from affectionate interactions on the one end to extreme abuse or murder on the other. All of the forms of occasional violence between parents and children would fall in the center of the continuum. Because the continuum model suggests that all parents are potential abusers and that abusive acts differ from nonabusive ones in degree rather than kind, it could have significant impact on this society's willingness and ability to eliminate abuse. The continuum approach to child abuse offers a valuable perspective because it implies that, depending on the particular familial and environmental circumstances, all parents are capable of abusing their children. Further, it suggests that child abusers cannot be dismissed as strange or psychopathic human beings; on the contrary, they are usually indistinguishable from parents who are never reported for abuse. That view of abuse is obviously threatening to most parents since child abuse is considered deviant behavior and, as research has shown, people usually try to distance themselves from those whom they perceive as deviant (Becker, 1963). Parents might feel threatened by the continuum approach, but the benefits of that perspective outweigh its potential costs.

First, the continuum approach forces parents to come to terms with their own potential abusiveness. While most parents would probably deny that they could ever intentionally injure their children, few would deny that on particularly frustrating days they toyed with the fantasy of how serene life would be without children. Some might even remember days when their temper snapped and they lashed out at their children in exasperation. Child abusers who seriously injure their children rarely intend to inflict such pain. In fact, many parents start out rather innocently using some mild form of punishment and end up, to their own horror, seriously injuring their child. By conceptualizing abusive behavior as part of a continuum of possible parental behaviors, people might be more empathetic toward abusers. Second, people tend to help individuals whom they feel share similar features to themselves and punish those whom they perceive as deviant or different from themselves. The continuum approach to abuse, by breaking down the distance between abusers and nonabusers, encourages people to support policies that prevent abuse or help abusers, since all parents are potential abusers and might one day benefit from such programs.

To date, this society has engaged in very few primary prevention efforts (defined as the prevention of abuse before it occurs) and the continuum definition of abuse might foster more widespread support for those policies (see Alvy, 1975, for discussion of primary vs. secondary prevention issue). This society's reluctance to invest in primary rather than secondary prevention of abuse is related to the fact that people are often more willing to treat a problem's symptoms than its causes. Current work in the child abuse area is no exception. In explaining "the major flaw that exists in current programs and current strategies of intervention," Gelles points out that

> they amount to "an ambulance service at the bottom of the cliff." Child abuse programs now are after-the-fact treatment of parents and children. What needs to be done is to "fix the road on the cliff that causes the accidents." Strategies should be developed that can deal with the problem before the child is beaten or killed. (1973, p. 620)

One explanation for the broader support for secondary rather than primary prevention programs is that it is very difficult to gauge the effectiveness of secondary prevention measures. For instance, predicting the number of parents who did not become abusive because they completed a special parenting education class is much more difficult than counting the number of abusive families served by a crisis day care center. The emphasis on secondary prevention is slowly changing. The 1978 research and funding priorities for the National Center on Child Abuse and Neglect (National Center, 1978) did not include any funding for primary prevention programs while the 1979–1980 priorities (U.S. Department of Health, Education and Welfare, 1979) subsidized grants for twelve state and community primary prevention demonstrations. Scholars could further bolster support for primary prevention efforts by emphasizing the continuumlike nature of child abuse.

A comprehensive definition of abuse that places it within a continuum of possible behaviors is valuable because it underlines the potential for abuse among all parents and dramatizes the pervasiveness of social support for violence between parents and children. However, such a broad definition may not be a useful practical definition for guiding intervention procedures. For the purposes of devising studies on the characteristics of abusive parents or abused children and developing guidelines for state intervention into families, a broad definition is too all-encompassing to be of any practical use. The definition of child abuse that is often used in those specific instances, and the one that will be used throughout this paper, unless otherwise specified, is "non-accidental physical injury (or injuries) that are the result of acts (or omissions) on the part of parents or guardians that violate the community standards concerning the treatment of children" (Parke & Collmer, 1975, p. 513). The narrow definition, therefore, can be used to pinpoint and isolate individual cases of abuse while the broad definition can provide a contextual framework within which long-range strategies for eliminating abuse can be developed.

The Incidence of Child Abuse

A number of factors make it very difficult to assess the incidence of abuse accurately. The lack of a standardized definition of abuse, as just discussed, has a dramatic impact on incidence data because statistics reflect phenomena ranging from the number of deaths from abuse to the number of children spanked each year. Further, incidence rates are often calculated based on the number of cases reported to the public authorities. Many cases of child abuse are never reported, so those statistics are, at best, a very rough index of the actual incidence of abuse. Studies have not yet determined the precise relationship between the number of actual and reported cases of child abuse in a community so researchers are relying more and more on interviews to calculate its incidence. Social class differences also compound statistical accuracy because studies have shown that reporting rates differ dramatically between classes. There are reasons to believe that private pediatricians are reluctant to report their patients to public authorities as abusers; that poor families may hide their knowledge of abusing families to protect them from the authorities; and that because poor families have more contact with social service agencies, they are more likely to be reported for abuse than wealthier families are. None of these hypotheses has been proven, but they all contribute to the unreliability of estimates of child abuse.

What then is the best, albeit imperfect, estimate of the incidence of child abuse in America? Gil conducted a national survey and estimated that between 2.5 and 4 million adults each knew of a separate case of child abuse (defined as deliberate injury of a child by its caretaker) in the preceding year (1970, p. 59). In a reanalysis of Gil's statistics, Light (1973) suggested that between 200,000 and 500,000 children are abused each year. In a household survey, Gelles (this volume) found that between 1,400,000 and 1,900,000 children were intentionally injured by their parents in the preceding year. It is hardly informative to state that the incidence of child abuse ranges from 200,000 to 4,000,000 cases annually. The estimate that the public hears most often is the one that was released by the National Center on Child Abuse and Neglect in 1975, which indicated that approximately one million cases of abuse are reported each year. Douglas Besharov, director of the National Center at the time the figure was released, maintained that the American Humane Association furnished the statistic, yet that organization reportedly claimed that it was "groundless" and "excessive" (Divoky, 1976, p. 18). Despite the figure's questionable reliability or accuracy, it has become the most commonly cited estimate of child abuse incidence to date.

The absence of reliable data has made it difficult for researchers to determine whether the incidence of child abuse has increased or decreased over the last century. Child abuse is not unique to twentieth century America. Throughout history, children have suffered from harsh physical punishment, the hardships of child labor, and strenuous living conditions. Incidence rates are sketchy and unreliable today, but they were nonexistent in America before state legislatures passed mandatory child abuse reporting laws in the mid-1960s. Estimating abuse rates for nineteenth and twentieth century America is virtually impossible. Comparisons are also difficult because the ambiguous definitions used today to determine incidence rates do not necessarily describe situations that were considered abusive in the past (see Ross, this volume). The number of child abuse cases reported to public authorities has increased over the last decade, which suggests that the problem is worsening. Many researchers, however, maintain that the actual rate of abuse is the same and that heightened public awareness has swelled reporting statistics (Bourne & Newberger, 1979; Kempe & Kempe, 1978).

Determining the overall magnitude of the problem may be impossible, but few people question the pervasiveness of intra-family violence in this society. By focusing time and energy comparing incidence trends, scholars debate an unresolvable issue. Quibbling over numerical niceties is nothing more than a prescription for inaction. Policymakers must make a firm resolution to devote a considerable amount of energy and money to the problem of child abuse because without that kind of commitment, the problem will never be solved. Moving away from a hesitation based on doubts regarding incidence trends, however, does not mean that workers should not continue to collect reliable data on the incidence of abuse. The National Center on Child Abuse and Neglect, for instance, ought to compile statistics on the total number of cases of abuse reported each year. In addition, researchers need to determine what, if any, relationship exists between reported and actual rates of abuse in different communities. Determining the magnitude and the demography of the problem can certainly help guide decisions about funding and service implementation priorities. A number of equally important avenues of research are also open for scholars to pursue that will enhance the effectiveness of programs aimed at curbing abuse.

Do We Have the Knowledge?

Theoretical and empirical research efforts in the area of child abuse, which still remain somewhat primitive and rudimentary, have improved both in quantity and quality over the last decade. The definitional dilemma posed, and still poses, a theoretical stumbling block that scholars must tackle in designing empirical studies. It is, obviously, difficult to study a problem that is undefined. Nevertheless, researchers have begun to explore new angles that may help isolate variables and factors that are linked to abuse. Research has moved beyond the point that characterized it only recently when, as Richard Gelles pointed out (1973), it abounded with tautologies that explained virtually nothing about abusive parents. John Spinetta and David Rigler, for instance, stated that "a general defect in character—from whatever source—is present in the abusing parent allowing aggressive impulses to be expressed too freely" (1972, pp. 300–301). Isolated adjectives describing abusive parents are, as Steele and Pollock pointed out, often uninformative because "they are so prevalent among people in general that they add little to specific understanding" (1974, p. 95). Such adjectives include "immature," "dependent," narcissistic," and "demanding." A particularly telling indicator of the improved quality of child abuse literature is that it is neither as circumscribed and fractionated nor as isolated from the mainstream of behavioral science research as it once was. Scholars have begun to cross-fertilize child abuse research with child rearing, attachment, and human aggression research. Such cross-fertilization enhances the sophistication of thinking in the child abuse field, broadening the knowledge and understanding of the roots of intra-family violence and subjecting it to the methodological rigor of procedures, approaches, and measures used in related areas.

By the same token, researchers in the more established fields of the behavioral sciences have begun to deal more explicitly with the problem of child abuse. Workers interested in socialization, who once gave little direct attention to child abuse, are beginning to apply their findings to that phenomenon. Even the more narrow literature on child rearing, once strangely silent on the phenomenon of abuse, has expanded and some of the basic principles uncovered by that work have been applied to explain abusive parent-child relationships.

It is difficult to pinpoint why child abuse research was isolated from the general socialization literature for so long. Perhaps that isolation reflects a distinction often made by psychologists between basic and applied research. Scholars working in the general area of socialization, who often view themselves as basic researchers, may feel that they will be sullied if they turn their attention to practical and applied problems like child abuse. On the other hand, researchers working directly in the area of child abuse, who consider it an urgent and pressing social problem, may feel that general socialization principles are too esoteric to be of much value. However, because child abuse is a phenomenon that is, at once, not only pressing and practical but a particular dynamic within the broader framework of human socialization, a cross-fertilization of basic and applied research can provide a broader knowledge base from which to tackle the problem.

Certain subareas of investigation in the behavioral and social science fields would have particular relevance to the study of child abuse. Light (1973) suggested that general child rearing studies might offer a valuable perspective from which to view abuse. A closely related area with value for work in child abuse is the field of attachment behavior and the nature of the parent-child bond. It would be almost circular to state that there is something unusual about the bond between a parent and child in those families where abuse occurs, yet few studies use the methodology of attachment literature to study that relationship in abusive families (see chap. 2, this volume). Konrad Lorenz, for instance, found that an inadequate parent-child attachment in early infancy is a major cause of aggression in general (Evans, 1975).

Scholars could use comparative psychology literature to examine instances in which infrahuman species' behaviors paralleled the behaviors found in abusive adults. Harry and Margaret Harlow, investigating whether abused monkeys grew into abusing parent monkeys, found that peer relations of monkeys had an ameliorative effect on the behavior of monkeys who experienced atypical child histories (1971). Their work suggests that similar studies investigating the relationship between abused children and their siblings or peers might be valuable. Comparative psychology literature offers a rich source of hypotheses for workers in the child abuse area, but scholars must use great caution in making definitive generalizations on the basis of inter-species studies.

Given the embryonic and limited state of knowledge that currently exists, it is not surprising that the literature is as replete with myths as it is with well-validated facts. Many of those myths have never been carefully researched, so their only claim to validity is that they are so frequently repeated. One such myth enjoying wide currency is that abused children are likely to develop into abusing parents. That correlation has become so widely accepted that it is now mentioned as fact in some introductory psychology textbooks (Zimbardo & Ruch, 1975). While there may be a modicum of truth to this myth, it is also true that abused children often do not develop into abusing parents. Researchers have not yet done careful investigations of the circumstances under which abused children do or do not become abusing parents, so any conclusions are highly speculative.

A number of dangers stem from the presence of so many myths in the field. Scholars often build studies on the basis of previous findings;

this can mean that undocumented or unvalidated myths distort the outcome of further research. In addition, a logical correlation exists between the knowledge base in an area of social policy and the ability of workers in that area to mount effective prevention and intervention programs. Government policy aimed explicitly at controlling child abuse is relatively new so policymakers do not have a long history of policy decisions to help inform current ones. In the absence of reliable research or past policy decisions, policymakers often rely on myths as guides for action. They base decisions about funding priorities and programs on "commonsense" ideas about the roots of abuse even though some of those "commonsense" ideas have no basis in fact. The presence of myths and the absence of extensive research have grave implications for the ability of policymakers to mount effective or far-reaching programs to eliminate abuse.

Workers in the child abuse area must handle the poor knowledge base in two complementary ways. Research to date offers some knowledge about the extent and causes of child abuse as well as realistic, though limited, ways of controlling it. Poor though the knowledge base may be, much of the information that already exists about effective intervention and prevention tactics has not yet been translated into social programs. Policymakers must put to use what information is available about the best ways to meet the needs of abusive or potentially abusive families. The knowledge base is still too limited to provide solutions, but it can point to policies that will help curb the incidence of abuse. Delaying all program and policy decisions until every last piece of scientific research is completed, or using the relatively poor quality of scholarship as an excuse for inaction, is absurd.

The importance of implementing policies to curb abuse despite the incomplete knowledge base is easier to understand than the importance of continuing research. The Child Abuse Prevention and Treatment Act of 1974 restricted research funding, and the National Center made further cuts in 1978–1979. These restrictions reflect the negative attitude toward behavioral science research currently in vogue in the Congress. When faced with a social problem as pressing as child abuse, it is often difficult for policymakers to remember that their ability to construct effective programs cannot out-distance the availability of valid information about successful approaches to the problem. It often seems more productive for policymakers to concentrate all funding on the establishment of services. At times, however, it is more productive for them to focus some of that funding on research. Social action efforts should not be halted entirely, but the child abuse area is desperately in need of hard facts about why abuse occurs, and how programs can be made more cost-effective. Given the fiscal austerity of the times and the public preference for funding practical rather than research projects, it is conceivable that research will continue to lose funding in the years to come. Because child abuse policy is in a relatively formative stage and is expanding rapidly, research is critical and should be given a high priority in funding. Again, the inadequate knowledge base as well as the society's failure to implement even those policies that research has shown are effective in controlling abuse are discouraging signs of this nation's ability to eliminate the problem of child abuse.

CHARACTERISTICS OF THE ABUSED CHILD

Though child abuse research is still relatively limited, some tentative information about the characteristics of abused children and adults is available. Increasingly, research aims to determine whether particular combinations of characteristics like a child's age, gender, birth order, temperament, physical development, and congenital features make it a likely candidate for abuse. Because those factors are highly interrelated, interpretation of findings remains somewhat speculative. Research has already *linked* certain characteristics to abuse, but the causality between the two is unclear and awaits further research.

Researchers have uncovered a number of physical and emotional characteristics of children that are associated with abuse. Premature and low-birth-weight infants are often the victims of abuse. The unusual circumstances surrounding the birth of a premature or low-weight infant may make the acceptance of the child into a family particularly difficult. Premature infants are separated from their mothers for a period of time immediately following birth, and research has indicated that the postpartum period is crucial in the formation and strengthening of the parent-child attachment bond (Mussen, Conger, & Kagan, 1970). The nature of premature birth produces considerable stress and anxiety in a family's life (Newberger & Hyde, 1975; Parke & Collmer, 1975; Stern, 1973), and this general stress phenomenon may mediate the relation between prematurity and child abuse. Further, the slow and difficult development of a premature baby places extra demands on a parent that may push a parent's patience beyond its limit. Studies have also shown that premature infants emit a high incidence of noxious behaviors such as crying and whining, which provoke parental abuse.

Scholars have documented a link between prematurity/low-birth-weight and abuse but that correlation is made after abuse has already occurred so it is difficult to isolate the particular aspects of prematurity and low weight that precipitate abuse. Some questions emerge from those general findings: Does the separation of the child from its mother immediately after birth inhibit attachment bonding and make it easier for her to abuse the child later on? Or, do the stressful circumstances surrounding a child's premature birth precipitate abuse? Do parents of premature infants have trouble interpreting their child's behavioral cues (like crying and whining) because they are unable to be with the child following its birth? Or are the behavior cues of premature infants inherently too confused and exaggerated for even the most sensitive parents to understand? Finally, are premature infants abused because of their unattractive behavior and looks? Or do the stressful circumstances surrounding the child's birth precipitate its abuse making it more unattractive and, consequently, a more likely target of abuse?

The link between mental retardation and abuse poses other problems of interpretation. Do parents physically assault a child because he is retarded, or does the child become mentally retarded as a result of the abuse he experiences? Again, a number of circumstances aggravate the early years of a family's adjustment to a mentally retarded infant so the mental retardation itself may not be responsible for later abuse. The birth of a mentally retarded infant is often disappointing to parents and that disappointment may be translated into frustration and anger as the child develops. Parents may not be aware of the special needs and developmental stages of retarded children so unrealistic expectations may lead to abuse. Further investigations might uncover ways to both ease parents' acceptance of a mentally retarded child and help them cope with the special needs of that child.

Examination of the quality of the bond between parents and children in abusive families holds promise. Until recently, researchers rarely used the methodology or principles of the attachment literature to investigate the nature of the parent-child bond in abusive families. Ainsworth has broken important ground in her investigations of the anomalous parent-child relationships that characterize abusive families. Parke and Collmer (1975) suggest a number of ways that the relationship between a parent and infant can be disturbed and strained (the child may present weak or confusing cues, he may have a genetic predisposition for physical contact, or he may react unexpectedly to parental attention and/or discipline). Further research might provide invaluable insight into how predisposing factors can distort the parent-child dyad to make the parent abusive.

Even completed research on the mother-infant bond is by no means in agreement on the characteristics of abusive relationships. Burgess and Conger (1978) studied the interaction patterns between parents and children in abusive families, neglectful families, and control families. They found that the abusive and control groups were remarkably similar. In another study, Ronald Rohner and Evelyn Rohner (1978) compared abusing and nonabusing families and found that remarkably few of the abused children aged 7 to 11 described their mothers as rejecting. That finding implies that factors outside of the relationship may disrupt otherwise warm and stable parent-child dyads to make them abusive. Age is another characteristic often associated with abuse. Gelles's finding (1973) that younger children suffer abuse more often than older children confirmed earlier ideas. Gil (1970) attributes this common finding to sampling bias so interpretation of that hypothesis awaits further research.

Another area of obvious relevance to the phenomenon of child abuse is the widely explored topic of human aggression. Child abuse is but one form of human aggression so the literature on aggression might enhance understanding of the roots of abuse. Some manifestations of child abuse seem consistent with the frustration-aggression formulation (Dollard, Doob, Miller, Mowrer, & Sears, 1939), which postulates that aggression is likely to occur following frustration. Expanding on that theory, Feshbach (this volume) suggests that adults often act less aggressively to accidental frustration than they do to intentional frustration.

Disinhibition theory (Bandura & Walters, 1963; Berkowitz, 1964) in the general field of aggression offers another promising area in which to explore the roots of abuse. Over the long course of socialization, individuals develop an inhibition against overt and naked violence toward each other, so research might explain what kinds of social stimuli cause this strongly entrenched inhibitory system to break down. As Feshbach points out (this volume), intra-species violence rarely goes beyond the display level so a biological basis for child abuse seems unlikely. Parental perception of a child's responsibility and intentionality in its behavior might be important antecedents to aggression. Parke and Collmer (1975) point out that pain feedback cycles usually inhibit adults from engaging in visibly violent behavior. Further research might illuminate how that pain feedback cycle breaks down in adults allowing them to abuse their children.

CHARACTERISTICS OF THE ABUSING PARENT

A considerable amount of work in the child abuse area has focused on the psychodynamic and sociocultural characteristics of abusing parents (Alvy, 1975; Bourne & Newberger, 1979; Garbarino, 1976; Newberger & Hyde, 1975; Parke & Collmer, 1975). This line of investigation traces back to Tardieu who, writing in France in the 1860s, described some of the behavioral characteristics of abusing parents and also identified sociocultural

18

conditions associated with child abuse (1868). As Hurt (1975) notes, much of what Tardieu reported is consistent with modern research findings. Isolating the psychological characteristics of abusive parents poses problems because it is almost impossible to separate the individual personality characteristics of parents from their sociocultural environment. Few researchers claim that any single characteristic of an adult will *cause* that adult to abuse a child. Some scholars imply that certain psychological characteristics of adults are warning signals of abuse. However, the bulk of current research suggests that the cumulative effect of different personality and environmental factors impact upon individuals in different and unpredictable ways. Increasingly, researchers have found that they must draw from a variety of models (psychological, sociocultural, and situational) to explain abuse.

Research during the early 1960s concentrated on pinpointing the individual characteristics of the abuser. Current investigations are moving away from the narrow perspective of individual pathology to consider the interplay between personality and environmental factors. The bulk of current National Center for Child Abuse and Neglect research studies, for instance, investigates the psychosocial ecology of abusive families (National Center, 1978a). Nevertheless, at a psycho-dynamic and somewhat tentative level, research indicates that abusing and neglectful parents often have poor self-concepts or poor self-esteem (Steele & Pollock, 1974). Alcoholism and drug usage are also reportedly associated with abuse (Kempe & Kempe, 1978; National Center, 1978a). Though research has isolated a few common characteristics of abusing parents, no one has yet developed a set of personality traits that consistently describes abusers.

Considerable converging evidence indicates that child abuse is frequently found in a single (female) parent home in which the mother is working (Elmer, 1967; Garbarino, 1976; Gil, 1970). Mothers in those homes often experience stress and feel a sense of isolation and separation from social support systems. Abusing parents (in both single and married families) rarely have close ties with their neighbors and most do not participate in any community organizations (Giovannoni & Billingsley, 1970; Kempe & Kempe, 1978; Parke & Collmer, 1975). Again, research about the correlation between social isolation and abuse is speculative, so it is difficult to determine whether parents become abusive because they are isolated from the community or become isolated from the community because they are abusive.

Also deserving of further investigation is the gender of the abusing parent in the intact home. Researchers generally focus more attention on the mother's role than on the father's role in intra-family violence. Psychological and sociological literature often underplays the father's role and influence on a child's development, which makes it difficult to contrast the father's relationship to children in abusive and nonabusive families (Lamb, 1975). Literature is inconsistent on whether the mother or the father is more likely to abuse a child. Gelles's survey (this volume) found that mothers are slightly more likely to abuse than fathers. Gil (1970), however, reported that by controlling for the varying rates of involvement that mothers and fathers have with their children, there is a higher incidence of child abuse among fathers.

Research is still inconclusive about the education level of abusive parents. Some researchers (Garbarino, 1976; Gil, 1970) maintain that parents with little or no secondary school education are most likely to act aggressively toward their children. Gelles, however, reports that adults with just a high school diploma are overrepresented in his abuse statistics (this volume). Studies have consistently shown that abuse is more likely to occur in families with four or more children (Gil, 1970; Parke & Collmer, 1975). The relationship between the size of a family's house and child abuse is unclear, but general sociological/psychological studies have shown that violence increases in dense, crowded living spaces (Mitchell, 1971). Research indicates that large families are prone to abuse, but a single child, often the youngest, is usually the target for parental aggression (Gelles, 1973).

Inconsistent discipline is also associated with abuse. Studies have shown that if power and responsibility over childrearing decisions are concentrated in one parent's hands, or if they shift too much from one parent to the other, the children often become victims of abuse (Gelles, this volume; Parke & Collmer, 1975). The reasons for that connection are unclear, but children who receive inconsistent disciplinary cues from their parents may become oblivious to all parental discipline.

Current research on child abuse has most consistently associated parent-child violence with stress rather than character and personality anomalies (Garbarino, 1976; Gelles, 1973; Giovannoni & Billingsley, 1970; Parke & Collmer, 1975; Rohner & Rohner, 1978). Because of the stressful and frustrating conditions under which many low-income families live, they seem like particularly likely candidates for abuse. Parke and Collmer (1975) dispute the claim that child abuse is more common in impoverished families and maintain that it is simply more well-concealed in wealthier ones. In the absence of reliable incidence data, the connection between class and abuse is difficult, if not impossible, to determine. If statistics bear out the prediction that child abuse is more common among poor families, the finding demands careful analysis and interpretation.

Given the difficult conditions under which poor families live and assuming that stress is a critical factor in abuse, finding more cases of abuse among low-income families does not mean that the poor are inherently more abusive than the wealthy. In fact, Gelles (this volume) found that stress is more likely to lead to abuse in poor- to middle-income families than it is in very poor or very wealthy families. Stressful circumstances or unexpected hardships (emotional, physical, or financial) may have a heavier impact on middle-income parents who are not used to coping with stress and who do not have the financial resources to ease them through a crisis. Ronald Rohner and Evelyn Rohner offer a social-situational model of abuse in which they posit that parental behavior depends on the personal characteristics of the parent, the personal characteristics of the child, and situational factors. They compiled a list of "risk factors" within each category and found that only 10 percent of the risk factors, when viewed alone, differentiated abusive from nonabusive families. The cumulative difference between risk factors in abusive and nonabusive families, however, was significant, and 64 percent of the abusive families had difficulties in all three categories (1978, p. 19). The situational stresses stemming directly from poverty are part of everyday life for low-income families. Assuming the validity of the cumulative stress model of abuse, it is hardly surprising that poor families are overrepresented in abuse statistics.

Scholars are often reluctant to make a connection between class and abuse because similar links have been made in the past as a means of disparaging the poor. While more studies are needed to show whether or not poor children are more likely to suffer abuse than wealthy children, important insights can be drawn from the information that researchers have already accumulated. Leroy H. Pelton (1978) disclaims the notion that child abuse is equally prevalent in all social classes and contends that the "myth of classlessness" diverts money from poverty programs. He maintains that child abuse does indeed occur more frequently in low-income families and that the current tendency of scholars and politicians to disassociate class from abuse dilutes the effectiveness of preventive and/or treatment efforts aimed at eliminating abuse. Researchers often conclude that child abuse is more common among poor families, but scarcity of analysis has made that information difficult to translate into nonpunitive policy. Programs often "blame the poor" for their poverty and, in this case, blame them for their abusiveness by trying to "help" poor parents adjust to their situation without offering any real solutions to the stressful circumstances that precipitate abuse. Because child abuse arouses such intense emotions, it is difficult to discuss the link between poverty and child abuse *without* people causally connecting the two.

PARENTAL EXPECTATIONS

The literature on the characteristics of abusing parents indicates that some parents have unrealistic expectations about an infant or young child's capabilities and/or a general lack of knowledge about child development (Alvy, 1975; Elmer, 1967; Gelles, 1973; Newberger & Hyde, 1975). As Philip Zimbardo and Floyd Ruch explain:

> By perceiving their children as far more capable and potentially responsible than they really are, abusive parents are more likely to interpret crying, soiling of diapers, or breaking a toy as a deliberate attempt to misbehave, to be spiteful and cause trouble. Since they are often "loners," the parents have no basis for social comparison (which could help correct their misconceptions) and also lack the support of friends or relatives in times of stress. (1975, p. 622)

Further, several investigators have found that abusive adults often lack parenting skills (DeLissovoy, 1973; Evans, 1970; Lauderdale et al., 1978). In terms of implications for effective intervention, courses about child care and child devlopment would probably help reduce the incidence of abuse.

It is difficult, however, to determine to what extent courses in parenting would reduce the incidence of abuse. Policymakers must determine the efficacy of implementing any social program, like parenting education classes, by measuring its demonstrated effectiveness, cost, and social acceptability. If unrealistic parental expectations are often a factor in abuse, the national implementation of parenting education courses would probably be an effective means of reducing child abuse. In addition, the cost of implementing those courses in schools is relatively small. Finally, scholars, professionals, child advocates, and parents themselves have championed parent education for many years and it appears that more and more people are prepared to support that effort. Young people themselves have reacted positively to such courses.

Some people will undoubtedly resist government subsidized education for parenthood programs because they will interpret it as yet another encroachment into family affairs. In order to protect parents' rights to raise their children as they see fit, courses must avoid the inculcation of values and emphasize instead basic information about the development of children. Those courses should explain the benchmarks of human development, realistic behavioral expectations of children at different developmental stages and ages, as well as the kinds of experiences that interfere with a child's optimal development.

Courses in parenting education would be offered to children from all racial and economic backgrounds. In this they would differ from other child abuse primary prevention programs, which are directed at a targeted segment of the population (people considered "at high risk of abuse"). Because parents of all backgrounds can have unrealistic expectations of their children, all young people should receive training in parenting skills. Even a middle-class parent's efforts to raise his child's IQ by twenty points is a form of abuse because it stems from unrealistic expectations of children's capabilities. Parenting education classes address some of the common problems faced by all parents and their effectiveness does not depend on any arbitrary distinctions between abusive, nonabusive, and potentially abusive parents.

INDIVIDUAL VERSUS SOCIAL APPROACH

Employing the individual or the social approach to child abuse has implications for the decisions that policymakers will reach in creating programs to tackle the problem. Child abuse can be conceptualized as a pathological phenomenon with roots in the character traits and/or psychodynamics of individual abusing parents; a sociocultural phenomenon in which the extremely stressful nature of the abusing parent's ecological niche precipitates abuse; or as a combination of individual and social factors whereby particular character traits of parents and children, when aggravated by situational factors, lead to abuse (Alvy, 1975; Belsky, 1978; Cottle, 1975; Daniel & Hyde, 1975; Galston, 1965; Garbarino, 1976; Garbarino & Crouter, 1978; Gelles, 1973; Gil, 1979; Hurt, 1975; Kempe et al., 1962; Parke & Collmer, 1975; Rohner & Rohner, 1978; Steele & Pollock, 1974). Poverty, isolation, and the lack of effective social support systems for parents are the forces commonly cited as having the most powerful influences on a family's stability. The controversy over how to conceptualize child abuse has echoes in the debate about whether psychological traits or situations are the primary determinants of behavior (Bem, 1972; Bowers, 1973; Mischel, 1969, 1973).

The use of the psychodynamic/individual approach to the problem of child abuse traces back to Freud's essay "A Child Is Being Beaten" (1919, 1959) in which he used his theoretical formulations to describe the dynamics of a child abuser. His individual pathological perspective demanded further refinement. Becker (1963), for instance, distinguished between a deviant behavior that indicates an underlying pathology and a deviant behavior that is the product of some recognized psychiatric entity such as psychopathy. Some proponents of the individual approach to child abuse treat the abuse itself as indicative of an underlying abnormal process or disease (Spinetta & Rigler, 1972).

Fewer and fewer people view child abuse from an individual psychological perspective. Yet there are aspects of the pathological approach that merit consideration. Certainly a small percentage of abusing parents are violent toward their children because of psychological impairments that can be defined in terms of psychiatric descriptions. Gil, for instance, found that "in over 46% (of child abuse incidents) the perpetrator was viewed by others as suffering marked mental and/or emotional deviations" (1970, p. 128). Some individuals engage in abusive behavior even if they are not living in a stressful sociocultural situation while other parents, no matter how much stress they are subjected to, never engage in abusive behavior. This finding suggests that in some cases psychological problems account for abusive behavior.

Pathology only explains abuse in a limited number of cases, however, so employing the individual approach will have limited success in controlling abuse for a number of reasons. From a practical point of view, psychiatric treatment for abusers is simply too costly to be considered a realistic or effective way of combating abuse on a national scale. Further, because emotional instability accounts for abuse in such a small fraction of the population, psychiatric intervention is incapable of solving the problem of abuse in the majority of cases. The individual approach implies that child abusers need help dealing with a particular abnormal personality trait. It suggests that the abusing parent is, in effect, addicted to child abuse in the same way that alcoholics are addicted to alcohol or gamblers are addicted to gambling. Research has shown that abuse, unlike alcoholism or gambling, has much broader and deeper roots in social and situational forces which the individual approach fails to recognize or address.

The emphasis on individual pathology or deviance among abusers led to the implementation of a number of intervention programs like hot lines and parents anonymous groups that had proven effective in tackling other types of addictions. While voluntary programs like the two mentioned above can be invaluable sources of support for abusive or potentially abusive parents, the current emphasis on the need for those services reveals a lack of understanding of the structural roots of abuse. It takes a great deal of sophistication for parents to recognize that the frustrations of living under a series of economic, emotional, and social strains often lead to violence. Parents who buckle under pressure and abuse their children often see themselves, and are seen by others, as inadequate parents who, because of their own individual failings, are incapable of raising children. Although self-help and self-reporting programs for abusers implicitly acknowledge that abuse stems from circumstances beyond a parent's control, they offer only individualized help to those parents who ask for it. Such services cannot combat child abuse effectively because they are based on an inadequate conceptualization of the problem and treat its symptoms rather than its causes. Programs that stem from the individual approach to abuse fall short because they do not have an impact on the sociocultural situation of abusers.

The Sociocultural Approach

The model that offers the most promising explanation of child abuse is an interactive one, which describes the child abuser as someone with particular personality characteristics who is part of a family that is itself imbedded in the social, economic, and political framework of a community. Seen from that broad perspective, child abuse is a symptom of a variety of stresses whose underlying social determinants are both difficult and costly to correct. The society's success in eliminating child abuse will be determined by its willingness to implement policies that address a variety of problems that, because they are woven into the fabric of the society, cannot be tackled in isolation from one another.

The social factors that might be considered causes of child abuse seem overwhelmingly difficult to correct at first glance. Many people feel that the physical structure of city apartments and the anonymity that many city-dwellers feel have made this society increasingly a nation of strangers (Packard, 1974; Lofland, 1973). Increased alienation, loneliness, and isolation are undoubtedly related to child abuse. In fact, the incidence of child abuse increases in the week before Christmas (Murphy, 1976), which can be interpreted as an indictment of the lack of effective social support systems for families. As Eli Newberger and David Hyde stated:

> Child abuse, like such other human troubles as suicides, disturbances in prisons and mental hospitals, and violent crimes, gets worse at times of year when people long for missing family supports and, in their desperation, may turn on their children when they make unacceptable nurturing demands. (1975, p. 706)

The loss of a sense of community and the breakdown of a supportive network of family and neighbors for parents has taken place over several decades and is due to a variety of factors related to modernization. These factors include the rise in commuting, suburban housing patterns, and the resultant split between the work place and the home; the demarcation of America's social activities along age lines; and the greatly enhanced mobility of many Americans. Increasingly, families move several times during their children's schoolage years and, as a result, parents often do not develop a sense of community and tend to keep social ties to a minimum.

Gil has found a positive correlation between mobility and the incidence of child abuse in a family (1970). Due to crowding and the increased density of living spaces in cities, families are more and more possessive of their privacy and hesitate to interfere in other families' lives. That reluctance has a certain appeal until families find themselves in a crisis and need help or support from friends and neighbors. Not surprisingly, a common theme running through many case studies of child abuse is that parents feel a sense of loneliness, isolation, and alienation from the surrounding community. The control of child abuse, therefore, might be as effectively tackled by beefing up the nation's general social service programs as it would by creating programs specifically directed against child abuse.

Improving the Social System

The ecological approach to abuse points to a number of changes in the family's ecology that might have particularly high payoff in terms of reducing the incidence of child abuse. For instance, in view of the finding (Gelles, 1973, Lauderdale, 1977) that unwanted pregnancies can lead to abuse, the expansion of family planning services might help reduce its incidence. In addition, making homemaker services available to families experiencing difficulties might ease stress in those families and help keep families intact and children out of the impermanence and insecurity of the foster care system.

The availability of a variety of child care services, ranging from day care centers to home visitors, would relieve parents of full-time childcare responsibilities and reduce the incidence of child abuse. The Final Report of the National Day Care Study summarized the benefits and costs of day care for preschool children. As Blandina Cardenas wrote, "parental needs for and government support of day care services are growing [and this report gives] . . . policymakers . . . a research base on which to shape programs of day care support and regulation for the 1980's" (Abt Associates, 1979, p. iii). Despite the current enthusiasm and support for the expansion of day care services, the White House Conference on Children (1971) named the need for quality day care for children of all classes a top priority for child advocates nearly a decade ago. Today, the situation remains little improved. Studies proving the benefit of providing quality day care services for families must be considered merely academic if government agencies and legislatures never act on that knowledge.

Decision-makers need to consider the potential impact of policies on the strength of families as a variable in cost-benefit equations that lead to the passage of one piece of legislation over another. For instance, convincing evidence has already shown that an unemployed or underemployed father in the home is associated with a higher incidence of child abuse (Garbarino, 1976; Gelles, this volume; Parke & Collmer, 1975). The government's calculated national unemployment rate of 8 percent reflects no commitment to strengthening the family or to curbing abuse. Decision-makers who believe that high unemployment is the necessary tradeoff to reducing inflation are not consciously bent on abusing America's children. In fact, they may feel that inflation is more detrimental to family life and therefore deserves priority over reducing unemployment. In the absence of data proving any empirical relation between inflation and child abuse, however, child advocates must continue to push for legislation to reduce unemployment rates because they know that it will have a positive impact on children's lives.

The ecological model provides the most comprehensive framework for conceptualizing abuse. The classic work of John Whiting and Irvin Child demonstrates the relationship between a culture's childrearing practices and its social norms (Whiting, 1963). This society has taken some tentative steps to correct environmental pollution. It has done precious little to correct the social pollution of many Americans' ecologies. Those polluted ecologies often drive parents to abuse their children. So long as the society attends only to the symptoms of child abuse and engages in the merely token efforts growing from that narrow concern, it will continue to avoid confronting the underlying social determinants of abuse that are much more costly to correct.

Pervasiveness of Social Support for Child Abuse

Just as child abuse narrowly considered cannot be completely understood without consideration of the social context in which families function, so too that context must be examined for the part it plays in socializing adults in their parental function. The structural roots of violence run deep in this society and because they affect both the nation's institutions and people's values, they have a powerful influence on parents and children alike. Parents often receive subtle and sometimes not so subtle cues telling them it is socially acceptable to behave aggressively toward their children. The society provides little outside support to bolster families, yet it provides plenty of support for behavior conducive to child abuse (Gil, 1979).

One of the single most important determinants of child abuse is the willingness of adults to inflict corporal punishment upon children in the name of discipline. Well over half of all instances of child abuse appear to have developed out of disciplinary action taken by the parent (Gil, 1970). All too often an adult begins disciplining a child with mild forms of punishment and ends up unintentionally harming the child. Parents often hurt children if they are unable to gauge their own strength and the physical vulnerability of young children and infants, or if they are unable to control their anger. Some parents are unaware that severe shaking can cause brain damage in young children. Parents are often shocked by the tragic outcome of an incident in which their well-intentioned desires to impose needed discipline on a child resulted in severe physical injury.

Who is the real villain in this common scenario? The child is certainly not at fault. Nor are the parents who believe that they are providing discipline in the name of love for their growing child. The real villain is the society that approves of corporal punishment as an acceptable means of disciplining children. Many scholars (Alvy, 1975; N. Feshbach, this volume; Gelles, 1973; Gil, 1970; Maurer, 1977) maintain that as long as corporal punishment remains an acceptable form of discipline child abuse will continue to be a problem in this society.

The widespread use of behavior modification is contributing to the increased acceptability of violent childrearing techniques. Behavior modification principles underlie many of the disciplinary techniques used in homes, schools, camps, institutions for children, therapists' offices, and psychologists' research laboratories. While no responsible adherent of behavior modification would counsel parents to use extreme physical punishment, its popularization by magazines and journals has led to widespread misinterpretation of the appropriate use of those techniques. Parents often distort its principles by equating behavior modification with discipline. They learn that behavior modification is an effective and easy way to reinforce positive behavior and punish negative behavior. So, for example, an advertisement for the book *Parents and Children, Love and Discipline* (Madsen & Madsen, 1975), written by two established authorities in the behavior modification field, reads:

> *Parents should take fast, positive action* when children misbehave. The authors . . . explain why long, involved analysis of a child's personality is unnecessary and probably counter-productive. This easy-to-understand, easy-to-use book tells how to teach children essential behavioral guidelines such as "If you do good things, good things happen to you." (*New York Times Book Review*, October 26, 1975, p. 43)

The not-so-hidden message is that children should learn that "if you do bad things, bad things happen to you." The danger of using "fast, positive action" to discipline children is that it often leads to severe injury or death; parents have more control over discipline if they measure their actions than they do if they lash out the moment the child misbehaves. Simplified and distorted versions of the behavior modification formulation have led to the view that physical punishment is an effective method of shaping children's behavior.

Schools and institutions frequently employ aversive behavior modification techniques to discipline unruly students or patients. Countless children are brutalized under the banner of behavior modification. Active and aggressive children pose a very real disciplinary problem to parents, teachers, and institutional guardians and many resort to negative reinforcement techniques because they are at a loss for other ways of handling them. The public misinterpretation of behavior modification techniques might be corrected if magazine articles and child development courses emphasized the value of positive reinforcement and the harmful effects of negative reinforcement. The widespread public acceptance of behavior modification techniques as a justification for violent discipline will not be easy to correct. It has been incorporated into people's values and child rearing practices in subtle and unconscious ways. Only a massive commitment to reeducate people about the value of nonviolent disciplinary techniques will counter the effects that years of socialization have had on the public's consciousness.

The widespread acceptance of physical punishment as an appropriate disciplinary technique implicitly condones the physical abuse of children. The highest repository of society's values, namely the government, actually engages in abuse and sets a very poor example in its treatment of children who reside in publicly funded institutions. Parents receive a very contradictory message when they hear the government condemn the use of physical punishment of children and simultaneously see the socially sanctioned abuse and neglect of children in institutions run by federal, state, county, and city agencies. Instances of the legalized abuse of institutionalized retarded children have been amply documented by Burton Blatt (this volume). The television documentary "This Child Is Labelled X" depicted the physical abuse of children in training schools for delinquent children as well as in hospitals for emotionally disturbed children.

The classic study by the National Council of Jewish Women, *Windows on Day Care* (Keyserling, 1972), was the first in a series of exposés documenting widespread abuse of children throughout the nation's day care system. Similar exposés uncovered other instances of institutional abuse and neglect and those studies sparked increased public awareness of the problem. The funding priorities for the 1979–1980 National Center on Child Abuse and Neglect programs include a proposal to gather data on the extent and the nature of institutional abuse in the United States. That project represents a long-awaited federal commitment to correct the problem of abuse in residential institutions. Tax dollars support public institutions that overtly engage in the abuse of their wards. Both the government and the taxpayers themselves are guilty of child abuse as long as their silence allows those abusive conditions to persist.

The legal and social sanctioning of abuse is not limited to the conditions in institutions for public wards. The use of corporal punishment by teachers is commonplace in schools throughout the nation. Schools are probably the most important socializing agent next to the family; socially sanctioned abuse in education has a profound and insidious effect on children's development. Nat Hentoff researched corporal punishment for the American Civil Liberties Union and in November, 1971 reported that corporal punishment was so widespread that "the brutalization of children appeared to be a part of the core curriculum" in many schools (quoted in Maurer, 1974, p. 617). Only Maine, Massachusetts, and New Jersey forbid the use of corporal punishment of students (Maurer, 1977).

Schools play a critical role in children's development. A school's practices not only reflect the values of American families but they also influence familial attitudes and practices. The abolition of corporal punishment in the schools might reduce the incidence of abuse by setting a positive example for parents to follow in their child rearing practices at home. The 1975 Supreme Court decision upholding the right of school personnel to physically punish children is a step backwards because it implies that corporal punishment is an acceptable and permissible mode of child discipline (Zigler & Hunsinger, 1977). That decision, made by the highest judicial body in the land, reflects an acceptance of violence and physical aggression as positive modes of human interaction. So long as violence, hostility, and aggression are tolerated and even glorified by public and private institutions and policies, children will be subjected to abuse both in school and at home.

The roots of violence and abuse run deep in this society's structures, values, and practices. The chances of eliminating child abuse when the problem is viewed within such a broad context seem discouragingly grim. This society needs a tremendous commitment of energy and money if it is ever to solve problems like institutional abuse and pervasiveness of violence as an acceptable means of discipline and interaction. Investing money in support services and parenting education classes will eliminate some of the individual cases of abuse, but money alone cannot transform the society's values. Because violence is so deeply imbedded in the values of the society and reflected in the behaviors of individuals within that structure, eliminating child abuse involves transforming the context in which people live rather than altering the behavior of individuals.

CONCLUSION

The problems discussed in the foregoing analysis lead to a pessimistic evaluation of this nation's ability to eliminate child abuse. The knowledge and the resources available are simply too limited to deal effectively with even a symptomatic treatment of abuse. Even the federal government's commitment to solving the problem of child abuse, which it theoretically demonstrated in 1974 with the passage of the Child Abuse Prevention and Treatment Act, is questionable. Ellen Hoffman pointed out that "the shapers of the bill deliberately accepted an incremental approach [because they knew] that adequate funding for a more comprehensive attack on child abuse was not forthcoming" (1978, p. 71). That "something-is-better-than-nothing" strategy necessarily reflected a compromise in goals but, because of the political climate at the time of the bill's passage, it was the only realistic tactic open to policymakers who wanted some show of Congressional commitment to the problem. History may one day prove that the bill was actually counterproductive. A twenty-million-dollar bill to fight child abuse in America amounts to little more than putting a Band-Aid on a cancer.

Congress cannot legislate away a major social problem like child abuse with a single bill. Social change occurs not by the stroke of a pen but by intensive and persistent efforts to restructure the human ecology within which the problem exists. Laws like the Child Abuse Act accomplish little and they may be destructive to social change. They give people the false sense of security that something meaningful has been done and, in so doing, interfere with later efforts to mount effective prevention or treatment measures.

Token bills like the Child Abuse Act may have other insidious effects, not the least of which is that they call into question the credibility of the federal government. The Act simply promises more than it can possibly deliver. As the Wirtz report stated:

> The American people today are deeply skeptical about any grandiose representation. They have been oversold for too many years on too many grand initiatives . . . the first demand on policy today is that it be totally credible. And the second demand is that it be fiscally responsible. (quoted in Reston, 1975, p. 15E)

The difficulties inherent in constructing or implementing a credible and fiscally responsible child abuse act seem overwhelming, given the nation's limited success in solving even relatively minor social problems. For instance, Elliot Richardson became interested in the cost of reducing lead paint poisoning among children during his term as the Secretary of Health, Education and Welfare. When the Assistant Secretary for Planning and Evaluation did a cost analysis on the problem and discovered that it would cost the nation billions of dollars to solve, Richardson had to conclude that such vast sums of money were simply not available to solve even a problem whose technological aspects posed no difficulty.[1]

Despite the pessimism that this nation can eradicate the problem of child abuse over the next few years, the emerging framework of knowledge offers promising directions for policy-makers to pursue. Research has uncovered a number of programs and policies that might curb the incidence of abuse and are worth trying because they will not hurt families or children. Those tactics include: (1) continuing research on the prevention and treatment of abuse and collecting data on its incidence, (2) expanding family planning services, (3) implementing education for parenthood programs, (4) reducing the number of premature births in America, (5) increasing the availability of homemaker services, and (6) increasing the availability of child care services in America. Individual and social alternatives must both be used in the nation's efforts to control and eliminate the problem of abuse. Finally, and perhaps most importantly, Americans need to reexamine and transform their values because child abuse stems from a general acceptance of violence and aggression throughout the society.

1. Personal communication.

II

THE PSYCHOLOGICAL
CONTEXT

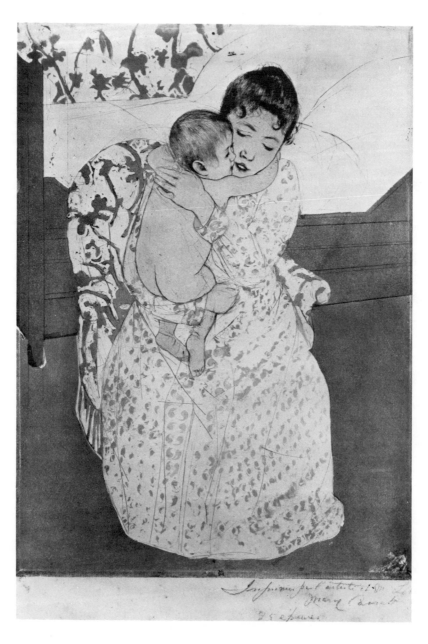

Mary Cassatt's "Maternal Caress," a color print etched in 1891.

2

Attachment and Child Abuse

Mary D. Salter Ainsworth

Very little research has been done on the connection between attachment and child abuse. Nevertheless, it seems likely that child abuse is related to anomalies in the development of attachment. These anomalies may be of two kinds. First, anomalies in the development of parents' attachment to the child may be hypothesized as crucial in the etiology of child abuse. Second, anomalies in the development of an abused child's attachment to his parents seem likely to result from child abuse and yet may themselves evoke further abuse.

The concept of "developmental anomaly" is drawn from the ethological-evolutionary attachment theory first formulated by Bowlby (1969). According to this theory, an infant is genetically programmed to behave in ways that have the "predictable" (i.e., probable) outcome of contact with or proximity to his caregiver. Such attachment behavior is assumed to have become part of the repertoire of the human infant because it increased the probability of his survival in the environment in which the species first evolved. When close to his caregiver the infant was more likely to be protected than when apart. Protection is thus conceived to be the biological function of attachment and of attachment behavior.

Provided that the circumstances under which an infant is reared do not depart too grossly from the environment to which his attachment behavior is genetically preadapted, he will form an attachment to the person who is principally responsible for his care. This person is referred to as the "mother figure"; it is most usually the natural mother, but not necessarily so. The infant is also likely to become attached to one or a few other familiar persons, usually including the father—but this discussion will focus on the mother figure.

The baby's attachment behavior is hypothesized to be preadapted to an environment that resembles the environment in which it originally evolved to become characteristic of the human species. Surely, an important part of that environment of evolutionary adaptedness is the presence of a responsive mother. Nevertheless, the infant's preadapted behavior is so effective that it is only under extraordinary circumstances that he fails to become attached to anyone. This failure occurs only when a baby has too little interaction with any one person to be able to focus his attachment behavior on anyone. This may happen in the depriving atmosphere of certain institutions in which an infant's care is fragmented among many persons. It may also happen at home when the mother figure is grossly unresponsive to the infant, and no one else takes her place (e.g., Ainsworth, 1962). The result, of course, is deprivation of maternal care—or child neglect, not child abuse.

Thus, provided that an infant has sufficient interaction with his principal caregiver he will become attached to her—or him. He becomes attached regardless of the nature of the interaction with that person (Ainsworth, 1979). Once attached, he directs his attachment behavior toward that figure in preference to others. Whenever pain, alarm, threat, or rebuff occur, he especially seeks to be close to her. There is good reason to believe that he tends to do so even when the pain, alarm, threat, or rebuff emanates from the attachment figure herself. Striking examples of this stem from Harlow's research with infant macaques. Infant monkeys are very alarmed by air blasts. When a surrogate cloth-mother, to whom an infant has become attached, emits air blasts, the infant, highly alarmed, clings tightly to the surrogate despite the fact that "she" is the source of the frightening stimulus (Harlow, 1961). Similarly, infants whose "motherless mothers" grossly abused them, nevertheless persisted in clinging to the abuser (Harlow, 1963). In addition, many clinical observations suggest that human infants and young children can and do become attached to an abusing parent.

Attachment theory suggests that maternal behavior is also genetically programmed. Such behavior is complementary to infant attachment behavior, and also has as its predictable outcome the maintenance of proximity, and, as its biological function, the protection of the infant. Maternal behavior became established as part of the groundplan of the species because it contributes to survival of the infant and thus indirectly to population survival. Because of the long time-gap between birth and parenthood, however, there is ample opportunity for developmental anomalies to occur.

Indeed, great variation in maternal behavior exists from culture to culture and from individual to individual. Only by taking a broad view can one detect the species' groundplan (Bowlby, 1969). Despite cultural and individual differences, parents do tend to maintain a reasonable degree of proximity to their infants, and themselves take drastic action to reinstate proximity when the infant is lost or threatened. Thus, in general, parents do serve a protective function. Obviously the groundplan has gone awry when child abuse occurs. An anomaly in the development of parental behavior may be inferred.

One major component of the original environment to which infant behavior is preadapted seems to be the presence of a mother figure who is responsive to infant signals and communications. To the extent that a mother is unresponsive or inappropriately responsive, it is reasonable to assume that the nature of the child's attachment to her will be affected. When developmental anomalies in the mother have interfered with the development of normally responsive maternal behavior, mother-child interaction tends to be distorted and developmental anomalies are likely to occur in the child.

RESEARCH ON INFANT-MOTHER ATTACHMENT

My research on the development of infant-mother attachment in the first year of life, which has been most comprehensively reported so far in a 1978 volume (Ainsworth, Blehar, Waters, & Wall, 1978), has implications for our understanding of child abuse. The project involved frequent, long observations of mother-infant interaction as it naturally occurred in the home environment, supplemented by observation in a controlled laboratory situation toward the end of the infant's first year. We called this controlled procedure "the strange situation" because it involved the strange in the sense of unfamiliar. This procedure has yielded a valid and reliable method of assessment of qualitative differences in the way a one-year-old has organized his attachment to his mother. The most crucial aspects of this assessment refer to how the baby responds to reunions with his mother after two separations in the unfamiliar laboratory environment. In the reunion episodes it is evident that the attachment behavioral system is activated at high intensity. In addition to our longitudinal sample, several hundred one-year-olds have been observed in this situation by various investigators in addition to myself and my associates. The results of these investigations have also been reviewed by Ainsworth et al. (1978).

The assessment of attachment yielded by the strange situation procedure rests on the patterning of the infant's behavior in this situation. A classification system identified three main groups. One of these may be identified as securely attached, and the other two as anxiously attached. Whereas the securely attached infants sought proximity, contact, or at least interaction with their mothers in the reunion episodes, the anxiously attached infants were conspicuous for mingling attachment behavior with behaviors antithetical to proximity/contact maintenance. Indeed in some infants such antithetical behaviors entirely overrode attachment behavior. For the most part the two anxiously attached groups were clearly discriminable. One, variously referred to as "ambivalent" or "anxious/resistant," mingled attachment behavior with angry resistance to contact or interaction. The other group was conspicuous for avoidance of the mother under circumstances that ordinarily activate attachment behavior at high intensity. This group has been referred to as the "anxious/avoidant" group or the "mother-avoidant" group. The mother-avoidant infants, discussed below, bear substantial resemblance to abused children.

Let us first consider, however, the relationship between strange-situation classification and mother-infant interaction at home. At home, throughout the first year, the two anxiously attached groups were obviously more anxious than those identified as securely attached. They cried for longer periods. They showed more distress in little everyday separations, and yet they did not seem glad to see their mothers return. They took less pleasure in being held by their mothers, and yet more often protested being put down. They were less cooperative with their mothers. They were clearly more angry.

Several studies have followed up infants, assessed in the strange situation at the end of the first year, into their second year—or beyond, even as late as the sixth year (e.g., Bell, 1978; Connell, 1976; Arend, Gove, & Sroufe, in press; Main, 1973; Main & Londerville, 1978; Matas, Arend, & Sroufe, 1978; Waters, Wippman, & Sroufe, 1979). Much the same kind of picture emerged. In comparison with securely attached infants, anxiously attached infants when observed later on had less harmonious interaction with their mothers, with more negative affect. They were less responsive to friendly but unfamiliar adults, less competent both in problem-solving situations and in interaction with peers, generally less cooperative with their mothers, and less "ego resilient."

The mothers of the anxiously attached infants, in comparison with the mothers of the securely attached infants, were less sensitively responsive to infant signals from the beginning. Not only did they delay in responding to infant crying, but generally this unresponsiveness was confirmed across many contexts. Maternal insensitivity to signals clearly made it difficult for the baby to build up expectations of his mother as an accessible and responsive person. It was difficult for him to establish basic trust.

It is especially interesting, however, to examine the differences between the mothers of the two anxiously attached groups of infants. The first distinction was that the mothers of avoidant babies were more rejecting than the mothers of merely anxious babies. From the rating scale that we constructed to assess acceptance-rejection, it emerged that the loving feelings of the rejecting mothers were more frequently overwhelmed by feelings of irritation and resentment. There was no implication, however, that loving feelings were altogether absent, or that these rejecting mothers were not bonded to their babies. Often these feelings of resentment were centered on how much the responsibility for infant care interfered with other maternal interests and activities.

Mary Main conducted further analyses of the mothers from our longitudinal sample. She found that *all* of the mothers of babies who eventually became avoidant had a deep-seated aversion to close bodily contact. They also tended to be less expressive emotionally, which she hypothesized to indicate a defense against overt expression of anger. She also found that they were more rigid and compulsive—traits which clinicians generally interpret as a defense against anger. In short, underneath their defenses they tended to be more angry than other mothers.

As for the mother-avoidant babies themselves, in comparison to those who were merely anxious, the most conspicuous difference was that, at home, avoidant babies more often evinced anger, although in the strange situation this anger was masked by avoidance. Furthermore, the avoidant babies were less positively responsive when in close bodily contact with their mothers than were other babies. In particular, they were rarely able to "sink in" against their mothers, totally relaxed, molding their posture to conform to the mother's body.

Our interpretation of the dynamics of the mother-avoidant babies is that they have a severe approach-avoidance conflict about close bodily contact with the mother. Like other infants, they want contact whenever attachment behavior is activated at high intensity. Yet their experience in the context of such contact has been one of rejection and rebuff—not always, perhaps, but often enough for the baby to distrust his mother's responsiveness should he again seek contact. To him it seems safer to avoid contact, and certainly avoidance defuses the strain. Yet it is reasonable to suppose that a baby's history of being unable to gain comfort and reassurance in close contact with his mother means that his attachment behavior is crucially frustrated. Such frustration implies that the baby is chronically angry.

Follow-up studies by Main (1973; Main & Londerville, 1978) and Matas et al. (1978) suggest that differences between mother-avoidant babies and the other two groups of infants persist at least into the second or third years—and perhaps longer, although no one has so far undertaken a longer follow-up. Babies who were mother-avoidant at one year continue to avoid the mother, and find it very difficult to cooperate with her when cooperation is needed. They engage in aggressive behavior that seems quite out of context. They are less willing to engage in interactive play with friendly but unfamiliar adults than are securely attached toddlers.

A Study of Abused Children

Although a number of studies reporting characteristics of victims of child abuse exist, the only one of these that I have encountered that compares these characteristics with those of a properly matched control group of nonabused children is that by George and Main (1979). Both the abused children and their controls were observed in regard to their behavior toward caregivers and other children in a daycare center. No observation of interaction with the parents was feasible in this study.

In comparison with the control children, the abused children approached caregivers less often, more frequently avoided both caregivers and other children, more frequently manifested signs of approach-avoidance conflict toward caregivers, and more often assaulted or threatened to assault both caregivers and other children. In addition, special features of their approach and aggressive behavior deserve special mention. It was particularly when a caregiver made a friendly overture that the abused children failed to approach. If, however, one did approach a caregiver upon invitation, he was likely to do so indirectly: from the side, from behind, or by turning about and back-stepping toward her. Harassment—defined as malicious behavior having the apparent intent of obtaining a distress reaction from the victim, who was usually the caregiver—was conspicuous among the abused children. Such behavior occurred spontaneously and without apparent cause.

In short, the abused infants of the George and Main study behaved toward caregivers in much the same way that our mother-avoidant babies behaved toward their mothers—only in exaggerated fashion. This finding suggests that the dynamics of abused and other mother-avoidant babies may be similar. Presumably, abused children have even more severe approach-avoidance conflicts about contact with a parent who has already caused them grievous bodily harm. Nevertheless, they may be hypothesized to want close bodily contact with an attachment figure when under stress— just as all infants and very young children do—but they have found this may be very painful. Like other mother-avoidant children, they may be assumed to be unusually angry, if only because their contact-seeking behavior is generally frustrated.

The avoidance reaction shown by a rejected infant when under stress has two interrelated outcomes: the baby avoids the painful rebuff that he expects he would receive should he seek contact with his mother; he also avoids the punishment that he expects should he express the anger he feels toward her. Main (in press, a,b) suggests a third outcome, namely that the avoiding baby nevertheless remains within proximity to his mother, seemingly engaging in exploratory play. Thus, from an evolutionary point of view but presumably unwittingly, the infant avails himself of the protective function implicit in proximity maintenance. It seems reasonable to assume that the avoidance shown by the abused child has similar outcomes.

When not under special stress, mother-avoidant toddlers tend to show more redirected anger than do other toddlers, behaving aggressively and even destructively toward inanimate objects in the environment, perhaps with some concomitant repression of angry feelings, for they do not appear to be angry (Main, 1973). Such redirection combined with inferred repression may well be more conspicuous with abused children who in a daycare center redirect aggression toward caregivers and other children. It seems likely that often enough such aggression, perhaps especially harassment, would be displayed with no apparent immediate cause and with no apparent show of anger—perhaps even "in fun."

In summary, there seems to be no essential difference save in degree between nonabused but mother-avoidant infants that we have observed (e.g., Ainsworth et al., 1978) and the young abused children observed by George and Main. Both overt behavior and inferred dynamics seem basically alike.

A STUDY OF ABUSING MOTHERS

So far, only one study of abusing mothers has come to my attention that has specifically based itself on evolutionary-ethological attachment theory—that by DeLozier (1979). She hypothesized that abusing mothers, having been anxiously attached to their own parents, would continue to show characteristics of anxious attachment as described by Bowlby (1973), and indeed would have had childhood experiences identified by Bowlby to be common in the histories of older children and adults who could be classed as anxiously attached. Conspicuous among the latter were not only severe experiences of separation in childhood, but even more important, threats of separation—of abandonment, being sent to an orphanage, or of parental death, including threats of suicide. Because of the significance of actual or threatened separation in Bowlby's account, DeLozier employed Hansburg's (1972, 1976) Separation Anxiety Test, as well as a structured interview and questionnaire focusing on early relations with attachment figures.

DeLozier found that abusing mothers, in contrast with a control group, had histories suggesting "severe attachment difficulties" in childhood, with an emphasis on both threats of abandonment and severe disciplinary methods. In other words, they themselves probably suffered anomalies in the development of attachment to the mother figure early on. As adults, these abusing mothers seemed extremely sensitive to separations, reacting with strong anxiety, anger, and feelings of rejection, and self-blame, low self-reliance, and feelings of low self-esteem. Some of them responded in the Separation Anxiety Test with response patterns indicating "detachment"—which we have hypothesized as a defensive reaction in response to separation bearing much similarity to mother-avoidant reactions of one-year-olds in our strange situation, and probably stemming from similar dynamics, namely, approach-avoidance conflict associated with experience that it is dangerous and painful to rely upon the mother figure to be accessible and responsive.

DeLozier's sample of abusing mothers did not differ significantly from the control group in terms of either prenatal or perinatal stresses of the usual sort identified in the literature, or in incidence of premature births. They did, however, score significantly lower in their perceptions of availability of significant helpful others, both in general and at the time of childbirth, and in their feelings of being isolated, unprotected, frightened, unhappy, or angry at the time of the baby's birth and immediately afterward. DeLozier pointed out that whereas, according to the ethological view, a mother just before, during, or immediately after giving birth is especially vulnerable and especially needs the support of her social group, these mothers felt isolated from support. This feeling could be attributable to their own anomalous development, which in turn seems largely attributable to the hostile and rejecting behavior of their own parents. This rejection prevented them from having normally close relations with attachment figures and from building up internal representations of attachment figures as being consistently accessible and responsive. Thus they were especially vulnerable when they themselves became mothers both because they did not expect "significant others" to be helpful and because they lacked the healthy self-reliance characteristic of those whose attachments are and have been secure.

In short, DeLozier's findings are congruent with the implications of attachment theory. They are also essentially consistent with the main thrust of the findings of the characteristics of abusing parents reported by Parke and Collmer (1975) in their excellent review of the literature. Abusing parents themselves had disturbances of relationships with attachment figures as children, and themselves experienced violence from severely punitive parents. Furthermore, it is noteworthy that they are essentially more angry in response to separation than are nonabusing parents. De-Lozier also noted the phenomenon of role-reversal among abusing mothers, who turn to the child (even when an infant) as to an attachment figure. Thus they feel angry and rejected in even mild separations from the child when, for example, he goes to bed or goes to school, and may interpret even normal infant behavior, such as crying, as threatening rejection or abandonment.

The Child Whose Behavior Evokes Abuse

So far the role of anomalous development in the parent has been stressed in accounting both for child abuse and for subsequent anomalous development in the child. Yet other literature suggests that the victim of child abuse may behave in such a way as to evoke such abuse (e.g., Parke & Collmer, 1975). There is evidence that certain types of infants are more likely to be abused than others, for example, infants who are born prematurely, or brain-damaged, or both. Furthermore, it has often been reported that child abuse is often triggered by the child's persistent crying. Leaving aside for the moment the obvious notion that each member of a dyad affects the interaction between them, let us discuss two major considerations.

First, it seems likely that any set of circumstances that makes it difficult for a mother to bond herself to a particular baby will adversely affect the meshing of her maternal behavior with the child's attachment behavior. Such a difficulty may occur in the case of premature birth. It is a reasonable hypothesis that the weeks of separation from the baby, while he is held in intensive care, might well affect the nature of the mother's caregiving behavior. Similarly, any condition in the infant that makes it particularly difficult for him to get his physiological rhythms stabilized, or which makes his signals difficult to interpret, seems likely to make it hard for his mother to respond appropriately. In other words, it makes it more difficult for her to approximate the kind of ready responsiveness to which infant attachment behavior is preadapted. Whereas such conditions and circumstances would be hard on any mother, they seem especially likely to present problems to those whose own development has followed an anomalous course.

Second, we must not ignore the fact that vicious spiral effects can become established in the interaction of parent and child, so that each contributes to the undesirable behavior of the other. For example, George and Main's study (1979) suggests the probability of such spiral effects, at least after abuse has become established. The fact that abused children physically assault the caregiver, and/or harass her without apparent cause surely suggests that the victim of child abuse may evoke further abuse, especially if, as generally agreed, the abusing parent has tenuous control over aggression. Furthermore, DeLozier's (1979) picture of the dynamics of the abusing mother suggests that she might find a child's reluctance to approach when invited, or even simple avoidance under stressful conditions, a demonstration that the child rejects her—does not love her—and this in itself might trigger abuse.

Crying has been singled out as a behavior that may especially activate an abusive reaction on the part of the parent (e.g., Parke & Collmer, 1975), whether because it is particularly aversive as the cry of a brain-damaged baby is judged to be (Wolff, 1969) or because it is especially persistent and resistant to efforts to stop it.

Yet a mother may herself contribute to an infant's persistent crying. Bell and Ainsworth (1972) reported evidence that mothers who tend to be unresponsive to an infant's crying during the first few months tend to have babies who cry more later on. Such persistent crying then tends to make an initially unresponsive mother even less likely to respond promptly and appropriately. It is easy to imagine that such spiral effects are especially apt to occur when both mother and infant contribute to them. Thus the infant might be one whose crying is particularly aversive (as in the case of brain damage) or one who is particularly resistant to soothing, for whatever reason. The mother might be one whose own anomalous development or present stressful circumstances make her especially insensitive to infant behavioral cues. The combination of such a mother with such an infant would be bound to produce a mismatch. If, in addition, the mother is herself full of smouldering resentment or otherwise finds aggression difficult to handle, child abuse is clearly possible.

PREDICTION AND PREVENTION OF CHILD ABUSE

Obviously the prediction of child abuse is complex and difficult. It implies the assessment of: (a) parental characteristics that may predispose her/him to abusing behavior, (b) infant/child characteristics that predispose him to be abused, and (c) circumstances that make it especially difficult for either parent or child to establish and maintain normally harmonious interaction. These circumstances have provided a convenient starting point for intervention programs designed to prevent abuse (and neglect). Similarly, infants judged to be "at risk" because of organic damage, low birth weight, and the like have provided another type of criterion for the institution of programs of intervention. The most difficult, and yet the most important, criterion for intervention is the identification of a parent as potentially abusing. Demographic information may provide some clue, but it is obviously inadequate. Child abuse is, fortunately, a *relatively* rare phenomenon, and even though it may be statistically more probable among certain socioeconomic, ethnic, or age groups than others, the demographic indicators are not significantly predictive.

From the studies reported in this paper it would clearly be desirable when there is any suspicion of risk of child abuse or neglect to be able to assess the parent in question for the psychological characteristics associated with such patterns. Unfortunately, the techniques and instruments ordinarily available for such an assessment are irrelevant, or at best blunt. It seems necessary to assess both childhood attachment experiences, positive and negative, and their outcomes in terms of relevant parental behavior and attitudes. DeLozier's work seems to be an excellent beginning in this complex task, but, in general, our personality assessments, except for the most skilled and sensitive clinical appraisals, fall short of what is needed. The development of new instruments of assessment seems essential, and naturally, my bias is toward the development of instruments based on attachment theory and research.

Another approach is to identify infants and young children who, because of their behavior, seem likely to be victims of distorted parental behavior. So far, in infancy, the failure-to-thrive syndrome, rare as it is, has been the chief indication that something is amiss in the interaction of the infant with his principal caregiver—usually insufficient interaction. As for child abuse, obviously the chief pointer has been actual physical damage to the child. Our "strange situation" provides a procedure for identifying children between the ages of, say, 10 and 18 months, who are "at risk" in their attachment relationships, but has not been used to date to identify children "at risk" of abuse. Its usefulness for this purpose is clearly suggested by the comparison of the mother-avoidant babies found in a presumably normal sample with the abused children observed by George and Main. The strange-situation procedure is, however, too elaborate and time-consuming for widespread use as a screening device. Perhaps its most appropriate use would be as a "marker-instrument" against which infant behavior in other situations (for example, the waiting room in a pediatric clinic) might be "calibrated," in order to develop more feasible assessment procedures. Furthermore, the strange-situation procedure is not directly applicable to children much older than 18 months, although recent research finds it predictive of later mother-child interaction, and thus suggests the possibility of future development of other "marker instruments" appropriate at later stages of a child's development.

Even without sophisticated, standardized instruments for assessing parent or child it is, of course, possible to undertake successful intervention with families who somehow have been identified as needing intervention. One such program has been instituted by Fraiberg and her associates (e.g., Shapiro, Fraiberg, & Adelson, 1976). Two salient characteristics of this program are that (a) it has been undertaken by a team noted for clinical acumen and experience, and (b) it has been sensitive to the implications of attachment theory and research. Such intervention is, of course, very expensive, requiring extensive interaction with infant-mother dyads in the home environment. Interventions involving home visits seem most likely to be effective in helping parents of infants and very young children to be more appropriately responsive in everyday situations. Obviously the more clinically experienced the interveners, the more likelihood of success. Nevertheless, a good grasp of attachment theory and research might well compensate for lack of formal clinical training.

Finally, it seems clear that parents who themselves were abused as children are more likely than others to abuse their children. Or, as previously suggested, a person whose own development has been anomalous tends to foster anomalous development in his or her own children. How can the vicious spiral be arrested? Recently there has been a surge of interest in training in parenting, even beginning with high school students. Surely such programs are worthy of support.

It is my conviction, however, that potential parents most at risk for child abuse need more individual help than that implicit in most programs for training in parenting. To provide such help in a timely fashion implies first screening to identify those who are likely to become abusive parents, and then motivating them to accept the help that is offered. These two steps seem to be both ethically and practically more difficult than the step of choosing the mode of therapy that is most likely to be useful. It seems most likely that screening could be most feasibly undertaken in clinics designed to provide prenatal or even immediately postnatal care, and it also seems likely that prospective or very new parents would be more likely to accept intervention than they would earlier. As to the type of intervention—whether this be individual, group, or family therapy—surely this would depend on individual needs and on the availability of various alternative modes in the community in question.

On the other hand, there seems little doubt that intervention could be most incisive after the new parents actually begin to cope with the reality of the baby, whether the intervention be some mode of psychotherapy, behavior modification, or home-based intervention such as undertaken by Fraiberg and her team—or, indeed, the kind of intervention undertaken by the Parent-Child Development Centers sponsored by the Office of Child Development—now the Administration for Children, Youth and Families. These latter were intended generally to give infants from disadvantaged families a particularly early "head start," but programs such as those of the New Orleans demonstration PCDC project (Andrews, Blumenthal, Bache, & Wiener, 1975), seem to achieve more than the purposes for which they were originally intended, namely, to facilitate cognitive development through improving the quality of mother-infant interaction. That improved interaction probably reduces the incidence of child abuse as well.

3

Child Abuse
and the Dynamics of
Human Aggression and Violence

Seymour Feshbach

Child abuse is a form of human aggression. This statement is self-evident for the most common type of child abuse, which entails the infliction of physical damage. The extent to which aggression is implicated in other types of abuse such as sexual exploitation and neglect of children is a more ambiguous matter. This latter question need not concern us here since for our purposes it will suffice to restrict the phenomenon of child abuse to situations in which the child has been subjected to adult attack.

Given that child abuse of the sort that we are considering here is fundamentally an act of aggression, it is possible that we may achieve a better understanding of this phenomenon by examining it from the perspective of the theoretical and research literature on human aggression. In this essay, we shall consider the relevance of the several mechanisms that have been shown to mediate aggression in the child abuse situation. Attention will be given to those aspects of child abuse that contribute to its singularity as well as those aspects which it shares with other manifestations of human aggression. We shall also attend throughout this discussion to implications for the prevention and reduction of child abuse. As an incidental note, the relationship between the analysis of aggressive phenomena and the analysis of child abuse is by no means unidirectional. Just as research and theory on more general problems of aggression bear on the specific phenomenon of child abuse, so will deeper insight into child abuse increase our understanding of human aggression in general.

Students of child abuse have, of course, paid considerable attention to a number of aggressive mechanisms that might be at work in abusive behavior (Curtis, 1963; Parke & Collmer, 1975; Spinetta & Rigler, 1972). Consequently, some of what is said here will be in the nature of a review and summary. However, we shall also take this opportunity to present some original theoretical views regarding mechanisms that may be particularly significant in the maintenance of aggressive behavior and that have special relevance for child abuse.

CHILD ABUSE AND THE ANTECEDENTS OF AGGRESSION

The antecedents of aggression can be categorized into three broad classes: (1) biological, (2) situational instigations, and (3) learned response patterns. The biological category includes genetic factors, hormones, cortical stimulation, physical constitution, temperament, and social stimuli that act as innate releasers of aggression. Given our present state of knowledge, biological variables, except in a very general sense, do not seem particularly germane to the child abuse problem. It may be that biologically rooted differences in temperament between child abusing adults and nonabusers will emerge, although research findings up to now have not reflected differences. It may be that neurosurgical interventions that have been used to treat some violent individuals (Mark & Ervin, 1970) will be proposed for some child abusers. Nevertheless, such biological considerations remain at best minor elements in the phenomenon of child abuse.

In fact, from a biological standpoint, child abuse is very much an anomaly. Intraspecies aggression for most animal species is regulated by a balanced system of aggressive threat and submissive inhibitory signals. Most aggression takes place primarily for display, and physical injury is infrequent. Human beings have exchanged the security of a relatively rigid innate signal system for the adaptive possibilities of a flexible response system. One consequence, as Konrad Lorenz has noted, (1966, p. 241), is the absence or fragility of stimuli that act as inhibitors of aggression. A fight between wolves will terminate when the vanquished offers up the unprotected throat to the teeth of the victor. The struggle between male deer during the mating season, engaged with locked horns in an apparent fight to the death, is concluded when the loser exposes his bare flanks to the now dominant winner. What are the inhibitory signals that the infant or young child can emit that stop the onslaught of a physical attack? Crying ought to be such an inhibitor but, as we know, the child's crying may have instigated or acted to release the parents' aggressive behavior, and may only serve to intensify the attack.

The helplessness of the young, like the submissive gestures of the vanquished, may have some biologically based inhibitory properties, but one cannot count on helpless displays to blunt the wrath of a child abuser. Involuntary controls have to be acquired and trained through the development of empathy, self-monitoring, and through social supports and sanctions. In addition, there are more possibilities with regard to the reduction of aggression and of child abuse than is suggested by a sociobiological model that sees aggressive behavior as the result of aggressive instigators and aggressive inhibitors. There is the possibility of fostering new behavior to stimulus situations that elicit child abuse—to which we shall return.

SITUATIONAL INSTIGATIONS OF AGGRESSION AND CHILD ABUSE

We turn now to our second category of situational instigating antecedents of aggression. This category includes experiences of pain, frustration, deprivation and threat—aversive conditions that frequently but not invariably elicit anger and aggression. These antecedents are well noted in the child abuse literature and are integral to the so-called sociological approach (Parke & Collmer, 1975) to child abuse. A number of authors have reported a higher incidence of child abuse among lower socioeconomic groups (Gil, 1970; McKinley, 1964). There is some debate in the literature as to the significance of these findings since reporting practices may underestimate child abuse in middle-class families. In addition, the data may reflect socioeconomic differences in childrearing attitudes rather than economic frustrations. However, there are other findings consistent with a frustration explanation. Thus job dissatisfaction (McKinley, 1964) and size of family (Light, 1973) have been shown to be significant correlates of child abuse.

Frustrations, of course, may arise from many sources other than demographically linked factors. And clinical reports of middle-class child abusive parents as well as lower-class parents indicate that assaultive incidents are often instigated by situational frustration and threat in conjunction with psychological insecurity and a history of frustration. For a better understanding of the role of frustration and threat in child abuse, we have treated frustration, threat, pain, and stress as if they were conceptually equivalent.

After the proposal of the frustration-aggression hypothesis, researchers soon recognized that frustration does not inevitably lead to aggression, and that this relationship is strongly affected by the particular motive that is frustrated and by the cognitive interpretation of the frustration. Thus, reactions to the same objective frustration will sharply differ depending upon the subject's views concerning the basis of the frustration. One significant cognitive parameter is the attribution of intent. Frustrations that

Studies of child abuse are also limited by the operational definition of "child abuse." Many investigators define child abuse as only those cases which are publicly labeled "child abuse." We have found in our research (Gelles, 1975a) that certain individuals are much more likely to be "caught" abusing their children than others. A selective process insulates upper-class professional families from being labeled "abusers" and increases the chances of poor or minority families being identified as child abusers, either correctly or incorrectly.

Rather than struggle with the impossible task of defining child abuse and rather than restricting our examination of violence toward children to only those cases that come to public attention, we have chosen to concern ourselves with the issue of family violence, and specifically with violence toward children. We investigated this phenomenon by conducting a survey of a nationally representative sample of American families.[1] The study of family violence was designed to examine the incidence, patterns, and causes of violence between husbands and wives, parents and children, and between siblings.

We do not view the issue of parent-to-child violence as distinct from other forms of violence in the home. As we shall point out below, violence in the family, whether between husband and wife, parent and child, or siblings is one interconnected issue. One cannot hope to understand or do something about parent-to-child violence without a full and complete understanding of the nature and patterns of all the forms of family violence.

DEFINING VIOLENCE

The national survey of family violence defined violence as "an act carried out with the intention or perceived intention of physically hurting another person" (Gelles & Straus, 1979). The "physical hurt" can range from slight pain, as in a slap, to murder.

A number of important issues had to be dealt with when we developed this definition. The definition includes acts that are not normally considered violent by most people, such as spanking a child. Our definition viewed spankings as violent for two reasons. First, a spanking can, does, and often is used to cause pain. Second, a spanking, if administered to someone who is not a family member, would be viewed as assault in the eyes of the law.

When we defined violence, we took into account that violent acts

---

1. The initial data on the incidence of violence toward children in the United States has recently been published (Gelles, 1978), and the complete survey of violence in the family appears in Straus, Gelles, and Steinmetz, 1980.

have a number of characteristics. Violence can be "instrumental" to some other purpose, or it can be "expressive" in which case it is an end in itself. Violence can be legitimate when it is culturally permitted or required, or it can be illegitimate when it runs counter to cultural norms.

 Our definition of violence does not consider the possibility of injury caused by the violent act. Many definitions of child abuse view an act as abuse only when it produces some harm or injury. Because harm or injury often depends on events or contingencies that are external to the behavior, such as: aim, size, and strength of actor and intended victim; luck; or availability of weapons, we chose to focus only on intended acts rather than outcomes.

SAMPLE

Response Analysis (Princeton, N.J.) was contracted to draw a national probability sample. They used a national sample of 103 primary areas (counties or groups of counties) stratified by geographic region, type of community, and other population characteristics. Within these primary areas, 300 interviewing locations (census districts or block groups) were selected. Each location was divided into 10 to 25 housing units by trained interviewers. Sample segments from each interviewing location were selected. The last step involved randomly selecting an eligible person to be interviewed in each designated household.

Eligible families consisted of a couple who identified themselves as married or as being a "couple" (man and woman living together in a conjugal unit). A random procedure was used so that the sample would be approximately half male and half female.

The final national probability sample produced 2143 completed interviews.[2] Interviews were conducted with 960 men and 1183 women. In each family where there was at least one child living at home between the ages of three and seventeen, a "referent child" was selected using a random procedure. Of the 2143 families interviewed, 1146 had children between the ages of three and seventeen living at home. Our data on parent-to-child violence are based on the analysis of these 1146 parent-child relationships.[3]

MEASURING VIOLENCE

We measured the incidence of violence in American families using a series of questions called the "Conflict Tactics Scales" (CTS). The CTS

2. The completion rate for the entire sample was 65%, varying from a low of 60% in metropolitan areas to a high of 72.3% in other areas.
3. For a complete discussion of the methodology, see Straus, Gelles, and Steinmetz, 1980.

were first developed at the University of New Hampshire in 1971. They have been used and modified over the past eight years in numerous studies of family violence in the United States, Canada, Israel, Japan, Finland, Great Britain, and British Honduras (data on validity and reliability of the scales are given in Straus, 1979).

All respondents were asked to consider two time frames. First, we asked them to consider conflicts that took place in the previous 12 months. Then we asked them to think back over the duration of their marriage or the lifetime of their children. The first time frame was used to compute annual incidence rates. Because we interviewed our subjects from January to April, 1976, these can be thought of as rates for 1975. More limited information on the violence that occurred over the entire marriage or the duration of the parent-child relationship also emerged.

The Extent of Violence toward Children

Previous research on child abuse and violence toward children have produced a wide range of estimates and figures on the extent of child abuse and violence. David Gil's 1968 survey of officially reported and validated cases of child abuse yielded 6000 cases (Gil, 1970). The Children's Division of the American Humane Society documented 35,642 cases of child abuse in 1974 (American Humane Association, 1974). In 1976, the American Humane Association found 26,438 reports of child abuse, 14,115 of which were proved valid in investigation. These reports, however, came from only the 31 states that participate in the American Humane's Child Abuse and Neglect Clearinghouse Project (American Humane Association, 1978).

David Gil's household survey, conducted with the National Opinion Research Corporation in 1965, produced an estimate of between 2.53 and 4.07 million individuals who knew of at least one case of child abuse (Gil, 1970). Richard Light (1973) revised that estimate to arrive at a figure of 500,000 children abused annually. Saad Nagi's survey of community agencies produced an estimate of 167,000 annual reports of child abuse and 91,000 cases that go unreported (1977). Other investigators have projected an annual rate of child abuse from as low as 30,000 abused children (De-Francis, 1973) to as many as 1.5 million cases (Fontana, 1973).

DEATHS OF CHILDREN BY VIOLENCE

The estimates of how many children are killed each year are equally variable. The low estimate is 365 (Pediatric News, 1975) and the high figure is 5000 deaths per year (United States Senate, 1973b). The estimates vary because there is no formally established tabulation of the number of children who are killed each year by a parent or caretaker. Even if such a tabulation were conducted, it would probably be somewhat biased, since many cases of lethal child abuse might be officially recorded as accidents.

IS CHILD ABUSE INCREASING?

The limitations of the data on the incidence of child abuse make it impossible to determine if child abuse is increasing. Certainly, if one goes by officially reported cases of child abuse, the evidence supports the claim that child abuse is doing so. However, official statistics are not valid data for answering the question. These data are affected by public media campaigns that aim at increasing the public's knowledge about and concern with child abuse and child abuse reporting. Official statistics are also based on varying definitions of child abuse. From 1968, when all 50 states enacted child abuse and neglect laws, until now, there has been a tendency to *broaden* the definition of "child abuse" and thus, more acts and behaviors are coming under the legal definition of child abuse.

A NATIONAL SURVEY OF PARENT-TO-CHILD VIOLENCE

Our survey of violence toward children asked about a range of acts, starting with the "normal violence" of physical punishment and ending with using a gun or knife. This was based on the belief that "ordinary physical punishment" and "child abuse" are but two ends of a single continuum of violence toward children. In between are millions of parents whose use of physical force goes beyond mild punishment, but which, for various reasons, does not get identified and labeled as "child abuse."

"*Normal Violence.*" The milder forms of violence were, of course, the most common. The minimum estimates[4] are that over half of all American children (58%) are spanked in any one year. At least 71 percent have been spanked or slapped at some time. Thirteen out of 100 children are hit with objects each year, and this is the fate of at least 1 out of 5 children at some point in their lives. Throwing an object was less common. Approximately 5 out of every 100 children have something thrown at them at least once a year and double this figure at some point while growing up.

"*Abusive Violence.*" The most dangerous types of violence were the least likely to occur. But even the figures for these extreme forms of violence yield an astoundingly high number of American children who were

4. We use the term "minimum estimate" because we feel that our figures understate how much violence there is in the family. We assume that there were interviews where the subjects did not report violence that actually occurred.

kicked, punched, bitten, threatened with a gun or knife, or had guns or knives used on them.

Approximately 3 children in 100 are kicked, bitten, or punched by their parents each year. Many more (8 in 100) have a parent do this at one time or another.

Slightly more than 1 out of 100 children are beaten up[5] by a parent each year, and 4 percent are beaten at least once while growing up.

Each year one child in 1000 faces a parent who threatens to use a gun or knife, while nearly 3 children in 100 have grown up with a parent who threatened them with a gun or knife in their lifetimes. The same proportions hold for children whose parents actually *used* a gun or knife on them.[6]

FREQUENCY OF VIOLENCE

With the exception of being threatened with a knife or gun or having a knife or gun used on them, children whose parents were violent to them experienced violence more than once. Children who had something thrown at them had it happen an average of 4.5 times that one year. Children who were pushed or grabbed or shoved experienced that 6.6 times over a twelve-month period. As expected, spankings and slappings were the most frequent; they occurred an average of 9.6 times a year. The average of kicks, bites, and punches was 8.9 times a year, while children were hit with objects 8.6 times. For those who were beaten, this was repeated almost once every two months—an average of 5.9 times over the year. If a gun or knife was used, it happened "only" once in the survey year.

The figures on how often a form of violence was used must be interpreted with care. For some items these frequencies seem to be low. Many people would expect that if a child is spanked by a parent, this would occur more frequently than once a month. But our data are based on children aged 3 to 17. Thus, the frequencies are the average for all children, 3 to 17, who are spanked by their parents. Obviously, older children might be spanked less often than once a month, while some younger children

5. The term "beaten up" was defined by its place in the list of violence items. Specifically, it came after the items dealing with kicking, biting, hitting with a fist, and hitting with an object, and before the items dealing with a knife or gun. Thus, it is something more than just a single blow, but the precise meaning of the term undoubtedly varied from respondent to respondent.

6. We do not know exactly what is meant by "using a gun or knife." In the case of the knife it could mean threw the knife or actually stabbed or attempted to stab. In respect to a gun, it could have been fired without anyone being wounded. However, the fact is that the respondent admitted employing the weapon, not just using it as a threat.

might be spanked weekly, daily, or in some families, hourly. In fact, 82 percent of the 3- and 4-year-olds had some mode of violence used on them, 82 percent of the children from 5 to 9 years old had been hit, two-thirds (66%) of the pre-teens and early teenage children (10 to 14 years old) were struck, and "only" a little more than one-third (34%) of the children 15 to 17 years old were hit by their parents.

INCIDENCE OF CHILD ABUSE

We were surprised—although perhaps we should not have been—to find that the extreme forms of parental violence are not rare, one-shot events. They occur periodically and even regularly in the families where these types of violence are used. If a beating is considered an element of "child abuse," then our findings show that child abuse is a chronic condition for many children, not a once in a lifetime experience for a rare few.

We estimated how many American children were "at risk" of being physically injured by means of a Child Abuse Index. This index combines all the items that have the highest probability of injuring or damaging a child (kicks, bites, punches, beatings, threats with a gun or knife, use of a gun or knife). Almost four out of every hundred children (3.6%) are at risk of serious injury each year because of their parents using at least one of these dangerous forms of violence. Assuming that any of these acts has a high probability of causing harm to a child victim, *between 1.4 and 1.9 million children* were vulnerable to physical injury from their parents the year of our study.

Being at risk of being injured is not the same as being a victim of child abuse. Many a child had been slammed against a wall, or punched and kicked by his or her parents, but did not end up with a concussion or broken bones. However, these figures may still be the best available for estimating how many children might be abused each year in the United States because they are the only statistics ever derived from a nationally representative sample using consistent measurement procedures. If they are a reasonable estimate of child abuse, then they offer new and surprising information:

First, the estimates are *at least 1.2 million children higher than the estimates published by the National Center on Child Abuse and Neglect (NCCAN).* The National Center on Child Abuse and Neglect estimates that a million children a year are abused and neglected. The physical abuse figure they publish is approximately 250,000.

Second, even these figures *underestimate* the true level of abuse for five important reasons. (1) They are based on self-reports of the parents. Underreporting is quite possible when sensitive questions such as "did you beat up your child?" are asked. (2) The survey examines only physical violence. It omits such categories as burning a child, torturing a child, sexual abuse, and other acts that are considered abuse but not violence. Also, because our interview schedule was limited to 60 minutes, we only included 7 specific types of violent behavior. (3) The data on violence toward children refers to violent acts of only one of the two parents. (4) The children we studied were only between the ages of 3 and 17.[7] Previous research suggests a large amount of child abuse is directed toward children between three months and three years of age, and these children are not covered in our survey. Had they been included, our figures would probably be higher. (5) We studied only "intact" families (husbands and wives who were living together).[8] The literature on child abuse suggests that abuse may be more common in families where only one parent lives with the child. Had we studied single parent families, we might also have uncovered a higher rate of extreme violence toward children.

All of the above suggests that the actual violence children experience is probably much higher than the figures we report here. Thus, while our figures are accurate (in terms of the parent-child relations we investigated), they only hint at a much more extensive incidence of the abuse of children in the United States.

Sex of Children and Parents. We found a small, but significant difference between mothers and fathers in the use of physical violence on children. Mothers were slightly more likely to use violence on their children than fathers. Mothers were also more likely to use abusive violence on their children.

One common explanation for why mothers are more violent than fathers is that men and women do not ordinarily share equally in the raising of children. In our society the primary responsibility for childrearing lies with women. They experience the majority of the rewards and costs of raising children, and they generally spend more time with their children than do fathers. But time at risk is only part of the story. Not only are mothers with their children more, they tend to receive most of the blame for their children's misbehavior. The combination of time at risk and the greater responsibility for caring for children delegated to women, irrespective of their interest or competence, probably explains the difference between the rates of violence for fathers and mothers.

7. Because the survey was a study of all forms of family violence, we had to choose "referent children" between the ages of 3 and 17 to obtain meaningful data on violence between siblings.

8. Again, because the survey was on family violence, we had to select intact families in order to study violence between marital partners. Although it would have been desirable to sample single-parent families as well, budgetary constraints precluded selecting a sample of single-parent families that would have been large enough to conduct meaningful analysis.

Boys were slightly more likely than girls to be victims of parental violence. Boys are also more likely to be physically abused in all age groups than are girls.

Age of Child. Our survey found that the children who were most vulnerable to physical abuse were the youngest (3 to 5 years of age) and the oldest (15 to 17 years of age). Previous research, based on clinical samples (Kempe et al., 1962; Skinner & Castle, 1969; Baldwin & Oliver, 1975), has found that young children are at the greatest risk. In fact, some investigations (Kempe et al., 1962; Bennie & Sclare, 1969) found that the children not covered in our survey—those under 3 years of age—were at the greatest risk of being abused. In part, this finding is probably due to the fact that young children are more likely to be detected and less likely to be confused with accidental injury (Laurer et al., 1974; Maden & Wrench, 1977). The oldest children in our survey were the most likely to face extreme forms of violence (beatings, guns, and knives).

Social Factors Associated with Violence toward Children

Popular explanations and conventional wisdom have been used in an attempt to explain child abuse and violence toward children. One school of thought, typically advanced by those who feel that abusive and violent parents suffer from personality or character disorders, is that social factors are *not* related to violence toward children (e.g., Steele & Pollock, 1974). A second, contradictory line of reasoning posits social factors as important; indeed, according to this theory, violent behavior is thought to be overrepresented among certain social groups such as the poor or people under stress (e.g., Gil, 1970).

Our examination of the factors associated with violence toward children focused mainly on social characteristics in order to determine if social factors were related to parental violence and to identify which individual or family situations produced the greatest risk that abusive violence would occur. For the purposes of this analysis we added the item "hit with something" to our "Child Abuse Index."

GEOGRAPHIC REGION AND SIZE OF COMMUNITY

The Midwest and (to a lesser extent) the West have the highest rates of violence toward children. Southerners have the lowest rates of violence toward their children.

Our most interesting finding, with respect to the geographic distribution of child abuse, is that Southerners are not the most likely to be vio-

TABLE 5.1: Child abuse by region

	Rate of Child Abuse (%)
Region	
Midwest (295)	19
West (188)	17
East (270)	13
South (378)	10
Residence	
Large city (210)	19
Rural (252)	14
Suburban (528)	13
Small city (141)	12

Source: *Behind Closed Doors: Violence in the American Family.* Murray A. Straus, Richard J. Gelles, and Suzanne K. Steinmetz. N.Y.: Anchor/Doubleday, 1980

lent toward their children. Previous research on homicide (Gastil, 1971) and official homicide statistics suggest the South has the highest rates of lethal violence. If ownership of firearms is an indicator of potential for violence, as is commonly assumed, Southerners have a high potential for violence as indicated by the fact that a higher percentage of Southerners own firearms than individuals in other parts of the country (Stark & McEvoy, 1970).

It is evident from our survey that the South's reputation for violence (Gastil, 1971) is far from accurate. Victimization studies (Ennis, 1967; Stark & McEvoy, 1970) find Southerners *reporting* the least punching and beating of other persons and about the same experience with knives and guns.

The question remains, why does the Midwest have the highest rate of abusive violence toward children? Do parents in Minnesota, Illinois, Indiana, and other Midwestern states dislike their children more? Are they under more stress? An analysis of data collected by the National Commission on the Causes and Prevention of Violence (Stark & McEvoy, 1970) reveals a mixed pattern of approval of violence across the country. Midwesterners were slightly more likely to approve of a teacher using corporal punishment on a student, but Midwesterners were half as likely as individuals in Eastern states to approve of a parent beating a child. Yet, respondents in the Midwest and West were most likely to approve of a boy having a few fist fights when growing up. One cannot, however, overlook the possibility that Southerners are less likely to report acts of violence to interviewers while residents in the Midwest and West are more candid and open about what goes on in their homes.

Our examination of the national rates of abusive parental violence finds that violence is not confined to one geographic area, but that violence is slightly more likely to occur in certain parts of the country. Our findings suggest that the need for services for abusive parents are slightly greater in the Midwest and West.

Families residing in large cities (population one million or larger) have the highest rates of abusive violence toward children.

One would expect cities to have more *cases* of child abuse, simply because there are more families residing in cities and because the social service network is better prepared to identify cases of child abuse. The key question is whether the *rates* of abusive violence are greater in large cities. Our national survey found that the rates for large urban areas were, in fact, greater than rates for small cities, suburbs, or rural areas.

There are a number of plausible explanations for high urban rates of violence toward children. One is that city life is characterized by a high degree of social isolation. The impersonal nature of urban living and the lack of close kin ties may make urban life more stressful and may provide urban dwellers with fewer interpersonal mechanisms to cope with the stress.

RACE AND RELIGION

There was no significant difference between blacks and whites in their acts of abusive violence toward children. Other minority racial groups (including Orientals and American Indians) have the highest rate of violence toward children.

Data from official reports of child abuse led us to expect that the rate of abusive violence toward children would be higher among blacks than whites (Johnson, 1974; Thomson et al., 1971; Gil, 1970). Certainly the fact that blacks are both economically and socially disadvantaged would support the expectation that blacks would have higher rates of violence. However, our survey results supported the findings of other investigators (Billingsley, 1969; Young, 1964; Elmer, 1967) showing that blacks do not have a significantly higher rate of child abuse and violence than whites. Cazenave and Straus (1978) have concluded from the national survey data that the aid and support in the care of children provided by the black extended family seem to reduce the risk of violent outbursts directed at children.

TABLE 5.2: Child abuse by social characteristics

	Rate of Child Abuse (%)
Race	
White (980)	14
Black (74)	15
Other: American Indian, Oriental, other (28)	18
Religion	
Catholic (585)	15
Protestant (1239)	14
Jewish (111)	6
Other (180)	19
None (140)	14
Age	
30 or under (264)	21
31 to 50 (746)	13
51 to 65 (112)	4
65 and older (3)	0

Source: *Behind Closed Doors: Violence in the American Family.* Murray A. Straus, Richard J. Gelles, and Suzanne K. Steinmetz. NY: Anchor/Doubleday, 1980

The same kin network may not be available to other racial groups that experience the same economic and social disadvantages. That lack may explain their high rate of parental violence.

Abusive violence toward children is unrelated to whether or not the parents consider themselves religious. Jewish parents have the lowest rate of violence, while the rate is highest among parents with religious affiliations other than Catholic, Protestant, or Jewish.

The rate of parental violence is lower when both parents have the same religious affiliation.

While no religious group is immune to using violence on children, there are differences between groups. These differences may be due to a number of factors, including the differing social and economic profiles of various religious groups and their differing religious and cultural values. Jews, by and large, are better educated, have higher incomes, and are more likely to hold a professional position. Minority religious groups may suffer the same economic and social disadvantages as members of minority racial groups. Thus, the difference in rates may reflect a difference in education, income, and occupation rather than religion.

With respect to cultural differences, Jews as a group may be less inclined to support the use of physical means of raising children. Other religious denominations may adhere more closely to teachings that give the parent a mandate to "bend the will of the child."

We found that mixed religious marriages had higher rates of violence toward children than marriages where the partners had the same religious affiliation. Why mixed marriages are more violent would seem to be related to the fragility of marriage and the fact that any additional conflict can be magnified by small differences. It is not that mixed marriages are bad, in and of themselves, or even that they should be avoided. It is simply that they cause more stress. This stress can be internal to the marriage, or it can be produced by people outside of the marriage, such as parents who oppose their children marrying people of different faiths and continue the pressure after the children marry.

AGE

The rate of abusive violence among parents aged 30 or younger is 62 percent, higher than the rate among those 31 to 50 years of age. Those 30 and under are over 5 times as violent as individuals over 50.

Younger parents are the most violent—but why? Since we only studied these families at one point in time, we cannot provide a definitive answer to that question. To explain adequately the differing rates of violence in each age group, we would have to follow people over twenty years of their marriage. Nevertheless, there are some plausible and disturbing possibilities to consider:

1. The higher rate of violence among young parents could reflect the fact that young people in each generation are more prone to violence. Certainly information on violent crimes confirms this idea. The highest homicide rate is for those between the ages of 18 and 24 and drops off rapidly after that (U.S. Department of Justice, 1976). Violent juvenile gangs are also evidence of a predisposition of younger people toward violent acts. Young people have more physical energy and go through more social, physical, and psychological changes, which may contribute to their high rates of violence.

2. A related possibility is that younger marriages are more violence-prone. The early years of a marriage demand that two people learn to live with and adjust to one another, while experiencing frequent and often drastic changes such as the birth of a first child. The exuberance of youth coupled with the tensions of building a marriage may contribute to violent modes of conflict resolution between parents and children.

3. Young parents have young children, and as we have already seen, young children are a high risk group for child abuse. The question is, is the abuse a product of the age of the parent, child, or both?

4. The most disturbing, though tentative, explanation is that our findings might indicate that violence in the family is increasing. Our study may have uncovered a violent generation under 30 years of age. This generation may remain violent as it grows older and be followed by yet another generation of violent adults and violent families. The under-thirty generation grew up during the Korean War, came of age during the riots, violence, and wars of the sixties, and was the first generation to grow up in an age when the majority of all American families watched television and its nightly dose of violence.

Our study clearly illustrates that violence is much more likely to occur in younger families. Whatever the reason, that conclusion merits close attention. If the United States is seeing the first crest of a wave of violent generations, we need to be aware of this and be prepared for future increases in the level and human toll of family violence. If this is not a generational phenomenon, but rather one that is due to younger people and newer marriages being most violence-prone, then we need to recognize that younger families require the most concentrated treatment and prevention resources if we are ever to reduce the level of family violence.

EDUCATION, INCOME, AND OCCUPATION

The most unexpected finding in our survey is that mothers and fathers who are high school graduates have the highest rates of abusive violence toward children. Men and women with less than an eighth grade education have the lowest rates of parental violence, as do those who have some college education.

We certainly did not expect to find that the rate of violence among men who graduated from high school would be 64 percent higher than the rate for men who had an eighth grade education or less. Gil's examination of officially reported and validated cases of child abuse found that abuse was more common among the least educated (1970).

One conclusion that we can draw from our survey is that a minimal education does increase the likelihood that an abusing parent will be *identified* and labeled as a child abuser. Beyond that we can only speculate why high school graduates have the highest rates of severe parental violence. Perhaps the complex relationship between education and violence may be explained in terms of a person's relative rather than absolute educational attainment. From what we know about education and violence,

TABLE 5.3: Child abuse by economic characteristics

	Rate of Child Abuse (%)
Education	
Husband:	
8th grade or less (126)	11
Some high school (188)	15
High school graduate (400)	18
College (407)	11
Wife:	
8th grade or less (95)	12
Some high school (206)	14
High school graduate (519)	17
College (306)	11
Family Income	
$5,999 and under (211)	22
$6,000 to $11,999 (762)	16
$12,000 to $19,999 (629)	15
$20,000 and over (315)	11
Occupation	
Husband:	
Blue collar (615)	16
White collar (491)	11
Wife:	
Blue collar (178)	16
White collar (301)	10
Employment Status of Husband	
Full time (1017)	14
Part time (11)	27
Unemployed (49)	22
Retired (11)	9
Disabled (37)	14

Source: *Behind Closed Doors: Violence in the American Family.* Murray A. Straus, Richard J. Gelles, and Suzanne K. Steinmetz. N.Y.: Anchor/Doubleday, 1980

we might argue that it is more stressful to an individual to have a moderate education than to have little education. Men and women who have been to high school, but not beyond, have achieved the average education in America (the median amount of schooling in 1970 was 11 years), but they still find themselves blocked from the high-status, well-paying professional jobs. In some instances, high school graduates find themselves working beside grammar school dropouts, earning the same salary and job status as their less-educated counterparts. Such situations probably cause more stress for the educated worker than the uneducated worker.

An inverse relationship exists between income and parental violence. Those with the lowest incomes (under $5999 per year) have the highest rate of violence, while families with incomes greater than $20,000 have the lowest rate of violence toward children.

Parents of all income levels use severe and abusive violence toward their children. But this *does not* mean that the rates are *equal* at all social levels. The fact that child abuse and violence occurs in all economic groups has recently led a number of professional and public commentators to claim that the frequency and severity of violence is unrelated to socio-economic status (e.g., Steele & Pollock, 1974). But, as Pelton points out, child abuse is not a classless phenomenon (1978). Evidence from official reports and our self-report survey of a representative sample show that the poorest families are the most likely to abuse their children. Despite the fact that the poorest families in our survey had rates of abusive violence that were twice as great as the highest income groups, it would be a mistake to infer that poverty is the sole cause of child abuse and violence. More than one in ten families where the total annual income exceeded $20,000 used abusive violence on their children during the survey year.

Manual workers (male and female) have rates of abusive violence toward children that are 45 percent higher than families where the husband and/or wife are white collar workers.

Part of the explanation for the difference in violence rates is the differential income earned by blue-collar as opposed to white-collar workers. Straus's examination of the national survey data supports the claim that low income and standard of living may relate to the higher level of parental violence in blue-collar families. Straus (1978) found that the child abuse rate for husbands who were dissatisfied with their standard of living was 61 percent greater than for other husbands (14.4% vs. 8.9%).

Another explanation for the higher rate of violence among manual workers may be the fact that they traditionally are more authoritarian with their children and believe that physical punishment is an effective child-rearing technique.

UNEMPLOYMENT AND UNDEREMPLOYMENT

In families where the husband was unemployed at the time of our interview, the rate of physical violence was 62 percent greater than for other families. In homes where the husband was employed part-time the rate was nearly double the rate of violence in homes where the husband was employed full-time.

Our findings are consistent with those of other investigators in finding that unemployment or underemployment is related to child abuse (Young, 1964; Steele & Pollock, 1974; Gil, 1970; Baldwin & Oliver, 1975).

Certainly it is obvious that not being able to hold down a full-time job or not having a job at all is a major problem for a man culturally bound to head a family. We recall one interview with a draftsman who had been laid off from a position with a shipbuilder. We conducted the interview a week after he was laid off. The layoff came on the very day that the man had signed a one-year lease for a new apartment. His wife was expecting a baby, and Christmas was only three months away. Although the man reported no violence, we wondered how different the interview might be if we returned in six months and he was still out of work.

STRESS

The more stress a family experiences in a year, the greater the chance that they will use severe violence on their children.

In order to measure how much stress the families we interviewed were under during the previous year, we asked questions about the types of problems they had encountered in the previous twelve months. There are, of course, an infinite variety of problems that a family can encounter. Moreover, something extremely stressful in one home might be considered a mild annoyance in another. To measure family stress, we administered a modified version of the Holmes and Rahe Stressful Life Events Scale (1967). Because of limited interview time, the scale was limited to the 18 items listed in Table 5.4.

There was a wide range of experiences among our 2143 families. Some individuals we talked to had encountered none of these problems in the last year. The maximum stress faced by our families was 13 out of a possible 18 stressful experiences. The average person we interviewed reported two stressful events in the last year.

We found that stress among the very poor and the well-to-do has no effect in terms of increasing the chances of child abuse within their families. But for the middle income families—those with earnings between $6000 and $20,000, increased stress does raise the risk of a child being physically abused.

The reason why stress does not increase the risk of child abuse among the poor and well-to-do seems to be their ability and likelihood of reacting

TABLE 5.4: Holmes and Rahe Stressful Life Events Scale (1967)

1. Troubles with boss	11. In-law troubles
2. Troubles with other people at work	12. Much worse off financially
3. Laid off or fired from work	13. Separated or divorced
4. Arrested or convicted for something serious	14. Big increase in the number of arguments with husband/wife/partner
5. Death of someone I felt close to	15. Big increase in hours worked or responsibility on the job
6. Foreclosure of mortgage or loan	
7. Pregnant or having a child born	16. Moved to a different neighborhood or town
8. Serious sickness or injury	
9. Serious problem with health or behavior of family member	17. Child kicked out of school or suspended
10. Sexual difficulties	18. Child caught doing something illegal

to stress. The poor, by virtue of being poor, encounter stress as a normal part of their lives. For the poor, stress is part of life; it is not a major crisis. An increase in stress is often considered inevitable. The rates of violence for the poor are already high. It would take much more extreme crises to push the rates higher still.

The well-to-do adapt to stress by using their financial resources to help alleviate problems. They can seek counseling for a personal or sexual problem. They can afford lawyers for a legal problem, and can cope with financial problems by drawing on savings or other resources.

This leaves us with the families making between $6000 and $20,000. They are the ones who struggle with every stressful event. Not poor enough to get welfare or food stamps, not well off enough to have financial security, they tend to resort to violence toward their children as a reaction to increased stress.

FAMILY STRUCTURE: CHILDREN AND POWER

Violence toward children varies by size of the family. Parents with two children have a rate of abusive violence 50 percent greater than parents with one child. The highest rate is among those with five children, while the lowest rate is for families with eight or more children (see Figure 5.1).

The largest families may be the least violent for a number of reasons. Perhaps parents with eight or nine children are simply too exhausted to raise a finger toward their children. But it may well be that the very largest families simply have less stress than five- or six-child homes. First, given that there is an average age span of two to three years between children, and that the odds of having twins and triplets are quite low, we can

FIGURE 5.1: Child abuse by number of children living at home

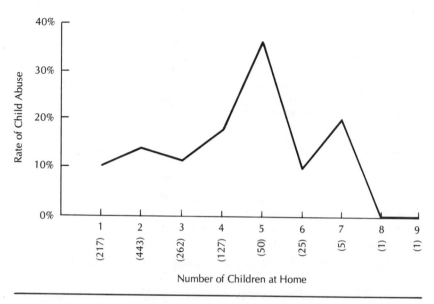

Source: Behind Closed Doors: Violence in the American Family. Murray A. Straus, Richard J. Gelles, and Suzanne K. Steinmetz. N.Y.: Anchor/Doubleday, 1979.

expect to find that a family which has an eighth child has at least one teenager at home. The oldest children may be a resource for the parents. They can baby-sit, help with the chores, bring in an additional income, and minimize the impact of the last in a parade of children. Another possibility is that those people who desire to have, and do raise such large families are so "child oriented" that they will be less violent no matter how many children they have.

Our most plausible explanation for the higher rates of violence among families with four, five, and six children, however, comes down to a matter of economic stress. Every new child means the family's economic pie is sliced smaller. As the strain on the pocketbook builds, parents' tempers tend to fray.

We found some important patterns when we examined the relationship of violence and the numbers of children among different income groups. Among the poorest families (annual family income under $6000), each additional child increases the likelihood of violence. The rate of abuse is 300 percent greater in two-child homes than in one-child house-holds. For those families whose income is between $6000 and $20,000 per year, the risk of child abuse increases with each child up to seven. In families with seven or more children living at home, there is no severe violence. Further, among well-to-do families who tend to have smaller families than those earning less money, there is no relationship between the number of children at home and the rate of child abuse.

FAMILY POWER

> *Violence toward children is more common in families where power (decision making) is concentrated in the hands of either the mother or father. In homes where power is shared, the rate of violence is half the rate for other families (see Figure 5.2).*

FIGURE 5.2: Child abuse by family power

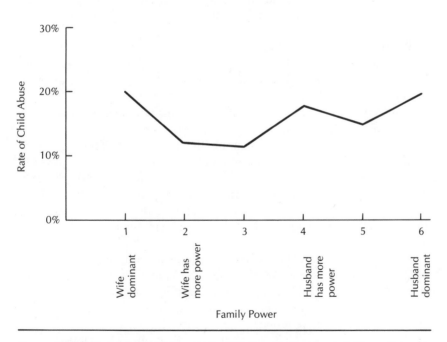

Source: Behind Closed Doors: Violence in the American Family. Murray A. Straus, Richard J. Gelles, and Suzanne K. Steinmetz. N.Y.: Anchor/Doubleday, 1979.

Democracy in the family tends to insulate the family from severe violence. Children who live with parents who share decision making are less likely to be abused physically than children in homes where either the mother or father make *all* the decisions. Clearly, the more inequality in a home, the greater the risk of severe parental violence.

EXPOSURE AND EXPERIENCE WITH VIOLENCE

"Children who grow up as abused children
will grow up to be abusive parents."

One of the consistent conclusions of research on abused children is the theory that being abused as a child increases the chances that a child will grow up to be an abusive adult (Steele & Pollock, 1974; Kempe et al., 1962; Gil, 1970). Unfortunately, the theory has often been misinterpreted. Many people see the theory as an example of "family determinism" and expect that *all* children who are abused will become abusing parents. Others, noting that not all children who are abused grow up to be abusers and also noting that some adults abuse children when they themselves were not victims of abuse, claim that the theory is not supported by the data.

We attempted to test the theory in our national survey of violence toward children. We asked our respondents how much violence they had experienced as teenagers (this age bracket was selected in order to increase recall of the experiences).

Eighteen and one-half percent of respondents who reported that their mothers had hit them more than twice a year reported using severe violence toward their own children during the survey year. This rate is 57 percent greater than the rate for respondents who experienced physical punishment less than twice a year—11.8 percent (Straus, 1978). Physical punishment by fathers made less difference. Respondents whose fathers hit them more than twice had a violence rate of 16.7 percent, while the rate for respondents whose fathers hit them less than twice was 13.2 percent.

It is clear from our data that children do learn to be violent to others by being victims of violence by their parents. While the relationship was not perfect (e.g., all children who are victims do not grow up to be violent), it is large enough to conclude that experience with violence as a child makes an adult more prone to use violence.

One of the surprises of our study was that observing violence was more important than actually being a victim of parental violence. Respondents who reported that they had observed their parents hit one another had a much higher rate of violence toward their own children than respondents who said they had never seen their parents hit each other (Straus, 1978).

Finally, we found that households where there was marital violence also had a high rate of violence toward children. The rate of severe violence toward children was 129 percent greater in homes where there was no marital violence—28 percent versus 12.2 percent (Straus, 1978).

There is no question that seeing or being a victim of violence in the home makes a difference in terms of later violent behavior. Moreover, the learning effect is probably enhanced by the insidious nature of family violence where, by and large, violence is used by people who claim to love and care for the child and also employ violence out of concern for the child.

The fact that observing and experiencing violence in the home increases the likelihood that an individual will engage in violent behavior should alert us to the negative effects of observing violence in other settings. There is reason, for example, to be concerned with how much violence children observe on television. One may not be able to prove that the learning is strictly imitative, but there is abundant evidence that children can learn to *approve* of violent acts and that approval of violence is a precondition of being violent. Secondly, we need to be concerned with the impact of children seeing and being victims of violence in other settings. The use of corporal punishment in the schools, behavior that is legally condoned by the Supreme Court, has the clear and present danger of creating, rather than preventing, violence.

CONCLUSION

Our study of violence toward children in the United States allows us to identify a number of factors that are associated with parents' use of severe violence toward their children. There were additional factors associated with violence toward children that are not covered in this paper and that are explained in detail in our complete report. Parents who swear and insult their children, are married less than 10 years, were physically punished by their parents as teenagers, have an above average level of husband-wife conflict, do not participate in organizations outside the home, have two or more children; and where the husband is a manual worker, the wife a full-time housewife, and where the husband is dissatisfied with his standard of living have the highest rates of severe violence toward children. Moreover, in families where none of these factors are present, there is *no abu-*

sive violence toward the children (Straus, Gelles, & Steinmetz, 1980, Chap. 9).

Our profile of violence toward children is useful for identifying the characteristics that are associated with abusive parental violence. But we must provide the caution that the profile is *not suitable for locating high-risk parents or predicting child abuse*. To use the profile as a predictive instrument would result in millions of instances of false labeling (in fact, more people would be incorrectly labeled than correctly labeled).

At best, our study has demonstrated which social factors are related to child abuse, and our study has the additional benefit of being generalizable to parents and children in the entire United States.

The findings reported here have clear implications for family policy. These include the need to reduce unemployment, the need to eliminate the devastating impact of being poor in an affluent society, and the need for community resources to alleviate the stress many families encounter. The study of violence toward children has advanced in recent years and we can speak with more assurance about what factors are related to parental violence. But the most important step, that of recognizing and implementing sound social policy that attempts to do something positive about the problem, will be more difficult and will take much more effort than the research enterprise that we report on here.

RECOMMENDATIONS FOR FUTURE RESEARCH

As we pointed out throughout the paper, the findings from our national survey of family violence are still tentative and require more refined analysis and interpretation. The survey did yield data from which inferences can be drawn and which are not confounded by vague definitions of child abuse and biased reporting practices.

We agree with Zigler's statement (in this volume) that knowledge about child abuse today is similar to the state of knowledge about mental illness in 1948. The present knowledge gap can only be filled if we apply more rigorous methods to the investigation of the causes of child abuse.

An important first step would be to forsake the endless search for the perfect general definition of child abuse and substitute specific nominal and operational definitions of specific behaviors. Two of the major roadblocks to knowledge building have been the general, all-encompassing definition of child abuse and for the purposes of research, the consideration of only those cases that are officially labeled as child abuse (Gelles, 1975b). If researchers were to move away from using only officially recorded cases of child abuse, the likelihood of selecting representative samples would increase. Presently, very little research is based on representative samples, and it has only been in the last few years that the majority of articles published on child abuse and family violence have included control groups in the sampling design.

One of the problems with our own survey was that it was cross-sectional. Because of this, we could not determine if the relationship between age and violence was due to a difference in generations or to a life-cycle difference. The same problem arose with assessing the relationship between number of children and violence; we could not determine whether the birth of a child increases the risk of abuse, or whether families that desire to have four or five children are abuse-prone. The only remedy to this problem, and the only way to reduce the number of plausible interpretations of the findings, would be to conduct longitudinal research on child abuse.

Lastly, there need to be more investigations that test theoretical explanations of the causes of child abuse. Too much of our present research is exploratory. Many of the explanations of the causes of child abuse are based on *ex post facto* interpretations of data (Spinetta & Rigler, 1972). We will only be able to improve our knowledge base with studies that set out to test empirically theories of child abuse.

We have come a long way in the past twenty years in the study of child abuse. Whereas the myths outnumbered the facts in the 1960s, research since 1968 has exploded many myths and replaced them with theoretically based hypotheses and sound empirical generalizations. Since we cannot hope to solve the problem of violence toward children until we understand the complex factors that cause parents to be abusively violent, it is imperative that we seek to advance and improve research on child abuse.

6

Primary Prevention
and Social Problems

George W. Albee

In considering how best to prevent child abuse, it seems important to examine the traditional models for prevention that have been developed to stem other plagues that have afflicted humankind. A number of difficulties become evident when child abuse is considered from an epidemiological point of view. Those difficulties attest to the problem of accurate prediction and assessment of behavior and to the crucial distinction between the prevention of disease and the prevention of psychopathological behavior. Difficulties stem, moreover, from entrenched social attitudes that characterize the thinking of the helping professions as well as of the general public.

It is essential to distinguish between primary prevention, on the one hand, and treatment or, in Gerald Caplan's terms, secondary prevention, on the other (Caplan, 1964). The literature on child abuse repeatedly confuses treatment with primary prevention. Public health doctrine holds that the mass disorders afflicting humankind are not eliminated by attempts at treating or intervening with each individual sufferer. While compelling humanitarian and moral arguments can favor one-to-one individual intervention—to ease suffering, to prevent contagion, to reduce or minimize the damaging consequences of the condition—only efforts at *primary prevention* have been demonstrated to be effective in eliminating a massive problem. This approach, usually referred to as the *public health approach*, may involve one of several possible strategies. One of them is finding the pathological or noxious agent and removing it. Removing or eliminating the microorganism causing an infectious disease may very well be the most important step in eliminating the condition. Adding materials to drinking water that kill disease-causing bacteria is an example of this approach. Thus, water purification has been a significant factor in eliminating several epidemic diseases. A second public health approach involves *strengthening the host*, and is characterized by raising the resistance of the population to the noxious or infectious agent. The ingestion of nutritious food, or vaccination with causative agents rendered inert or attenuated, such as the polio vaccines, helps the body build up its resistance (see Albee & Joffe, 1977).

PRIMARY PREVENTION AND MENTAL HEALTH

Professionals in mental health have employed related strategies in the field of mental and emotional disturbances. For example, efforts at controlling the level of environmental stress reduce the number and seriousness of emotional disturbances that result from such stress. Raising the capacity of large numbers of individuals to cope with stresses also has a preventive effect.

Serious efforts toward the primary prevention of child abuse must involve programs aimed at large population groups who do not yet show any evidence of child abuse. Working with parents or with others who have already been recognized as child abusers is not primary prevention, but *treatment*. This is important and humanitarian work and can reduce the damage to the child that might otherwise ensue, but it will not help to safeguard children who have not yet experienced harm. Epidemiological studies may locate *high risk groups* and focus prevention efforts on them, but when the focus is on individuals who show the disorder to be prevented, treatment, not prevention, is involved.

In 1977–78, the Task Panel on Prevention of the President's Commission on Mental Health (1978b, Vol. 4, Appendix) reviewed the research literature on primary prevention. The panel developed a fairly uncomplicated model that organized most of these data. It suggested to the President's Commission that the incidence of emotional disturbance and distress is related to five more or less separate and discrete factors. For descriptive purposes these five elements were put into a fraction. The equation goes something like this: An increase in both *organic determinants* and in *stress* increases the incidence of the disturbance; these two factors were put in the numerator of the fraction. Increases in *coping skills*, in *self-esteem*, and in available *support groups* reduce the incidence of emotional distress; these three factors were put in the denominator of the fraction. Each of these factors can be applied to child abuse.

In considering *organic conditions* that might be related to child abuse, a variety of factors may directly influence the basic health of parents and, indirectly, such variables as their frustration tolerance. Research with both animals and people has shown quite clearly that an inadequate diet, insufficient sleep, and overcrowding all stimulate aggressive behavior. A number of Swedish studies (see Carlestam & Levi, 1971) have shown the relationship between overcrowded living conditions and sleep deprivation. Poor people simply do not get as much sleep as the affluent. They often live in overcrowded housing, in noisy and physically uncomfortable surroundings. An excess of heat in summer and of cold in winter characterizes housing conditions in city ghettoes and rural slums. No insulation mutes the noises of the city streets, the blaring radio, the crying baby. Lack of money, lack of transportation, and lack of storage facilities all doom the poor to crowded quarters and to quickly prepared nonnutritious food. All of this, combined with deprivation of rest and sleep, constant noise, and the lack of a place to withdraw to, jangle the nerves and lower frustration tolerance and the threshold of aggressiveness. Clearly, most of the physical and organic conditions just described can also be interpreted as stressful. There are numerous other sources of *stress*: unemployment, discrimination, and the denial of basic human rights. Each is stressful and all are cumulative.

As an individual's or group's coping skills *increase*, emotional distress *decreases*. Poverty reduces a person's repertoire of available adaptive coping resources. The middle-class family, living in suburbia, can send children to nursery schools or to summer camp; it can afford babysitters and the expense of recreational leave-time. A fenced-in suburban backyard reduces the necessity for constant vigilance of the parent over the young child. The dwellings of the poor are not well adapted to child care, especially of young children. Lack of money makes preschool and babysitting impossible. Crowding exacerbates frustration and stress, and builds its intensity.

Increases in support systems and in self-esteem have been shown to reduce psychopathology. Poverty and unemployment, membership in minority groups, being female in a sexist society, all reduce self-esteem and natural support systems (Albee, 1979). Child abusers frequently are described as isolated, lonely people with poor self-esteem (Wooden, 1976). The evidence that these variables influence the incidence of other forms of psychopathology would suggest they are also related to rates of child abuse (see Albee & Joffe, 1977).

There is reason to believe that the preventive benefits of putting fluoride in drinking water will reach most persons in an area and will affect all, including those at high risk for tooth decay who constitute a large portion of the population. But because the prevention of child abuse unquestionably will turn out to be more complicated than the prevention of tooth decay, and the number of cases unquestionably is a smaller percentage of the total population, primary prevention would be appropriate for groups identified as high risks.

The Danger of "False Positives"

If the figures in the literature are accurate, one child in 100, at most, is subject to parental abuse each year and the rate may be as low as one in 1000 (Zigler; Gelles, this volume). But there is a statistical problem in trying to predict which parents will be abusive: the smaller the group to be identified, and the lower the reliability of the technique, the more "false positives" will occur. In other words, there is a danger of labeling as potentially abusive a large number of parents who indeed will turn out to be nonabusive (Light, 1973).

Predicting at random which parents will be abusive raises grave issues involving the important freedom of persons to be left alone. It also raises the danger of labeling a potentially abusive parent erroneously. The problem is very similar to the problem of predicting *dangerousness* in mental cases. For a great many years our society has used the allegation that these individuals are potentially dangerous to others and that society must protect itself by locking them up so they cannot carry out their predicted dangerous behavior as an excuse for incarcerating persons with "mental diseases." Nearly every textbook describes, as one of the criteria for labeling a person as mentally ill, the probability of dangerous acts. However, when we look at the literature concerning the prediction of dangerousness we find that successful prediction is rare. It turns out that mental patients as a group do *not* commit a large number of dangerous acts. Even those committed to hospitals for the criminally insane have relatively modest rates of dangerous behavior—and this is true even when they are transferred to other mental hospitals for administrative or social reasons. "Former mental patients" commit no more crimes than other persons from their own socioeconomic groups who have never been hospitalized or identified as mental cases.

Alan Stone, a Harvard psychiatrist and attorney, has reviewed the research evidence on the prediction of dangerousness. He concludes:

It can be stated flatly on the basis of my own review of the published material on the prediction of dangerous acts that neither objective actuarial tables nor psychiatric intuition, diagnosis, and psychological testing can claim predictive success when dealing with the traditional population of mental hospitals. (1975, p. 33)

This inadequacy leads to the statistical problem of "false positives." Because the rate of dangerousness among mental patients is relatively low, and because the accuracy of our techniques for its prediction are relatively weak, the prediction of dangerousness is itself a dangerous activity because of the many false positives involved. Some figures illustrate the problem well. If the test to predict dangerousness is 90 percent accurate (and no test exists with this high level of accuracy), and if the rate of dangerousness among mental cases is only one in one hundred, then of one thousand persons tested for dangerousness, nine of the ten actually dangerous persons in the group will be correctly identified, but we will *mislabel* as dangerous ten percent, or one hundred of the one thousand screened. So to find ten dangerous persons, one hundred will be incorrectly stigmatized.

Obviously, the rarer the rate of the condition to be identified and the lower the reliability of the test used to identify it, the more "false positives" who will be incorrectly labeled and thus stigmatized in the process. We must be wary of identifying future child abusers. Many will be unjustly labeled, and we may stigmatize the innocent and even cause self-fulfilling prophecies.

An argument immediately comes to mind. It suggests that we only deal with those persons who have *already* demonstrated that they are child abusers. Why not focus our work on the parents whose children have been beaten or otherwise abused? I can only point out that this approach is *not* primary prevention. As soon as individual, one-to-one intervention with identified problem-individuals begins, the process engaged in is treatment. While few would oppose the importance of this kind of personal intervention, it is *not* primary prevention. The number of children who are abused, according to the United States Office of Child Development, lies somewhere between 50,000 and 500,000 a year. But even if we use the largest estimate, this means that the number of abused children is no more than one in 100, and with the low reliability of our methods of early identification, we are squarely in the bind of erroneous prediction of false positives.

The Defect Model

There is another significant danger implicit in planning the primary prevention of child abuse. Experience with other social problems has identified the danger of locating the source of behavioral problems like child abuse as an individual defect *inside* the perpetrator. The widely used *defect model* comes in several convenient forms. The origin of child abuse may be attributed to a defect in the personality structure of the parent, or the tendency to abuse children may be explained as a genetic, or biological, weakness or inferiority. Defect explanations have in common an enormously reassuring quality. They absolve society, and the prevailing social institutions, of any responsibility. They suggest that prevention take the form of individual medication, genetic counseling, mutual support groups, and so forth. Whatever else, they inhibit any serious consideration of a reorganization and revolution in the structure of our social and economic institutions. William Ryan describes the process in *Blaming the Victim* (1971). Ryan shows in clear detail how social science has been able to explain away low educational achievement, high rates of out-of-wedlock pregnancies, and other forms of social pathology in the poor as a result of faults to be found *in the victim*.

INSTITUTIONAL ABUSE

It is also very easy, with the best intentions, and apparently the best will in the world, to work up a sense of wrath, indignation, and anger at parents who mistreat and abuse their children; but what justification do professionals have for their punitive views held toward abusive parents when they all participate in a conspiracy that brutalizes and abuses at least as many other children, in situations that they have the power to change or influence but where they rarely lift a finger to make changes? More specifically, on any given day there are 8000 to 10,000 juveniles held in adult jails in the United States (Wooden, 1976). Each year more than 100,000 young people spend time in adult jails or police lock-ups. In the majority of cases these children are locked up with adults who often abuse and exploit them. Most of the jails in the states that detain juveniles with adults have no supervisory personnel to protect the children from rape, brutalization, and molestation. Thousands of other children are locked up in institutions for "juvenile offenders," although many of the "offenses" these children commit involve only invoking the disapproval of their very existence by parents, schools, and law enforcement officials. Many of them are guilty of no crimes. In many states children have no rights to legal counsel and often institutions enjoy strong political patronage and protection. Children are sent to them at high maintenance and treatment costs, not because they are helpful, but because of politics and profit. The institutions have ways to encourage political protection and support. Efforts at closing them or modifying institutional practices almost always run into the vested interests of proprietors, employees, and the communities in which they are located. Frequently the institution provides the major source of employment and commerce for a particular town or county. Any effort at changing their programs, or closing the institution, elicits immediate community rage and political action that result in the continuation of the institution and of the barbaric and abusive practices that are so common in them. There are unwritten sweetheart contracts between elected officials and heads of these institutions. Children are incarcerated who clearly do not belong behind locked doors but who are delivered for expensive care that turns out to be only dehumanizing and brutal (Wooden, 1976; Forer, 1977; Richette, 1969).

This whole system of institutionalization is a major source of child abuse that is ripe for preventive action. Several recent books such as Kenneth Wooden's *Weeping in the Playtime of Others* document the problem in detail. Read it and weep. For years major newspapers throughout the country have exposed the horrible and inhumane conditions in the juvenile penal system. Professionals have read about physical beatings, sexual abuse, solitary confinement, brutal punishment. Social critics like Burton Blatt (this volume) have exposed the sadistic guards, the political payoffs, the overcrowding, yet all of these conditions continue. Most of us have also read of the thousands of youthful runaways, many of them between the ages of eleven and fifteen, who get into the clutches of exploiters, of vultures—the pimps and the chicken hawks—who subject these children to the most unbelievable abuse. If the "helping professions" are seriously interested in the prevention of child abuse why have they not taken concerted action on all of these kinds of child abuse? How long are the "helpers" going to remain silent while major tranquilizers are given indiscriminately to incarcerated children (Forer, 1977)? Those seriously interested in the prevention of child abuse should be actively involved in efforts at reforming the whole entangled legislative-judicial-incarceration system that does so much damage to children (Richette, 1969).

Indeed, this situation suggests that each of our professions determine the extent to which it participates in the widespread application of the *defect model* and its damaging consequences. Professions have a history of finding ways to justify the exploitation and neglect of groups of people by labeling them defective. The defect model has existed for a very long time. It suggests that there are large groups of people who, by virtue of their membership in a class that is tainted or defective, do not deserve the kind of respect or treatment accorded to the fortunate classes. Examples of the defect model abound in the history of our disciplines and our society. It has been used to justify slavery, to explain the higher rates of idiocy and lunacy among the immigrant Irish (and subsequently to explain the higher rates of idiocy and lunacy among every other immigrant group arriving in our cities), and as an excuse for discrimination against women. A hundred years ago Edward Jarvis (1855), one of the leading psychiatrists of his day, and one of the best known names in the field and in the history of psychiatry, had this amazing report on the high coincidence of poverty and idiocy and lunacy among the immigrant Irish:

> In this connection it is worthwhile to look somewhat at the nature of poverty, its origins, and its relationship to society. It is usually considered as a single outward circumstance—the absence of worldly goods; but this want is a mere incident to this condition—only one of its manifestations. Poverty is an inward principle, and rooted deeply within the man, and running through all his elements; it reaches his body, his health, his intellect, and his moral powers as well as his estate . . . hence we find that, among those whom the world calls poor, there is less vital force, a lower tone of life, more ill health, more weakness, more early death, a diminished longevity. There are also less self-respect, ambition, and hope, more idiocy and insanity, and more crime, than among the independent. (p. 52)

Those who shrug off this statement as something written more than a century ago will have to explain away Moynihan, Jensen, Shockley, and Eysenck, all of whom have found defects in the blacks, or the poor, to account for their lower IQ test scores, or their poverty, or their social pathology (see Albee, 1979).

The defect model continues to be used to account for schizophrenia and most other forms of "mental illness," which the organicists in psychiatry say are all due to genetic defects, or to biochemical dysfunction; the defect model continues to be applied today to account for the lack of educational and economic achievement by blacks, Puerto Ricans, Chicanos, and other minority groups, as well as to explain lower levels of achievement in women. How many times have we heard, subtly or blatantly, that each of these groups is biologically different—their brains are smaller, less convoluted, different: "They" are incapable of abstract thought, of creativity, and so forth. We cannot treat them, the argument goes, because they are defective. So we lock them up: in ghettoes, in back wards, in the kitchens and bedrooms.

If we have learned anything from widespread use of the defect model to account for differences in achievement or economic success, we should look with great suspicion on the application of this same explanation in the field of child abuse. Epidemiological evidence is cited throughout the literature to show that child abuse is more common among the poor, among the dehumanized, the down-trodden, the exploited, and the disadvantaged. It is just a short step to the conclusion that abuse is inherent in the nature of "these people." A very great danger exists that we will continue to find a *common principle* to explain both poverty and child abuse. "The reason you are poor," some may say, "is that you are inferior. The reason you are abusive is that you are naturally brutal."

Twenty years ago Paul Goodman argued prophetically in *Growing Up Absurd* (1956) that the problems of children and youth reflect problems in our political and economic system and that only social change will improve the lot of youth. This is a threatening message because it places blame on a dehumanizing social structure rather than on inherent defect. Obviously the remedy will require a redistribution of power, and power, as we all know, is not given up voluntarily. It is better strategy to kill the messenger!

Abrogating social change threatens the common value assumption underlying both psychiatric and psychological defect model explanations of delinquency, lunacy, and idiocy. The accepted assumption holds that persons who are not members of the middle-class and upper-class, Protestant-ethic, Nordic groups are clearly inferior. The higher rates of both idiocy and lunacy in these inferior groups are a result of constitutional defect. The defect is not limited, however, to members of these inferior races and cultures. It also applies to women. As a result, our treatment efforts have neglected these groups. The report of the President's Commission on Mental Health (1978a) belies any suggestion that this accusation is unjustified or of only historical relevance. The unserved and underserved are identified as children, adolescents, the elderly, blacks, Hispanics, Indians, migrant farm workers, persons with alcohol problems, with learning disabilities, the mentally retarded, the physically handicapped. In short, of the 35 million Americans with serious problems, only 7 million a year are even being seen in all our mental health facilities.

Mordechai Rotenberg (1978) at Hebrew University has written extensively and insightfully about the similarities between the Calvinist religious model of predestination that divides people into the saved and the damned and the models we use in the psychiatric field that separate people into the treatable and the defective. Clearly, we neglect those who are different, damaged, inferior—in short, the damned! The alternative to a Calvinist model is one that explains people's emotional problems as originating in their social environment and therefore as preventable through social change.

A Social Learning Model

A social learning model to account for child abuse would require social change as the road to prevention. It suggests that people are in large and significant measure a product of their social environment. This approach has different kinds of implications from a defect model. If people are indeed a product of their social history, then prevention of many of the conditions with which our professional fields have been concerned means changing the social conditions. But this idea threatens economic arrangements that are very profitable. Moreover, it threatens the psychiatric establishment because it suggests that even battered children may become parents who are loving and supportive if their social worlds are more supportive and lead to improvements in self-esteem and competence. It implies that abusive parenting is not caused by internal defect but rather by the lack of access to jobs, housing, and educational opportunities controlled by those who control the system.

We should seriously consider the connection between the self-esteem of adults and the way they treat their children. We find little research bearing directly on this hypothesis, although there is much that supports it indirectly. A strong possibility exists that those with a low level of self-esteem do not esteem others, including their children. Their children are the recipients of some of the aggression that characterizes their attitudes toward themselves and their miserable lives. A cross-cultural study reported by James W. Prescott (1979) has some relevant data here. He found that in those cultures where a large amount of affection is bestowed on infants there is relatively low physical violence by the adults in the society. On the other hand, in those cultures where infants are *not* dealt with affectionately, the adult society is highly aggressive. In the cultures that did not follow this common pattern the significant variable seems to be related to sexual permissiveness. Cultures that repressed and forbade many sexual activities tended to be more violent than those with considerable sexual permissiveness. From his study of 49 different societies Prescott concluded that physical pleasure inhibits physical violence. Social and political changes that give everyone greater self-esteem, a greater sense of personal worth, and more relaxed and enjoyable sexuality are threatening to a Protestant ethic that values hard work, exploitation for profit, and sexual repression.

Child Abuse and Oppression: The Weak and the Strong

The topic of child abuse evokes deep feelings, passionate concern, and ardor. Why is this so? Elsewhere I have argued how three million years of natural selection in the course of human evolution led to a deeply in-grained human need to nurture children. If natural selection is a meaning-ful concept, then it is hard to argue against this trait as a profoundly im-portant part of human nature. The long infancy and child helplessness of the human animal simply means that survival occurred only for those who had parents who were nurturant and supportive. If the need to care for and support infants is an important component in human nature, then dis-tortions and perversions of this need might be expected to elicit feelings of repugnance and revulsion.

But there is a more psychological explanation for our deep emotional reaction to child abuse. A significant part of the emotional reaction may be a displacement of feelings that reflects our deep concern and guilt over other patterns of exploitation and oppression in which *we are ourselves involved* on the side of the exploiters and the oppressors. Perhaps our in-tense feelings about child abuse, our anger at the abusers, are somehow deflections of our hatred of ourselves for being responsible for many kinds of abuse of the powerless.

What is child abuse but the heartless wreaking of damage and de-struction by the powerful on the powerless? It is not even a contest. The powerful parent, or other adult, who abuses the helpless child is relatively safe from retaliation. But most exploiters and manipulators act out of low fear of retaliation. Perhaps someone can explain the symbolic difference between child abuse and rape; between child abuse and the exploitation of migrant farm workers; between child abuse and incarceration of hun-dreds of thousands of those hapless and hopeless mental cases locked in the hellholes we call mental hospitals; between child abuse and genocide; between child abuse and torture of political prisoners—the terrible, unfor-givable things that brutal persons everywhere do to their victims. There are so many examples of the exploitation of the weak by the strong, that a continuing recitation would soon leave the reader refractory and numb. These exploitations are such an integral part of our culture that we have developed a callousness, a blindness, as a defense against our own aware-ness of our own participation.

When we remain silent in the face of any kind of oppression of the weak by the strong; when we tolerate the cynical manipulation of public opinion, the hucksters and influence peddlers; when a veil falls over our eyes as we see the exploiters respected; when we see evidence that the meek will never inherit the earth, or anything else, we are like the child abusers. What a cathartic experience it is to feel righteous indignation and wrath against child abusers. Do not misunderstand. Child abuse is a terri-ble thing, but so is every other form of tyranny. Where is this argument leading? It suggests that child abuse is part of a much larger problem of exploitation of the weak by the strong.

In his brilliant paper on the social responsibilities of psychology Kenneth B. Clark (1974) pointed out that "any form of rejection, cruelty, and injustice inflicted upon any group of human beings by any other group of human beings *dehumanizes* the victims overtly and in more subtle ways dehumanizes the perpetrators" (p. 144). He called on his colleagues to stop avoiding the moral and survival problems of the human race and to try to enhance the human capacity for creativity and progress. He argued that it is imperative for us to seek to mobilize our methods, research, and practice to understand more precisely and to reinforce the nature of the positives within humankind and to control the destructive forces within society.

After a long review of the literature of primary prevention, Kessler and Albee (1975) concluded about power:

> It is tempting to search for a simple formula to cover all of the complexities of environmental stress in causing disruptive behavior and emotional problems. It is tempting to suggest an extension to the human environment of Lord Acton's (23) dictum: "Power tends to corrupt—absolute power corrupts absolutely." Everywhere we looked, every social research study we examined suggested that major sources of human stress and distress generally involve some form of excessive power. The pollutants of a power-consuming industrial society; the exploitation of the weak by the powerful; the overdependence of the automotive culture on powerful engines—power-consuming symbols of potency; the degradation of the environment with the debris of a comfort-loving impulse-yielding society; the power struggle between the rich consuming nations and the exploited third world; the angry retaliation of the impoverished and the exploited; on a more personal level the exploitation of women by men, of children by adults, of the elderly by the youth-worshiping society—it is enough to suggest the hypothesis that a dramatic reduction and control of power might improve the mental health of people.

Similarly, Ryan (1971) writes: "We have failed to understand the nature of humanness and to provide for its nurturance; we have restricted people's ability to act effectively on their own behalf" (p. 242–243).

Do we want to prevent child abuse? Do we want to prevent sexism? Racism? Ageism? Or other forms of victimization? If we do, we must redistribute social and economic power. It is as simple, and as difficult, as that.

7

Child Abuse:
A Comparative Perspective

Alfred J. Kahn and Sheila B. Kamerman

Cross-national study in any field of social policy can provide a valuable perspective and an understanding of alternative policy options. Such perspective is badly needed in the child abuse field in the United States. Recent Congressional hearings suggest that federal funds may have created a large new "industry," but not necessarily more responsive intervention and more effective prevention (U.S. Congress, 1977).

Since cross-national studies must be precise and specific to be of use, they have the effect of reducing the hysteria that has resulted from high abuse rates based on loose counting and shifting parameters. The problem of child abuse is important, but no one knows if it is growing; no one has a good count; everyone knows that advocates of more provision in the United States often play a loose numbers game.[1]

PROTECTIVE PROGRAMS: THE HISTORICAL BACKGROUND

All industrialized countries take account of children who are abused and neglected. Early social services for children probably began with dependent or homeless children and turned later to the neglected when society was willing to intervene more often in inadequate family situations. The same mechanism, however, dealt with both categories and often failed to distinguish sharply between them. The current variations among countries in

1. This article draws heavily from Alfred J. Kahn and Sheila B. Kamerman, 1976. The countries covered in this study in addition to the United States are: Canada, United Kingdom, Federal Republic of Germany, France, Poland, Yugoslavia, Israel.

response to abuse and neglect can be explained by varying definitions of the problem, varying responsibility for intervention, and the nature of this intervention.

Basic shifts have occurred, historically, and continue to occur as values change. What was once defined as acceptable behavior often becomes unacceptable, over time. When children are no longer considered as the sole property of parents, to do with as they wish, society begins to assume an obligation to protect children against grossly inadequate care and (in some places) to ensure the adequacy of the care they receive. The definition of adequacy changes constantly. The central question is that of criteria for assessing adequacy or inadequacy of care and the specific nature of the protection provided.

Services for abused and neglected children, then, are services designed to protect children. Indeed, in all countries the relevant basic policies and programs are described as "protective" services, the very core of traditional child welfare services, and only in a very few places is any effort made at distinguishing abused from neglected children or from maltreated children generally. In even fewer countries are there laws and programs specifically designed to intervene in the problem of child abuse per se. To provide the proper context for discussing child abuse, it is helpful to examine protective services across national lines. "All agencies concerned with child welfare," according to a leading American work on child welfare services,

> may be said to be protective agencies. In the more specialized use of the term, the protective agency is an agency that is given special responsibility in cases of child abuse, exploitation, and neglect. Such agencies are often delegated, usually by charter, some specific authority to act for the community in its collective expression of concern for children. (Kadushin, 1967, p. 204)

Protective agencies or services have in common several major attributes. The client is generally there involuntarily. The agency action is initiated by a person other than the client, or by a community agency. The agency's actions are legally sanctioned. The focus of service is usually an adult, even though primary concern may rest with the child. Finally, protective service agencies use a wide variety of services in their efforts to help families deal with problems. Protective agencies traditionally have two sets of tasks: they monitor and administer rules of employment and related statutes to prevent exploitation and mistreatment of children; and they seek out or receive reports of mistreatment of children and intervene to prevent, punish, rescue, or treat.

Protective services for children emerged in the late nineteenth century in the United Kingdom and the United States. They grew from a specific concern for abused and neglected children. All seven countries studied now have some legislation that identifies parental obligations and responsibilities regarding the care of children. That legislation specifies penalties or consequences for failure to provide adequate care when there has been mistreatment.

Initially, protective programs removed children from neglectful parents and placed them in institutional care. Later, children considered neglected or abused entered long-term foster care or were adopted. One initial distinction in court cases was whether the child suffered from a parental "omission" or from "commission." Warning, advice, practical help, counseling, and, later, court review or administrative processes occurred before final action. Slightly later financial aid, including mothers' pensions in early twentieth-century America, or children's allowances in post-World War II Europe, became "preventive" tools and social assistance came to be viewed as an aid in treating families.

The 1960s: Activists Rally
to the Cause of the Physically Abused Child

Since the mid-1960s there has been particular concern in the United States with one subgroup of children in need of care, the physically abused children, always technically subsumed under child protection. Increasingly, these children have received special attention in law and policy, and special programs have been instituted to intervene in this problem. Some reformers declared traditional child welfare services inadequate. A special category of services for abused and neglected children that evolved in the United States provides the entry point for discussion of these services generally, cross-nationally.

The special and heightened concern with the subcategory of services for abused and neglected children emerged in the United States during the 1960s through the combined efforts of pediatricians, lawyers, and social workers. Concerned physicians made the phenomenon of child abuse more visible by distinguishing a separate "battered child" syndrome, characterized by the presence of severe, nonaccidental injuries in very young children. They felt that traditional child welfare measures had not protected these children. Hospital emergency room case-finding disclosed need for new alertness. New diagnostic and case-finding techniques were invented and publicized for hospital use in distinguishing accidents from battering. At the same time, the civil rights movement in this country and its lawyer-advocates noted that the rights of children, a politically powerless group, were inadequately guarded. Those advocates wanted more child protection and, at the same time, less agency arbitrariness.

Highlighting the inconsistencies and nonspecificity of existing legislation, and the inadequacies and fragmentation of services, these doctors and lawyers were joined by groups of social workers and others in related human services. Concern with improved case-finding and child protection emerged at the same time as a strong movement against the unnecessary removal of children from the homes of their natural parents for reasons of poverty, ethnic or social group membership, or inadequate housing. Children's advocates focused on the inadequacy of funding and manpower resources available for protective services, the lack of attention to the growing body of knowledge regarding children's needs and the factors contributing to wholesome child development, the failure to implement laws and regulations designed to protect children, and the absence of sanctions or authority for integrating the multiplicity of services needed by deprived families. The movement for children's rights and the campaign for improved programs for the abused and neglected were thus mutually enforcing, even though their real connections and even full consistency are not necessarily clear.

Protective services continue to play an important role in the general personal social services system. Insight into how other countries handle the problems of child abuse and neglect and the extent to which those services are viewed as subcategories for service delivery is important to consideration of social service delivery strategies.

DEFINITIONS OF CHILD ABUSE

Although conceptual definitions of child abuse and neglect exist, there are as yet no clear, consistent, agreed-upon, operational definitions of these phenomena. Abuse is sometimes defined as one broad problem category encompassing several subcategories of problems (physical abuse, sexual abuse, emotional deprivation, negligent or inadequate care); sometimes as one narrowly defined problem (the battered child); sometimes as two separate and distinct problems (abuse and neglect). Some definitions are oriented toward the behavior of the perpetrators (parents) and some toward the consequences of such behavior (the child's symptoms). Some include actual behavior (or consequences of this behavior) only; others include potential for abusive behavior as part of the problem. Certainly, how the problem is defined determines perspectives on size and gravity of the problem(s), as well as on policy, program, and the whole range of efforts involved in solving it (them).

The major United States federal legislation passed in 1974 defined abuse and neglect as a single entity and focused on both the behavior of the child's caretaker and the consequences of the act, but ignored the question of intent. Despite that broad definition, encompassing both abuse and neglect, most attention in the recent campaign for case-finding and service innovation focuses on one aspect alone: the physical abuse of children.

Most European countries have tended to view child abuse and neglect as part of the general problem of maltreatment of children, although the recently publicized United States initiatives have led to clear cultural diffusion, through the activity of national and international committees, commissions, and task forces. Nevertheless, European policies still seek to combat child abuse within the framework of protective services for children. This view is reflected in the British delineation of a continuum that includes "cruelty, ill treatment, and neglect" of children, with physical abuse defined as only one aspect of the problem, albeit the most severe and most visible. In Poland and Yugoslavia the problem is defined even more loosely: in Yugoslavia, as inadequate care of children by parents, and, in Poland, as a problem of children deprived of good care.

Canada and the Federal Republic of Germany report a distinction similar to that made by David Gil between child abuse (the "intentional, nonaccidental use of physical force, or intentional, nonaccidental acts of omission on the part of a parent or other caretaker" [Gil, 1970]) and child neglect (the unintentional acts that result in harm to a child). Both, however, acknowledge that it is nearly impossible to act upon this distinction since it depends on an accurate assessment of the perpetrators' motivations. Moreover, in these countries as well as in several others, one other question is raised, related to the difficulty in distinguishing "reasonable parental discipline and punishment" from child abuse. This gray area exists in the United States with regard to corporal punishment of children generally, both at home by parents and at school by teachers.

Obviously, the variations in definition affect estimates of the size and gravity of this problem. Nowhere are there firm data regarding the incidence of abuse or neglect although, in the United States especially, some spokesmen have given the impression of precision. On the contrary, all countries acknowledge that only loose and wide-ranging estimates exist and that such figures are probably meaningless. Similarly, although in some countries the problem is described as apparently more prevalent among the poor, all reporters insist that even where this seems to be the case (United Kingdom, Israel, Canada), the probability is that this population is more exposed to public view and to public authorities through social agencies. Therefore, incidents are more likely to be identified and counted among the lower classes than among the middle and upper classes. Reports from the United States, the Federal Republic of Germany, and France fail to indicate firm evidence of class differentials regarding the absolute incidence of abuse.

LEGISLATION

As mentioned earlier, all seven countries studied have some kind of legislation designed to protect children against abuse, neglect, and maltreatment generally. Only in the United States, however, and in some Canadian provinces, is there legislation to deal with the specific problem of child abuse as distinct from all other aspects of ill-treatment. Legislation passed in 1975 in the United Kingdom in response to public arousal about child abuse following several publicized and upsetting cases did supplement the laws by requiring the appointment of a guardian ad litem to represent the child's interests in court cases involving maltreatment, and to protect the child's rights where questions of care are concerned. In Great Britain, as in the United States, the direction of reform in foster care and adoption is to introduce legal protection for the child's interests apart from those of parents, agency, or substitute parent; to give authority to measures which protect or reconstitute the natural family; and to avoid placement if possible. At the same time, the intent is to make termination of parental rights easier if that is in the child's interest or if family reconstitution is obviously unlikely, and to simplify for foster parents the transition to adoption when "in the best interests of the child." (These are, of course, hardly simple matters and often reflect interests and motives in conflict.)

Policy in the United Kingdom continues to emphasize nonlegal intervention. In this system it is not enough to prove that a child is neglected, ill-treated, or receiving inadequate care. For a court to justify legal intervention, it must be convinced that adequate care would be "unlikely" without judicial intervention.

Although all these countries permit court intervention under certain circumstances, it in fact occurs relatively infrequently. In France, the court may intervene if a child is in clear danger, but there is no automatic implication of parental guilt if such intervention occurs. In the Federal Republic of Germany, the rights of parents are still considered paramount although legislation passed in the mid-1970s reflected a trend toward greater concern with children's rights here, too. Parental rights are forfeited if and when a parent is sentenced to prison for at least six months for a crime against his (or her) child. As a result, judges rarely impose a sentence of more than 5 months. In general, few parents are convicted of child abuse in the Federal Republic of Germany, which is one of the few countries in this group still specifying punitive action against parents in problems of abuse.

The initial major reflection of concern with the problem of abuse is enactment of mandatory reporting legislation. Again, only the United States has legislation in all its states mandating reporting and protecting those who do so. Some provinces in Canada mandate reporting, and interestingly enough, there does not seem to be any noticeable difference in reported incidence between provinces that do and do not mandate reporting. Reporting is also mandatory in France and in Yugoslavia, but in the latter country there are no penalties for failure to report suspected abuse. In Israel, the Federal Republic of Germany,[2] and the United Kingdom, reporting procedures exist, but their use is not mandatory, although there is some discussion about making them so.

Mandatory reporting, it may be noted, is intended to protect professionals against legal liability, improve case-finding, and create general public awareness of the problem. All that is certain thus far is that case totals or rosters increase as a result.

Special services for abused and neglected children as well as protective services generally involve a variety of services administered and operated under the aegis of different service systems. In all countries, responsibility for setting policy as well as developing and operating programs is under some combination of welfare and judicial auspices. In most countries, the health and educational systems are involved as well. Although the voluntary agencies play an active role everywhere, the public sector is predominant either directly, through provision of services, or indirectly, through the funding of the relevant voluntary agencies. In all countries except Yugoslavia the national government sets some (usually limited) policies (Canada, Federal Republic of Germany, United States) or determines much of what will occur (United Kingdom, France, Poland, Israel), and the local authorities—or voluntary agencies as surrogates—actually operate programs.

More specifically, in the United States, most legislation directed at the problem of abused and neglected children is enacted at the state level, and rests in the domain of the child welfare departments of social service agencies. The Canadian provinces and regional court systems provide an exact parallel. Although some special federal legislation has been enacted in the United States, its intent is to create awareness and exchange of experience. It is devoted largely to the funding of research and demonstration

2. In contrast, reporting is mandatory in the German Democratic Republic.

projects around the country and does not mandate any activity. Several research centers, clearinghouses, and publications have been subsidized, as have conferences and training activities. Federal legislation assigns a lead role in this activity to a national center located in the Administration for Children, Youth, and Families in the Department of Health, Education, and Welfare.

Although several countries carry out public educational programs concerning abuse, designed to improve recognition of its manifestations and to increase the reporting rate, no country distinguishes between protective services programs generally and the mechanisms for dealing with child abuse. And all are concerned by the gap between educational efforts and policy, on the one hand, and effective implementation, on the other.

PROGRAMS AND SERVICES

Legislation and funding in the United States have led to a variety of experiments with special subcategorized services for dealing with abused children. Although Canada, Israel, and the United Kingdom have a few demonstration projects that are similar to the newer American programs, the approach in most countries we studied has been to improve and enhance protective service programs by sensitizing staff to the problem of abuse, but not by establishing new symptom-specific services.

The ignorance and lack of knowledge that almost inevitably accompany a phenomenon as deeply implicated in the complexity of social values and social change as child abuse characterize all efforts at intervening in abuse cases. Social workers and physicians discuss prevention, but can do little regarding so vaguely delineated a phenomenon outside of supporting good social policies for families and children (adequate income, housing, employment, health services) and good opportunities for socialization. The French, in particular, stress the importance of family policy and public policy explicitly designed to support and benefit families with young children. Several other countries emphasize the importance of such services as: family planning services; parent and family life education, intended to teach parents what to expect, realistically, of their children and to advise them on child rearing; extensive child care programs to relieve mothers of the constant physical and emotional stress of child care.

Secondary prevention, or early case-finding followed by needed treatment and rehabilitation, is the focus of most programs. In effect, this means programs designed to: locate and identify cases of abused or neglected children (case-finding); report such cases to the appropriate agencies and authorities (reporting and registries); investigate and diagnose such cases; arrange substitute care for children and/or treat and follow up cases to avoid recidivism.

The United States has established special child abuse case-finding programs, either community "hot lines" to facilitate citizen or professional reports (usually to general social service staffs who will investigate and follow up) or hospital-based emergency room programs to sensitize hospital staff to symptoms of child abuse. Except for Canada, this type of program does not exist in other industrialized countries, because most already have institutionalized case-finding as part of various types of national child health programs.

In the United Kingdom, for example, health visitors are required to visit every newborn infant at least once, and in cases identified as high risk, several times, during the first year. Although mothers may refuse these visits, few do so, and coverage of mothers with young children is very high. A free medical service is available to both mother and child, and regular check-ups are provided to schoolchildren.

In France, the maternal and child health program is described as the cornerstone of the family welfare program. Regular check-ups are effectively mandated, since parents lose their family or child allowance payment if a scheduled check-up is missed.

Similarly, in Israel, the national network of locally based, universal, free or low-cost mother and child clinics provide the basic case-finding device for all sorts of child welfare problems. Moreover, an incentive is provided to influence mothers to give birth in a hospital rather than at home, to assure good care at such time. (A free layette of considerable worth is provided for each child born in a hospital in Israel.)

In Poland, too, universal free child health programs exist throughout the country, while in the Federal Republic of Germany national health insurance provides for seven free medical examinations within the first four years of a child's life. These are voluntary, however, so instances of child abuse can be missed; but most mothers avail themselves of this right.

In addition to these child health services, preschool programs and related school health services also offer a base for case-finding. These programs provide greater coverage in most European countries than in Canada and the United States. In Israel and the United Kingdom, compulsory education begins at age five, and the school health services assure medical examinations of all children regularly during the year. Furthermore, in France about 95 percent of the children between the ages of three and school entry (five or six) are in preschool, participating in regular check-ups. Even in Poland where coverage for this age group is only 50 percent, and in the Federal Republic of Germany where it is 75 percent, and Israel where it is over 85 percent, almost all children attending preschool are in public programs that have school health services.

Undoubtedly, some cases of abuse and neglect are missed even in these countries, but it seems likely that the extensiveness of child health programs and the high coverage of child care programs for preschool children (with concomitant school health services) assure far greater efficiency in identifying and locating cases of abuse and neglect through normal routines. The special case-finding programs established in the United States are only a poor substitute—at least in this respect—for a national health program in which all children are seen. Undoubtedly, there has been pressure to develop special reporting programs for lack of better alternatives in the United States. The rapid expansion of United States preschool coverage for three- to six-year-olds offers new opportunity there, too.

As noted, the United States, France, and some Canadian provinces now mandate reporting. Most countries, in fact, have some reporting procedures but do not legally require it. However, the trend is toward mandatory reporting in a good number of other countries.

Mandatory reporting appears to attract legislators, executives, and the public as they seek a policy response. However, it is not clear what the effects of such reporting would be as compared to the widely prevalent voluntary system. Technically, mandatory reporting frees professionals and laymen of liability if they report and the case is not sustained. It avoids personal decisions regarding how it will affect a relationship with a patient or client. It locates responsibility for negligence. On the other hand, one finds little evidence of any inclination actually to impose penalties for noncompliance, and professionals apparently remain concerned about the effects of frequent case reporting on clients and on their own community relationships and images. Moreover, on a more basic level, there are not yet available analyses of experience that establish reporting reliability and validity as large groups are brought into the network. Nor is it known with what effectiveness intervention takes place when reports are found to be valid.

Certainly, diagnostic services, including X-ray analyses, for assessing cases of physical child abuse or child battering are becoming more sophisticated as a consequence of the growing concern and involvement of pediatricians and other medical personnel. Beginning in the United States in the mid-1960s, and spreading to Canada, the United Kingdom, Israel, and France, such procedures have become well-known and apparently are highly valued. However, problems of neglect and inadequate care—except physical battering of infants—are diagnosed through the system described as case-finding.

Because of the specialized approach to child abuse and neglect that characterizes policy in the United States, this country has developed the widest range of treatment and follow-up programs and the most comprehensive and integrated service delivery packages in its special child abuse and neglect demonstration programs. These programs stress extensive, multiple interventions provided by a multidisciplinary team. The services are closely integrated, and continue for as long as needed. No one of the interventions included, however, is unique. Nor are these programs readily available. Nor are the services they provide able to reach all the children who need them.

Child welfare programs in Great Britain and France, in contrast, are integrated into more traditional child protective services. Rather than aiming at the problems of abuse and neglect, these problems seem to be moving toward the improvement of all services, for all children in need of help.

LITTLE SUPPORT FOR A SEPARATE CHILD ABUSE SERVICE

Except for the most enthusiastic proponents of special detection and intervention programs, usually those focused on physical battering of infants, few experts advocate a response system for child abuse truly separate from that for neglect. The fundamental task is to strengthen protective services, a component of child welfare, while encouraging case-finding in medical, educational, and community settings. Criticisms of separating child abuse and neglect from general social welfare systems for children by no means deny some need for research and experimental facilities to add to knowledge or interventive skill for dealing with abuse. Nor do they deny the need for short-range measures until overall provision of protective services improves. The real issue, then, is the strengthening of the system of case services responsive to children's and child-parent or family problems. The real choice, and it is a difficult one, relates to the degree of age-categorization desirable in a developing personal social services system.

THE IMPORTANCE OF GOOD PARENTING

Before turning to these programming dilemmas, it may be useful to place the entire abuse/neglect question in somewhat broader perspective. To begin, one is not talking about massive intervention into families and taking over parental prerogatives for defining the broad outlines of their behavior with their children. Societies continue to assume that for the most part parents know best. Nothing else could be the case, for there is little consensus regarding what is meant by "good parenting." There are no universal criteria for assessing adequate parenting and child care, nor willingness in any of these countries routinely to judge just how well parents care for their children. It is doubtful that a firm knowledge base for such assessment could be said to exist. A democratic country would in any instance be hesitant to endorse a specific behavioral requirement repertoire for parents or to organize such surveillance and intervention. Thus, it is only when care is grossly inadequate and the negative consequences overwhelmingly obvious that the problem comes to the attention of the public authorities. The services under discussion are targeted at such circumstances.

Two preventive strategies, however, are fairly widespread. First, many experts believe that parenting is more likely to be impaired when children are unwanted. Family planning services are stressed everywhere as contributing to the birth of desired children—and therefore children less likely to be neglected. A related development is the spread in several places of family life and parenting education programs. As yet no clear evidence shows that these programs improve the care parents give their children, but the enthusiasm they are generating is considerable.

THE IMPORTANCE OF BASIC SOCIAL POLICY

More fundamentally, while not specifically tied to the problems of abuse and neglect, there is growing discussion of the importance of basic social policy in minimizing factors clearly implicated in the inadequate care given children: poverty, poor housing, parental unemployment, hazardous physical environment, inadequate medical care. Several European countries have explicit family policies in which the well-being of families with young children is a criterion by which all policy development is assessed. Other countries are debating the value of such policies as underscoring and making visible what is, and what is not, being done for families with children.

Comparative data indicate that no country can deal with abuse or neglect or, indeed, meet its responsibilities in the field of child development without several key provisions; those include: (a) a maternal and child health, or child health insurance program that ensures case finding, health visiting, regularly scheduled check-ups, close linkage of child care centers and child health; (b) a universal preschool for the group aged three to five; (c) publicly assured maternity benefits; and (d) suitable income transfers to provide at least a guaranteed living level minimum for children (Kamerman & Kahn, 1979a, b).

Here, too, however, one cannot document any direct correlation between the nature of public policy and the quality of parenting and child care. In fact, one difficulty may be that standards and expectations regarding care may be higher in those countries that work at family policy, thus confounding comparisons. "Neglect," "deprivation," and "inadequate care" may be too amorphous as concepts to be rigorously assessed across national or even regional boundaries without more precise definitions.

IMMEDIATE INTERVENTION IN INSTANCES OF PHYSICAL ABUSE

The consensus seems to be that physical abuse is the most visible form of maltreatment of children as well as the one most urgently needing intervention. As such it warrants priority attention. Moreover, the emerging view is that the public sector must by the very nature of its responsibility carry the primary role in protective services, involving, as they may, use of legal sanctions and intervention into parental prerogatives. While voluntary agencies will continue to function in this field, their primary role tends to be public education and research, with some provision of services, often on a demonstration project basis. In those places where the voluntary agencies have a major direct-service role, they are financed by public funds and thus are or should be accountable to the public sector.

Along with increased concern, experimentation, and some growing service provision, a general consensus away from punitive, even legal, measures against parents has developed. This is a relative matter, of course, varying by country; to a parent even the entry of a public agency, no matter how supportive and treatment-minded it wishes to be, may appear to be a punitive community act.

The emphasis on treatment and rehabilitative work with the family, and the component policy of minimizing child removal in these cases, does increase physical risk to children. Several widely publicized "horror cases" in West Europe and North America inevitably resulted in fluctuation of public moods between parent support and treatment (and child risk) versus child protection and a less considerate involvement of parents. The delicate balance varies over time but leads to a clear consensus: if the child is to remain at home and a maximum effort made to work with parents, the service with responsibility for abuse and neglect cases must have proved capability for guaranteeing its ongoing "presence" in the case. This involves assurance of a social worker with a clear mandate as well as access to such resources as visiting homemaker services or day care facilities.

Access to flexible resources and emergency aid is essential. In brief, these are demanding situations and inspire the question: Can existing child welfare services be modified and improved to respond adequately to the pressure for services in all countries as the needs and demands for helping children and families increase? Or, must new, special programs of the kind already emerging be designed to meet these needs?

The Israelis identify a dilemma common to many countries. Most of the services described as essential are provided within—and by—the regular child welfare services, and not as a distinct program. Yet almost all these countries face a major difficulty in delivering these services because the system cannot meet the expanded demands for services. This gap between demand and supply leads to public and professional pressure for particular solutions—in effect, a highly specialized program to meet the special needs of a limited child abuse or abuse-neglect group.

But one danger of a special program for the abused child is the expansion of services for these children at the expense of child welfare service generally. The result would be more resources, better trained staff, and a richer assortment of treatment options for the few children suffering from abuse/neglect. However, the vast majority of children in need, whose need may not be less acute or less visible, would be deprived of help. In effect, such an approach implies that help is available only in situations of extreme severity or crisis. In fact, we already see signs of this in the United States, where new funding is made available for special programs but not for child welfare services generally. (As we go to press, the Congress is considering more adequate funding for child welfare generally—for the first time in many years.)

A second danger is that not only will there be special programs, but that to keep public attention, "abuse/neglect" will be defined so loosely and so broadly that the label and category will be meaningless. There have been indications of this development in the United States, also, where a government official recently was quoted as identifying parental efforts at early toilet training (6 months) as an illustration of child abuse.

One can argue that children who are in imminent danger of losing their lives, or of being severely hurt, should receive priority care and attention. To say that this care cannot be provided in a program designed to protect all children but rather only in a program for a limited, special group is to imply a basic lack of concern for children. Moreover, if one supports this position, inevitably there will be those who argue that every problem that children suffer from warrants a special program.

The heart of child welfare has been and is the identification and care of dependent (homeless, parentless, deprived) children and those who are abused and neglected. This was the recognized role long before the addition of certain developmental and socialization tasks. It is indeed a strange concept to argue that a special system is needed for a subgroup, the allegedly abused.

The real need is to improve personal social services for children generally. Services are fragmented now, and the establishment of multiple specialized programs under independent authority can only add to the problem. Abuse, neglect, handicap, retardation, child disturbance, or any number of other potential subcategories will not be dealt with adequately if each strives to build the needed comprehensive system around itself, inevitably at the expense of some of the others. Each complex case requires the coordination of diverse efforts and resources—and the pool of resources and skills needed for each of the categories overlaps substantially with the pool needed for the others. Whatever the special knowledge components and interventive specifics, they are overwhelmed by the shared elements. The choice is between further fragmentation, diffusion, competition (each exploiting potential public responsiveness and support), and an effective shared system. An integrated system will maximize the general resources, accommodating special expertise, equipment, or service as necessary.

Personal (some prefer the term "general") social services could help create a "common green" of shared expertise and provision in case services for children. The capacity for integrating case activity and the assumption of case accountability where there is "clear and present danger" would form the heart of that service role in protective cases. Case integration and drawing upon special expertise and resources are critical. The protective service presence must be constant and the drawing upon diverse resources continuous. The case manager or case integrator function is clearly a front-line personal social service function as it is developing in the United Kingdom and elsewhere in the world. Child abuse cannot and should not be programmatically separate from neglect, but is best conceived as essentially indivisible from the rest of child-oriented personal social services.

IV

THE LEGAL CONTEXT

8

Too Much Reporting,
Too Little Service:
Roots and Prevention of Child Abuse

Albert J. Solnit

Tragically, the violent, physical abuse and murder of children by adults, often parents, is as old as recorded human history; and sad as it may seem, most of us would not want to live in a society that was able to prevent every single instance of child abuse because that could only be carried out in a prisonlike state. At the same time, all of us would like to prevent as much child abuse as is possible to prevent in a relatively free society in which the democratic values of family privacy and the pluralism of differing life styles are protected and supported.

Historically, in the United States, the famous case of Mary Ellen in the late nineteenth century (Coleman, 1924; Bremner, ed., 1971) was not the first incident of child abuse to receive national attention; "Nor was it evident . . . that there were no laws to protect children from parental abuse; but because of the unusual publicity it received, it shocked many people into a greater awareness of this serious human problem, and it sparked the beginning of a massive crusade against child abuse" (Hiner, 1979). Precipitated by the reactions to what happened to Mary Ellen in New York City, realizing that children should have at least as much protection as domestic animals, the New York City Society for the Prevention of Cruelty to Children was organized in December 1874. Ironically, it

Supported by the Edna McConnell Clark Foundation; Maternal and Child Health Training Grant, DHEW Bureau of Community Health Services; the NIMH Training Grant in Child Psychiatry; and the Department of Children and Youth Services, State of Connecticut.

   With warm thanks to Joseph Goldstein and David B. Solnit for conceptual and editorial assistance.

was the American Society for the Prevention of Cruelty to Animals who responded effectively to the previously thwarted efforts of a New York charity worker, Mrs. Etta Angell Wheeler, to remove and protect Mary Ellen from her abusing parents.

Much as in the new era of concern about abused or battered children in the 1960s and 1970s, the crusade in the 1870s was dedicated to making certain that *existing* laws prohibiting cruelty to human beings should be enforced and that children should be protected. The movement grew quickly, for the nineteenth century—though not as quickly as it again grew when rediscovered in the 1960s. By 1905 there were 400 societies working to prevent cruelty to children or to intervene protectively when it was discovered. "In 1908, E. Fellows Jenkins, secretary and superintendent of the New York Society for the Prevention of Cruelty to Children estimated that 'almost ¾ of a *million* of children' (Jenkins, 1905, 1908) had been involved in the investigations of *that society alone*" (Hiner, 1979).

The rediscovery of the abused or battered child was ushered in by a radiologist, Dr. John Caffey, who initially reported it in 1946 as a new syndrome in which subdural hematomas in infants were often associated with atypical fractures of the limb and ribs (Caffey, 1946). It was not until 1962 when C. Henry Kempe referred to "The Battered Child Syndrome" that the medical profession and the public allowed itself to undo its denial of child abuse and to overreact by treating that continuing tragic human condition as though it were a new discovery (Kempe, 1962). The "Battered Child Syndrome" became a new style of human behavior that was to be blotted out by new laws that mandated how and by whom the reporting should be required and how the reporters are to be protected.

The roots of human violence that culminates in parents and other adults physically assaulting children, especially young children, represent a part of our biosocial heritage that has gone awry. Violence is aggression that has broken out of the socialization channels that the community accepts and supports when adult aggression is modified and transformed in the service of providing safe affectionate care for children. Because our society assumes that parents will nurture and safeguard children, it has constitutionally guaranteed parental autonomy in providing care for their children. Such guarantees also protect the integrity of family life associated with the privacy, intimacy, and richness of emotional exchange in a healthy family.

The child is entitled to feel wanted in the continuing care of affectionate parents who provide him with emotional nurturance and stimulation, guidance, and a safe social-physical environment. In connection with the violent, physical, and sexual abuse of children by adults, especially their parents, we are confronted with a breakdown of an acceptable standard of parental care. Our society no longer tolerates physical abuse of children by parents. Beyond the violation of humanitarian considerations, such abuse represents a threat to the well-being of a community and to the values we place on children in our society. The violence that is unleashed when adults assault children and the imminent threat of physical damage to children when adults fail to safeguard them from physical harm represent the activation of potential violence toward children of which each and every adult is capable. This human potential is highly charged and highly unacceptable as adult behavior, which clarifies to a significant extent why adults either deny the existence of child abuse or overreact in order to demonstrate that they are opposed to children being the victims of such inhumane and cruel behavior.

Psychological Roots

The psychological and biological roots of children's instinctual drives, as differentiated from their regulatory, mediating capacities, the ego, are best understood in terms of the human infant's helplessness at birth. Helplessness is a magnet for nurture, for attention, and for action; it is also a painful reminder to the adult of his own earlier helplessness, and perversely can be a magnet for attack (violence). The protracted helplessness and dependency of the young child dictate a biological and psychological requirement for survival; they also represent, inevitably, the needs of the helpless child to be cared for by an adult. Newborns may not survive if adults are not aggressive and loving enough, that is, if the adult is not active enough in protecting and nurturing the child; or infants may not survive if the adult's aggression becomes transformed into violent behavior. Such destructive effects may be evoked either by the adult's incapacity to invest the child with affectionate care and expectations or because the adult loses control and becomes violent and assaultive. Such loss of control may be the repetition of earlier experience, having its origins in the past when the adult as a child was the object of violent destructive assaults by his or her own parent or parents.

These close biological and psychosocial ties become the basis for survival beyond the individuated development of each child. The parent-child relationship is the matrix for the child's emerging socialization as a member of the family. The family, in turn, is a basic social unit of the community. In the context of institutionalized social behavior in the community, children and adults form group relationships across families and we are able to compare the standards of child care within the family to those that represent the standards of the community.

The child mediates, as he is able, the outside pressures to produce or conform to the social demands or opportunities. At the same time he is responding either directly or indirectly to his own inner pressures and tensions. Before the young child is able to mediate these competing, interacting demands, an adult, the parent, is the mediator. This adult protects the child from too much or too many environmental stimuli or demands. As an affectionate regulator the parent buffers the inner drives and tensions by soothing and providing gratifications that enable the dependent child to reduce the fluctuating tensions. In psychoanalytic terms, the parent is an auxiliary ego for the young child who is not yet sufficiently mature to have such self-regulatory capacities. Among the child's most dynamic sources of power are his impulses, his drives, and his unfolding capacity to become a unique person who has borrowed attitudes and behaviors from many models and yet retains his own individuality, whether dramatic, ordinary, or uncommon. As he mobilizes his inner resources and responds to the pressures of the social environment, the child helps to change and form the emotional climate of his own world. The child's behavior is derivative of inner impulsive energies interacting with the demands and channeling impact of the social environment, established largely for young children by their parents and siblings.

From the viewpoint of psychoanalysis and child development, the violence of the individual represents a social derivative of biological, psychological, and cultural interaction. It is, however, necessary to clarify the difference between subjective and behavioral aspects of violence. Violent feelings and thoughts are not the same as violent behavior. Thus, as the poet Stephen Spender (1976) suggested:

> The thought perhaps—the wish to kill,
> That I can understand, but really
> To do the deed. Ah no, that beats me.

When violent subjective states are curbed and transformed into nonviolent, socially constructive behavior, child care can be sound and can lead to healthy, safe development. Conversely, when the adult's aggression is expressed without the binding, modifying influence of affection (or sublimated sexuality), the child frequently becomes the target of violent assaultive damaging behavior associated with serious bodily injury.

FAMILY AND DEVELOPMENTAL PERSPECTIVES

In the family the child is safeguarded from violent assaults and the imminent risk of serious bodily injury by the care and guidance of ordinary devoted parents who provide protection against outside dangers and demands as well as buffering the child's own violent impulses through their affectionate attachment and concern. The parents and child influence each other toward social accommodation and satisfaction by virtue of their primary, mutual parent-child relationship, the basis of family integrity and by feeling valued as individuals and as a family.

The nuclear family, however, is changing in its structure and functions though it is still the mainstay of social organization and support for children and adults. Certain social indicators characterize some of the main changes, especially the divorce rate, the number of children raised in single-parent families and those raised in families in which both parents work. For example, in the United States, 45 percent of the mothers of children aged 3 to 6 years of age and more than one third of the mothers of children under the age of three worked in 1975, and most worked full time (Kamerman & Kahn, 1976). Are these changing indicators associated with child abuse? Are parents less able to protect and nurture their children in such a changing social environment?

Childrearing can be seen as a matter of parents regulating the nurturance, the stimulation, and the frustration that their children receive. A closer consideration of the meaning of nurturance reveals its importance at every phase of development. The human child is born helpless and perishes if he or she is not nourished, protected, soothed, and stimulated by an older person capable of providing such care on a continuing basis. What begins as biological helplessness leads to social and psychological attachment as a result of the interaction of the infant and the maternal person or persons. The infant progresses from biological dependency to psychological and social attachment in which the child craves affection, approval, and predictable dependable responses from the caretaking adults. This craving, or "social addiction," is the "stuff" out of which social development emerges as a result of identifications with the primary psychological parents. Through these close relationships, the child acquires and internalizes parental attitudes and expectations. These identifications are the core of the unique personality of each child.

In a sense we are endowed and challenged by this psychological and social "addiction" for the rest of our lives. The gradual transformation of the addiction leads to the need for social closeness, friendship, companionship, and eventually to the reestablishment of another family group. It also is the source of a need for privacy and independence. As with many of the lines of development, passive experiences such as being fed or bathed become the basis for actively taking care of oneself and later of others. Many of our neurotic and developmental deviations stem from the failure to turn passive experiences into active, self-initiating capacities, unique to the individual, but influenced to a significant extent by how the child identifies with his parents and older siblings.

These identificatory processes may entrap the child in conflict or may be his pathway to a unique and well-functioning personality. How the parents nurture and how they serve as advocates for health care, schooling, and participation in the life of the community all are vital influences on the developing child's personality and sense of self.

If parents are depressed or suffer from the long-term effects of deprivation in their own childhood, they may lack the capacity to stimulate, nurture, protect, guide, and support their children. They transmit to their children what they themselves had suffered. In this way, certain deficits and deviations may be transmitted from one generation to the next through the dynamics of the family interactions. When such parents turn what they experienced passively into an active mode of behavior, doing to their children what had been done to them in their childhood, they and their children also may be entrapped in the repetition of a past interactional pattern that distorts and limits their normal development and capacities.

Of course, a significant number of such parents resolve their difficulties by making as certain as they can that their children will not suffer what they suffered. They interrupt the transmission of the identification with the aggressor and master the residue of their past deprivation or abuse by doing for their children what had not been done for them. They are active in providing sustained affectionate care and guidance, safety, and assistance in helping their children come to grips with the real world in a socially constructive and satisfying way. To a significant extent, the later outcome of childhood deprivation can be influenced by the alternatives available to the child, adolescent, and young adult in the form of attractive, voluntary opportunities for sound health care, education, and employment that can make a difference in how the child becomes a future parent. Similarly, the continuity of cultural ties, social options, and pride in one's family or neighborhood represent supports for individual mastery of earlier deficits, deprivations, or disruptions of primary psychological relationships.

Because privacy is essential in creating the intimacy necessary for family integrity and fostering the development of primary psychological relationships in the family, our society provides legal and societal guarantees to safeguard family life. What are the grounds for putting these guarantees aside?

Since there is little or no agreement on what constitutes emotional and psychological neglect, the dividing line between respecting and intruding into family privacy should be physical abuse of the child or neglect that represents the imminent risk of serious bodily injury to the child. Other forms of child neglect should be a challenge to the development of attractive, accessible voluntary services, not the basis for intruding into the privacy of the family. It is crucial in assuring parents of support for their nurturing functions to respect the intimacy and privacy of the family. Such respect meets with our value preferences in a free, democratic society. These preferences also converge with children's developmental needs for affectionate closeness, continuity, and the establishment of the primary psychological relationships between parents and children.

Subjective feelings can influence parental behavior and increase the complexity and sensitivity of these mutual relationships. A young child's behavior is or can be experienced differently by various adults or by the same adult at different times according to differing moods. For example, an adult can respond to the same manifest behavior of the particular child as playful at one time, as irritating and provocative at another time, and as demanding and tyrannical at another. Such complexity is commonly observed between parents and their young infant during fussy periods, especially the paroxysmal fussiness of the first months of life when: one parent or set of parents may experience their child's fussy behavior as normative; they will rock, soothe, and stay with the child patiently; another parent may experience such behavior as illness in the child and call the pediatrician or discuss it with the visiting nurse; yet another parent or set of parents may experience the fussy behavior as violently and provocatively demanding, and they react to it by their felt need to survive—to not allow the "tyrannical" baby to destroy them. Obviously, in the case of younger children the chemistry of violence is one that incorporates the behavior of the child and the parent's tolerances of and reactions to the child's behavior.

REDISCOVERY IN THE PRESENT

Specific instances can be even more complicated. An autistic psychotic child, age 6, engaged in violent self-mutilating behavior and at other times in attacks upon household materials and occasionally on his parents and siblings. The parents understood these acts as the behavior of a sick child. They tried to curb it through a well-structured and simplified environment, through the elimination of environmental hazards and through the use of psychological and pharmacological treatment. They were able to mitigate all but the violent self-destructive behavior in which the child cut himself with any piece of glass he could find and break to form a sharp or pointed edge. The mother described how the child could detect pieces of glass in the yard that had been overlooked despite the family's extensive effort to eliminate the hazard. The boy had an extraordinary sensitivity to bright, flickering lights, which such pieces of glass exhibited when the sun was out. Finally the parents adopted the recommendations of the National Society for Autistic Children's paper (1975) on behavior modification, which carefully delineates the way in which to use painful aversive conditioning as a teaching method—not a treatment—to rapidly bring under control behavior which "threatens the child's safety or his survival in an optimum environment. Such aversive conditioning may involve spanking and electric shock." These parents were able to help their son in the least detrimental way. Thus, the question of physical abuse in childhood can be seen as a relative one that requires an awareness of the complexity involved.

As mentioned earlier, after World War II the condition of the battered child was first called to our attention by a pediatric radiologist, Professor John Caffey (1946, 1950, 1957) of Columbia University, College of Physicians and Surgeons. Why such an obvious condition could first be noticed as a radiological syndrome is an acknowledgment of how we can individually and collectively deny what we do to children. It is protective of children for adults to be reminded regularly that as much as adults need and cherish children, they also resent and fear them as competitors, replacements, and as consumers of limited resources of affection, energy, privacy, space, food, and valued materials. Following a world war, ironically, we were able to "rediscover" adults' inhumanity to children only if it was first presented in a radiological journal as an esoteric report of a new and puzzling syndrome.

As the awareness of child abuse spread, like a delayed virus, the studies revealed what appeared to be a large number of undetected cases of abused children. Some workers perceived or interpreted these findings to represent an epidemic of violent injuries and destruction of young children by their parents. The theory of delayed virus infection, as in multiple sclerosis, is heuristically useful; that is, parents who, as children, were deprived, abused and battered carry a "virus" that may be activated as a pathogenic virus—or may produce an antibody to prevent the repetition—when those individuals have their own children. If the virus is activated by the child's particular pattern of behavior and development, then there is a high risk of the parent's past experience being repeated, but now with the child as the object of the adult's violent behavior. Conversely, the child's behavior and the parent's reaction to having been violently abused as a child may ward off the risk of battering or physical abuse being transmitted from one generation to the next.

In the 1950s and 1960s, laws to protect against legal risk those who reported child abuse and neglect, and to require such reporting swept through fifty states faster than any state-by-state national legislation has ever been passed in the United States. Unfortunately, these child abuse and neglect reporting laws were not intended primarily for, and probably have contributed little to, protecting children. They were designed mainly to safeguard the conscience of our adult society and the legal vulnerability of those adults who were encouraged or mandated to report suspected cases of neglect or abuse. Although the reporting laws provided immunity against legal risk, they rarely, if ever, provided more preventive, therapeutic, or protective resources for such children and their families.

Indignation translated into such legislative action was a mixed blessing. The positive aspects of it were that we all became more aware of the problem. We were encouraged to develop an orderly way of reporting child abuse, and we began to plan for and institute protective, educational rehabilitative services. But such legislative impulsivity can beget chaos. The negative aspects have been that family privacy has frequently been coercively invaded following false reports based on life style differences and on prejudice against minorities, single-parent families, and low-income families. The concept of emotional neglect has been used as a basis for coercive inquiry when there is no consensus of how to define emotional neglect operationally so we can distinguish emotional disturbance from emotional neglect. Finally, the epidemic of reporting has not been matched by proportionate, appropriate services to help the child and family; instead, we often permit the state to point the finger of suspicion or accusation when the state does not have adequate resources to help the child and his family. This lack of services has often contributed to a greater risk for such children than before mandatory reporting of suspected abuse was instituted. Thus, inquiry and identification are a threat and a promise; if the promise cannot be kept by appropriate and sustained services, there is the threat of more risk of violence to the vulnerable child.

Mandatory reporting or/and reporting of neglect and abuse that guarantees legal immunity has swelled the number of complaints for neglect and abuse that must be investigated by the state. There continues to be an alarming increase in the reporting and in the efforts to investigate such reports. In most, if not all states (Nagi, 1975; Cohen & Sussman, 1975), this epidemic of reporting has thrown out a wide net bringing in, along with the reports of serious life-threatening cases of physical abuse, instances of suspected neglect and false reports that are harmful or at least not helpful.

In most states a third or more of the reports on neglect and abuse do not involve any physical or sexual abuse and do not involve the imminent risk of serious bodily injury (see Monthly Reports of Connecticut Department of Children and Youth Services, April and May 1979). Investigations into the one-third who are so reported constitute unwarranted intrusion into family privacy, weakening the integrity of the families involved. At the same time, such a deployment of resources creates a pattern of providing too little too late for those children already abused or those who are at serious risk of imminent physical injury. Our national policy of mandated reporting has not been accepted in the Netherlands, The State of Victoria in Australia, and many other regions. We are all trying to find an acceptable balance in preventing child abuse between mandated reporting and voluntary programs launched to prevent child neglect and abuse.

Our epidemic of mandatory reporting spreads a net that does not distinguish sufficiently clearly between those who can be helped through identification and those who may be harmed by it. It does not put sufficient emphasis on how to strengthen the family by voluntary support services. The registries and reporting figures it has created satisfy the alarmists, but do not necessarily create or effectively encourage or support services.

Indiscriminate reporting makes available services less effective and puts an emphasis on *too much reporting and too little services*. For example, there has been a tendency to expect state services to provide the resources and mechanisms for those children who are suspected of being neglected whereas private agencies have been used for direct clinical services. Prevention has fallen through the cracks. In fact, we have it all backwards. Instead of looking into antecedent factors, such as how to support families with voluntary services before they are in trouble, we report on them after they are having difficulties. By encouraging, even mandating, indiscriminate reporting, we arrange to misuse the available preventive and direct clinical services in three ways:

1. We spread them out with less and less services for more and more children and their families. The new idol we are invited to worship is short-term treatment—the briefer the better, regardless of whether it is effective or appropriate.
2. We impose clinical attention on children and their parents, a contradiction of threatening proportions. Clinical care, i.e., diagnosis and treatment, depends on a voluntary engagement in trying to help yourself by understanding yourself, and all of it rests crucially on feeling secure in the confidentiality of the engagement. If a child and parent know ahead of time that what they discuss with the helping persons will be communicated to the state (court

or department), then the capacity to reflect upon and cope with fears, anger, frustration, ghosts from the past, or any other feelings, acceptable or unacceptable, is sharply limited and significantly distorted. The damage done can be even worse when they find it out after the fact.

3. We identify those children who are abused or at imminent risk of serious bodily injury and then often fail to provide them with the services that would protect their bodies and lives. We often put them into multiple placements that destroy their personalities, and defer a plan that would either terminate parental rights and allow children to be adopted or would allow them to return home as the least detrimental alternative.

The diffusion of services due to our inability to establish priorities for the services we do have leads to a failure of services. This is associated with the step-by-step destruction of the child's body or/and personality as we fragment our concern, planning, and utilization of the services we do have or could have for children at risk.

Indiscriminate, mandated reporting leads to over-reporting which, in turn, demands more services than states are willing or able to provide. This increases the danger to those already at serious risk and encourages the coercive intrusion into family privacy and a weakening of family integrity when it is not necessary.

Thus, the present system constitutes a mockery of protective services, often exposing children who are physically abused or at imminent risk of serious bodily injury to greater danger than before they were reported. In the long run, these children's needs can best be served by bringing attractive voluntary services into action earlier. Such services include health care in the neighborhood, homemaker services, social service guidance, employment counselling, and, most often, assistance in finding sound day care that is affordable. Such services can often effectively prevent the conditions that later require coercive intervention to protect the child's life and physical integrity.

RECOMMENDATIONS

A number of recommendations for social policy grow from this analysis of the roots of and solutions to child abuse. First, the state must be prepared to inquire and intrude coercively when there is the report of physical or sexual abuse of children or the imminent risk of serious bodily injury. Second, coercive inquiries must be backed up by adequate and appropriate services, including sustained homemaker, social work, psychiatric, emergency foster and medical care assistance, with the highest priority for those children at greater risk of serious bodily injury. Third, neglect of children not associated with the imminent risk of serious bodily injury should no longer be included in mandated reporting. Neglect that does not seriously threaten to do bodily injury should not be a basis for coercive intrusion into the privacy of the family or for the removal of children from their family homes to state-supervised shelters, foster homes, or other institutions. Finally, state and private agencies should assume responsibility for preventing childhood neglect and abuse. They should study documented cases of child abuse to see how the particular community in which that child lived has failed earlier to provide voluntary services that were available, accessible, and attractive to those families whose children were abused. This is based on the presumption and findings that in each instance of child abuse there were earlier evidences of a family voluntarily seeking assistance that was not available, accessible, and attractive to them. The needs they express can range from parents who want to give their child away for adoption to those who find it difficult to feed or arrange for preventive physical health care for their child. Joint sessions between state and private agency staffs should be systematically planned and implemented to facilitate: in-service training; exchange of experiences and lessons learned; the understanding that both services are responsible for all the children in their region; coordinated efforts at providing preventive, curative, and rehabilitative services for children in their families with a minimum of fragmentation; and joint planning and evaluation of services for children in the particular region. These fundametal changes in priorities for service, treatment, and intervention would begin to resolve the dilemma of "too much reporting, too little service."

9

Save Them from Their Saviors:
The Constitutional Rights of the Family

Rena K. Uviller

A number of factors complicate the task of the court when confronted with cases of child abuse. It might seem that protecting the abused and punishing the abuser would be a simple task, but the application of the law is influenced by conflicting societal messages concerning what is right—even in the face of such an obvious wrong as child abuse. Parents' rights to the care and custody of their children and to a large measure of privacy in rearing them are firmly established by legal precedent. In recent times, however, the rhetoric of children's rights has contradicted this key element of our cultural tradition. The rights of parents have been implicitly attacked from two opposing points of view. The first involves the individual child to whom a liberationist ideology of self-determination is applied. The second is that of the state which, it is assumed, can in its wisdom determine what is good and sufficient care of children. The state and the helping professions seek to apply the principle of the so-called best interests of the child, which often leads to needless separation of parents from children. The rendering of justice in matters concerning families is made all the more difficult by the lack of reliable statistics concerning the incidence and nature of child abuse, and by the sensational treatment of the subject in the media.

CHILDREN'S RIGHTS

Public concern over child abuse inevitably calls forth rhetoric about "children's rights," an ambiguous and misleading concept with contradictory meanings. When some people speak of children's rights, they mean the right of children in a normative sense to the goods and services that enhance their welfare—a good education, health care, clean air, and non-abusive parents. Beyond the merely hortatory, the term children's rights often signifies a coercive state paternalism—the state's *parens patriae* power to impose benefits and disabilities upon children for their own protection, whether or not they or their parents want those services. Finally, children's rights can mean something quite the opposite: the right of children to control their own destinies free from state as well as from parental interference. This child's liberationist view protests the child's status as his parents' chattel and likens children to other historically oppressed groups. It argues for children's emancipation from both state and parent (Holt, 1974).

The liberationists are probably right as far as adolescents are concerned. The age of legal emancipation is too high. Sound public policy might enable adolescents to act independently at a younger age than they now do. But children in the first years of life—those most subject to abuse—can have no rights independent of their parents. Inherently and developmentally, young children are dependent—physically, psychologically, economically, and morally—upon the adults around them.

For young children there is no issue of "rights." For young children there is only one issue: On whom will they be dependent? Who will control them—their parents or state-designated caretakers? In the context of child abuse, the issue is not one of children's rights but of parents' rights, and the circumstances and conditions under which the state may abridge parental rights in the exercise of its duty to protect children.

The rhetoric of the children's movement, insofar as it suggests that young children do have "rights" independent of the adults who care for them, is entirely specious and misleading. Just as specious is the concept of child advocacy or the protestations of various individuals or groups purporting to represent children. They do not represent children. Rather they are parent advocates or state advocates. The former urge that parents retain or augment their control and authority over their own children. The latter urge that the state, through its various welfare agencies and the juvenile court, assume a greater responsibility for the care and rearing of children.

THE RIGHTS OF PARENTS

The right of parents to the care and custody of their own children is not expressly stated in the Constitution. A long line of Supreme Court cases, however, has firmly established that family privacy and the rights of parents to raise their own children are fundamentally protected by the Bill of Rights. In 1923, the Supreme Court in the case of *Meyer v. Nebraska* held unconstitutional a state statute that banned the teaching of the German language in public schools after a group of German-speaking parents challenged the act. The state argued that the statute was designed to protect school children from public ostracism stemming from the anti-German mood following World War I. Reversing the conviction of a teacher who defied the statute, the Court ruled as well upon the right of parents to guide their children's education. The Court declared that the due process clause of the Fourteenth Amendment includes the right of the individual "to marry, establish a home, and bring up children."

In *May v. Anderson*, in 1953, the Court held that a sister state need not honor a Wisconsin custody decree that had been obtained *ex parte* by one parent against the other. One of the most precious personal liberties, the Court emphasized, is a parent's "immediate right to the care, custody, management, and companionship of . . . minor children."

In the past decade the Court has elaborated upon the scope and nature of family freedom and parental rights. In *Stanley v. Illinois*, the Court in 1972 declared unconstitutional Illinois's neglect and dependency statute, which deprived unmarried fathers of the custody of their children upon the death of the mother. Rejecting the state's argument that the statute served the "child's best interest," the Court observed that it had

> frequently emphasized the importance of the family. The rights to conceive and to raise one's children have been deemed "essential," "basic civil rights of man," and "rights far more precious than property rights." It is cardinal with us that the custody, care, and nurture of the child reside first in the parents, whose primary function and freedom include preparation for obligations the state can neither supply nor hinder. The integrity of the family unit has found protection in the Due Process Clause of the Fourteenth Amendment, the Equal Protection Clause of the Fourteenth Amendment, and the Ninth Amendment.[1]

The *Stanley* case made clear that the mere assertion by the State of a protective interest in the child is insufficient to warrant abridgement of

1. In a variety of other contexts, the Court has forcefully acknowledged the constitutional stature of parental rights and family autonomy, e.g., *Moore v. City of East Cleveland* (1977); *Smith v. Organization of Foster Families for Equality and Reform* (1977); *Loving v. Virginia* (1967). The constitutional protection accorded family life has also been expressed in terms of the rapidly developing right of privacy, especially as it involves reproductive freedom. See, e.g., *Roe v. Wade* (1973); *Cleveland Board of Education v. LaFleur* (1974); *Eisenstadt v. Baird* (1972); *Griswold v. Connecticut* (1965).

parental rights. The potential harm to the child at his parent's hand must be significant and the steps taken in the exercise of *parens patriae* to protect the child must be tailored to effect the narrowest possible interference with the family.

In *Yoder v. Wisconsin,* also a 1972 case, the Court again stressed that the state's intrusion upon parental prerogatives must be necessary to protect against a real harm and not one that is only subjectively perceived, even when the subjective perception is widely shared. In *Yoder,* Amish parents challenged the state's requirement that their children attend school beyond the eighth grade. The state argued that it had a duty to prevent children from "growing up in ignorance." Nonetheless, the Court ruled that in the absence of any real threat to the children's safety, the state could not interfere with individual parental judgment, however dubious that judgment might appear to well-intentioned outsiders.

When the Court has accorded constitutional protection to minors, those protections have harmonized with parental interests: children have not been granted rights in conflict with those of their parents. Indeed, in the cases heralded as landmarks by children's advocates—*In re Gault* (1968) and *Tinker v. Des Moines School Board* (1969)—it was the parents themselves who advanced their children's cause: In *Gault,* the right of minors accused of crime to certain procedural safeguards, and in *Tinker* a child's freedom to express opposition to the Vietnam war by wearing a black armband to school. Significantly, Justice Black, dissenting in *Tinker,* observed that the majority did not vindicate children's rights but rather accorded to the parents (who were vocal opponents of the war) the "right to make martyrs of their children." (See also *Alsager v. District Court,* 1975; *Roe v. Connecticut,* 1976; *Sims v. Texas Department of Welfare,* 1977.)

The Supreme Court has not yet considered the question of parents' rights and family privacy in the context of a child neglect or abuse case, but it will doubtless do so soon. Several cases now in the lower federal courts may well reach the highest tribunal in the near future. When the Supreme Court does pass upon the issue, it will be asked to assess its concern for family privacy and parental authority in a climate of considerable public misperception, if not hysteria, about child abuse. The public and professional perception of that subject needs calm and considered reflection.

INACCURATE STATISTICS AND MEDIA DISTORTION

The public has been besieged with ominous reports that over one million children are abused and neglected in this country every year. Efforts to verify this statistic are unavailing since no reliable data are available on either the local or national level. Recent reporting legislation makes federal childcare funding contingent upon the maintenance of computerized child abuse reports. But these records do not reflect which abuse reports have been verified and which have not. The one million figure that is bandied about by the media is inflated by unsubstantiated and anonymous reports.

The media further distort the subject by suggesting that future child abuse can be predicted and can be prevented if the authorities moved in on families early enough. In line with this idea, many hospitals rely upon child abuse profiles; nurses are trained to scrutinize new mothers as they interact with their newborns in order to identify a future abuser. It is not uncommon for rural fairs to have booths that teach techniques for discerning abuse in one's neighbor's children. Yet future violence cannot be predicted or anticipated. Criminologists who make that claim have been thoroughly discredited (Ennis & Litwack, 1974; Okapu, 1976). Nevertheless some child care experts, abetted by the media, are now making the same false predictive claims regarding future parental violence to children.

NEGLECT AND THE "BEST INTERESTS OF THE CHILD"

The most pernicious distortion of the subject of child abuse, however, is the failure to distinguish between actual physical abuse and the wholly amorphous category of "neglect." The media abet this confusion by highlighting and sensationalizing tragic (and hence newsworthy) cases of actual physical abuse and then reporting that there are a "million such cases a year" ("The Short Unhappy Life of Ruben Almeyda," New York Times, Sept. 6, 1977). Even the greatest alarmists estimate that no more than 4 or 5 percent of all reported cases of abuse and neglect involve actual physical harm to children; the rest involve "emotional neglect." Yet the public perceive hordes of humanoid parents who cannot be trusted with the lives of their own children. The media have constructed the perception of a "child abuse epidemic."

Child neglect, as distinguished from actual physical abuse, is one of the most subjective and amorphous concepts known to the law. The term encompasses any parental behavior or familial situation of which a state official disapproves. When the term "neglect" is applied to poor families, it typically involves a dirty home, the subjective perception by a social worker or judge that the parent is intellectually dull, or that the family's daily life is distastefully disorganized. For poor families, "neglect" is also often a code word for parental hostility to the host of social workers and other state agents under whose scrutiny such parents disproportionately fall.

The less frequent cases of middle-class child neglect usually involve the subjective assessment of a psychiatrist, psychologist, or social worker that the child is not "thriving" or "living up to potential." Child rearing is perhaps one of the most emotional and value-laden of all human endeavors. Especially where members of the "helping professions" identify with a child of their own class in the sense that they can imagine it as their own, the danger of subjectivity is great. Passing judgment upon the childrearing values and norms of others can become a treacherous exercise for those invested with official authority.

In essence, the term "child neglect" is only a variant of the equally subjective and amorphous "child's best interest" standard. Such formulations allow highly subjective and value-laden official judgments about the parental capacity of others. They are a feint for those who would have the state make decisions about who may be a parent.

Lately, it has become fashionable to render these subjective judgments under yet another formulation—one with a patina of psychiatric validity. "Psychological parenthood" is the catchword for this new standard. Child care professionals no longer speak of "neglect" or "best interests." Rather, they would deprive a parent of custody if the child has developed a close attachment to a third party—that is, to a person who has become the child's "psychological parent."[2] This formulation, which would terminate parental rights in the absence of any parental wrongdoing, embraces the worst features of both the "best interest" philosophy and "emotional neglect" standards. It is as subjective and relies heavily upon prediction of a child's future emotional adjustment.[3] Its operation is more insidious, however, and must be understood in its functional context.

Typically, a parent is faced with an emergency—often the mother's illness—and cannot care for the child temporarily. Because of poverty or other reasons, the parent has no option but state foster care. The agency places the child in a foster home remote in distance and circumstance from the parent, rendering visits arduous both physically and emotionally. Often, the child is moved from one foster home to another. Not only is the parental bond strained, but the child is subjected to the trauma of unfamiliar surroundings and parental loss. When the parent seeks the child's return, she is discouraged by the agency, which advises her that she

2. For an exegesis of the "Psychological Parenthood" theory, see Goldstein, Freud, and Solnit, 1973.
3. For a definitive repudiation of the psychological parenthood theory, see Strauss and Strauss, 1974.

is "not ready." Or she may be refused outright because the child is "thriving" or "doing better" with the foster parent. By the time the parent initiates legal proceedings, given the law's inordinate and inevitable delay, the child *has* developed a close attachment to the foster parent.[4]

Whether rationalized by the "best interests" argument or because the foster parent has become the "psychological parent," the cumulative effect of agency and court decision and indecision is to sever the parental relationship. The state's own dilatory tactics, combined with an invidious comparison between the natural parent (typically poor or in strained emotional circumstances) and the foster parent, combine to deprive a nonabusive parent of her own children. The state becomes the *de facto* judge of who may be a parent.

As noted earlier, the United States Supreme Court has not yet addressed the substantive rights of parents in the context of neglect proceedings or other third party custody claims. Several lower federal courts, however, have ruled that the constitutional rights of natural parents cannot be casually abridged by the state unless the child's need for protection is demonstrably great and unless stringent procedural norms are observed (see Mnookin, 1973). Thus it has been held that parents have a right to a lawyer in any proceeding at which they are charged with being unfit. They also have the right to confront those who charge them with being unfit and to cross-examine them. It has also been held that children may not be taken from their parents involuntarily even on a short-term emergency basis unless a hearing is held within seventy-two hours to determine if an emergency really exists.

The crucial issue, then, is the substantive definition of neglect. What standard of care must parents satisfy lest they lose their children? Will neglect be confined to actual physical harm? Or will "emotional neglect" with all of its definitional, value-oriented, and predictive infirmities be sufficient? Several lower federal courts have held that such standards as "child's best interest" and its "emotional neglect" equivalents violate due process of law. They violate due process, the courts have reasoned, because the standards are too vague and imprecise. In order to satisfy due process, parents must be given written advance notice of the specific acts or omissions that will deprive them of their children; general conclusory terms won't do (see Mnookin, 1973). More important, the courts have held that vague and conclusory standards violate due process because they interfere with parental rights without sufficient justification. That is, the kind of deprivation typically identified as "emotional neglect" simply does not

---

4. For an extensive critique of foster care, see Mnookin, 1973.

signify enough harm to children to warrant the state's abridgement of their parents' constitutional rights. The state must demonstrate a sufficiently high and necessary need for child protection before the Constitution will tolerate a drastic interference with family privacy.

Indeed, since 1977 the Supreme Court has itself admonished, albeit in dicta, that the family unit may not be destroyed "without some showing of unfitness and for the sole reason that to do so was in the children's best interest" (*Smith v. Organization of Foster Families for Equality and Reform*, 1977; *Quilloin v. Walcott*, 1978). The Court's disapproval of the "best interest" standard suggests that it *will* reject a soft, subjective standard when it eventually resolves the rights of parents in this kind of case. At the very least, the Court's language indicates a concern for the erosion of family privacy and parental autonomy authorized by most state statutes and juvenile courts.

As for so-called "voluntary" placement of children into foster care and their subsequent imprisonment within the system, reform has been initiated by Congress and state legislatures. Recent congressional and state bills would withhold funds from child care agencies that unnecessarily prolong a child's foster placement. Other legislative proposals penalize agencies financially for failing to provide in-home services to natural parents that would have rendered placement unnecessary in the first place. Limitations upon the use of foster care and the availability of other options through meaningful community supports will over time help stem the erosion of family integrity and parental autonomy.

THE NEED FOR RESPONSIBILITY

In the meantime, the media have an obligation to address the tragic problem of child abuse responsibly. It must abandon the gross distortion that has characterized its treatment of the subject. Unfortunately, that change does not seem imminent. A recent media conference on child abuse at the Annenberg School of Communications announced a major network's intention to "mainstream child abuse into the entertainment model." A screening of projected programs depicted "the Hulk," the hero of a popular television series bearing the same name, crashing into a suburban home in order to save a screaming child from his brutal parents. Public consciousness will also be raised, a network spokesman proudly declared, through tunes, jingles, and spot announcements, in the same way that subjects like alcoholism and breast cancer have been treated by the network.

This sort of communication does not expand the public's knowledge or create a thoughtful civic response. Instead, it trivializes a tragic problem. Worse, it panders to the public's hysteria and sentimental fantasies of dramatic rescue. It is extremely dangerous. Those familiar with juvenile courts report the impact upon judicial decisions of lurid and distorted reporting of child abuse. Judges overreact out of fear of public criticism, separating children from their parents without any real necessity.

Most thoughtful observers will agree that child abuse is one by-product of alienation and poverty, typically within successive generations of the same family. Unfortunately, society's underclass and its manifold crises are not attractive subjects for television programs or news stories. The public is weary of the interdependent problems of those on the bottom and the failures in our social and economic system that keep them there. It is easier to attract audiences by simplistic indignation over an isolated feature of life at the bottom: the physical abuse of children.

There is no simple solution to child abuse, but this heartbreaking symptom of social malaise will never be alleviated without a more rational view on the part of the general public of its genesis and its incidence. Most important, unless Americans develop some awareness of the dangers of precipitous state action and a greater concern for the welfare and interests of families and not just of children, the treatment will be worse than the disease.

10

The Involuntary Child Placement Decision: Solomon's Dilemma Revisited

J. Lawrence Aber, III

Perhaps the first adjudicated child placement decision concerning a child-at-risk in recorded history was made by King Solomon. In biblical times such decisions were referred to more simply as "judgments," but they were probably reached no more simply or easily. The First Book of Kings, Chapter 3, describes this famous judgment in detail. This story provides a unique bridge across the centuries and reveals the almost existential character of the child placement decision in western society.

The story captures four essential aspects of the child placement decision that are as true today as they were in King Solomon's time. First, the adult members of society most likely to be brought before a judge for a child placement ruling, then as today, are over-stressed, isolated parents, and often labeled as socially deviant ones at that. The women arguing over custody in Solomon's judgment were both working prostitutes. Parents before juvenile courts' judges today are drawn disproportionately from the AFDC population. Second, the child placement decision is determined

This research was based upon data originally collected by Timothy Howland under the supervision of Dr. Eli H. Newberger, Director of the Family Development Study, Children's Hospital Medical Center, Boston, Massachusetts. The author wishes to thank Mr. Howland for permission to analyze data; Dr. Newberger and his staff at the Family Development Study, especially Drs. Jessica Daniel and Milton Kotelchuck for their technical guidance, support, and encouragement; and Mr. Jack Hagenbuch, previously of the Massachusetts Department of Public Welfare and Judge Francis Poitrast of Boston Juvenile Court for permission to review and reanalyze welfare and court records. Finally, special thanks go to Dr. Victoria Seitz and Professor Edward Zigler of Yale University, for consistent and strong intellectual and personal help throughout preparation of this study.

not by an established body of substantive or procedural law, but instead by the judge's unique talents and ingenuity in ferreting out the child's true parent in each case: a true parent is defined as the parent most able to pursue the child's best interests. Third and perhaps most revealingly, the specific strategy adopted to identify the true parent has changed instruments but not its essential character over the intervening centuries. Today as in biblical times, the true parent was identified by the nature of her response to the proposal by the judge that the living child be split in two, divided equally between the two contesting parties. The true parent, it was reasoned, would relinquish its custodial rights to the child to avoid the child's otherwise impending death. The main difference between biblical and modern times appears to be that Solomon planned to use a sword and juvenile court judges instead use a foster care system. Finally, the irony that even while such attention and care is brought to bear in individual cases to protect a child from injury at the hands of his parents, large groups of children are regularly sacrificed to make society as a whole run just a bit smoother. In Solomon's time the sacrifice required was literal. At the behest of his foreign wives, Solomon built altars to Chemosh, god of the Moabs and Milcom, god of the Ammonites, gods for whom the highest form of worship was child sacrifice. In modern America, despite the concerted effort of our most dedicated citizens, many children are still sacrificed to the cruel gods of poverty and racism in the mistaken belief that it will help win our national battles against inflation and recession. In our efforts over the centuries to protect children from injuries, truly the more things change, the more they remain the same.

THE "INVOLUNTARY" CHILD PLACEMENT DECISION

The decision to remove a maltreated child from his or her family is perhaps the thorniest problem facing any child welfare agency or juvenile or family court in America today. For the purpose of this discussion I will define an "involuntary child placement decision" as a judgment authorized by a court of competent jurisdiction to remove an allegedly maltreated child from the custody of his or her parent(s) despite their objections in order to place this child in the care of another guardian. This decision should be distinguished from many other types of child placement decisions that child welfare agencies and courts make on behalf of the state, including:

> the adjudicated placement by courts of a delinquent child in a juvenile placement facility;

the voluntary placement by parents of a dependent child or a child with special needs in such diverse settings as specialized foster care homes, group care facilities, and institutions for the emotionally disturbed, physically handicapped, and mentally retarded; and

the contested or uncontested custody arrangements for a child by separating or divorcing parents.

In contrast to these child placement decisions, an involuntary child placement decision entails fewer procedural protections of children's and parents' rights and a diminished presumption of parental competence to pursue the child's best interests. These two characteristics combine to make involuntary placement the most powerful, least restricted form of modern state intervention into the heart of family life.

Each decision to separate a maltreated child involuntarily from his or her parents raises a series of important, seemingly intractable problems for the presiding judge. Legally, the rights of the child, the parents, the family, and the state are so poorly articulated in case and statutory law— and often conflict to such a degree—that it is nearly impossible to forge a solution that is at once just and protective of the child. Moreover, given the overrepresentation of minority and poor children and families referred to courts on child maltreatment complaints, most cases raise the problem of ethnocentric, majority-culture intervention into minority-culture family life. Psychologically, the judge is required to make an extremely difficult prediction based upon scarce and often unreliable information about which of the two placement alternatives will prove least detrimental to the child's ongoing development. Returning the child to his or her family runs the risk of continued maltreatment, which could result in serious physical or emotional harm. Removing the child from his or her family breaks the continuity of care that the child receives and can result in emotional harm caused by both the separation from the primary caretaker and the impermanence of caretaking in the foster care system. Each case exposes the judge to competing interests and concerns. The involuntary child placement decision is truly a modern Solomon's dilemma.

Unfortunately, involuntary child placements do not arise in just a small number of difficult cases. The dilemma is becoming increasingly common. Today in America approximately one million cases of child maltreatment are reported annually.[1] State child welfare officials handle the vast majority of these cases without petitioning a court. For better or worse, critical decisions regarding the validity of the report, the provision

1. The term "child maltreatment" is used in this study to cover a wide variety of categories, including gross neglect and failure to thrive as well as physical or sexual abuse per se.

and acceptance of services, and ultimately the placement of the child are routinely settled by child welfare agencies without invoking the authority of the courts.

Nevertheless, juvenile and family courts still hear over 15,000 of the most controversial cases alleging child maltreatment each year. And the best available data indicate that one-third to one-half of these proceedings result in removing the child from the home over parental objections and placing him or her for an indefinite period of time in foster family, group, or institutional care. Each year 50,000 to 75,000 cases result in involuntary child placement. Jane Knitzer and her colleagues at the Children's Defense Fund recently estimated the total number of new children placed in residential out-of-home care each year at nearly 200,000 children (Children's Defense Fund, 1979). And this number appears to be growing at a rate of 4–5 percent a year. Court proceedings alleging child maltreatment, then, are the source of approximately 25–38 percent of all new residential, out-of-home placements of children each year.

Despite the frequency of child placement decisions we know little about why judges decide to separate some children from their families and reunite others at the end of the contested legal proceedings. The few studies conducted of the court's decisionmaking process rarely distinguish between case-specific determinants (such as the nature of the maltreatment or age, race, or wealth of the parents) and those larger structural constraints on the decision common to all cases in a given jurisdiction (such as the relative availability of preventive services or variations in the wording of a child abuse reporting statute). For the most part, case-specific determinants become a part of the court's decisionmaking process while the structural constraints lie outside the process. This paper is based upon a conviction that a careful analysis of both of these types of influences on the court's placement decisions can lead to substantial improvements of the child placement decisionmaking process.

STRUCTURAL CONSTRAINTS ON THE INVOLUNTARY CHILD PLACEMENT DECISION: A PARTICIPANT OBSERVER'S REPORT

During my work as a child advocate attempting to influence protective service policies and practices in Massachusetts during the mid-1970s, I became increasingly aware of the way in which structural constraints indirectly affect large numbers of involuntary child placement decisions by shaping the larger context in which court decisions are made. Structural constraints exist in a number of areas, which will be examined on the following pages.

LAWS

The most obvious factor influencing the involuntary child placement decision is the state law that authorizes courts and child welfare agencies to separate children from their families under various conditions. Prior to the passage of Public Law 93–246, the National Child Abuse Prevention and Treatment Act in the early 1970s, state laws varied more than they do today with regard to the mandating of reports of abuse and/or neglect to child welfare agencies and a requirement of counsel for parent and/or child in proceedings. HEW regulations implementing Public Law 93–247 required much greater conformity among states in reporting both abuse and neglect allegations. But the precise legal standard or test used by child welfare agencies and courts to investigate allegations of abuse or neglect or to place the child over the parental objections still varies significantly from jurisdiction to jurisdiction (National Center on Child Abuse and Neglect, 1978b). Some standards make it more difficult to remove children permanently from their parents, some less. Some of the substantive as well as procedural standards are notoriously vague and offer social workers and judges little guidance in this crucial decision (IJA/ABA Juvenile Justice Standards Project, 1977). In many jurisdictions, children only recently have become entitled to their own counsel during abuse/ neglect proceedings. Consequently, the placement decision often has been less influenced by the application of clear legal standards than by the personal values and inclinations of the social workers and judges.

POLICY REGULATIONS

Laws that direct executive branch actions are usually implemented through the promulgation of policy regulations. Thus, in most states, the child placement decision is influenced less directly by the statute than by the implementation of the statute by the public child welfare agency through "policy and procedure regulations" (Mintzer and Casaly, 1977). For instance, while statutes may explicitly provide legal safeguards for families of children "involuntarily" placed by the state, the task of distinguishing between "voluntary" and "involuntary" placements is left up to the executive branch of government through its policy regulations.

Are parents who decide to "voluntarily" place their child in foster care for fear of financial or legal retribution making a voluntary placement? This is the type of issue that a close review and critical analysis of regulations reveals as a major but hidden determinant of the placement decision. Other issues that are often addressed through policy regulations and that exert an influence on placement decisions include:

the range of service alternatives that the state must explore prior to deciding to remove the child from the home (e.g., provision of fiscal support, homemaker or day care services) and to place the child into foster care (e.g., placement of the child with extended family members or neighbors);

concrete and specific criteria for the removal of the child from the home, criteria for return of the child to the home, and criteria for the termination of parental rights to custody;

the form and process of establishing a placement agreement between the state and the parents which would specify concrete description of the reasons for removal, services provided by the state targeted to address reasons for removal and lead to the return of the child, the rights of the natural parents, child, foster parents, and the state at various points in the placement at various points in the decision-making process, and specific time-frames to reach a permanent decision concerning the child's placement.

COMMUNITY SERVICE RESOURCES

Some jurisdictions may require the state to specify alternatives to placement that agencies have considered and experimented with to protect the child without resorting to the drastic action of removal from the home, or specify reasons why these alternatives failed. But many communities' services, aimed at reuniting placed children and their natural families, may inadvertently weaken the indigenous family support systems and overtax the child welfare system: the availability of support service representatives to place children in foster care as a precaution against injury if they can't visit or support the family enough to guarantee protection for the child in the home. In general, however, the lack of service resources at the community level exerts a striking influence on the child placement decision by limiting the number of options that the community, child, welfare, and other service agencies, and courts can consider before placement.

CHILD WELFARE FISCAL POLICIES

The relevant policies affecting the involuntary child placement decision are promulgated primarily at the state and federal levels. Their effects are experienced directly by individual families, and indirectly by large groups of similarly situated families (Children's Defense Fund, 1979). Two examples will suffice.

Although the exact percentage varies significantly from state to state, an unrepresentatively high percentage of families in America reported as allegedly abusive or neglectful are AFDC recipients. When the children of AFDC recipients are placed out of their homes, the state discontinues child support payments. These families find themselves at a severe disadvantage if they wish to improve conditions so that their children can be returned to them. Increased rent for an apartment with an extra bedroom, transportation money to visit a child in placement, sitter money to care for other children while visiting a child in placement—all these financial aids are jeopardized when the child is placed. Recently proposed legislation in Massachusetts calling for continuation of AFDC payments to eligible families during the temporary placement of their child is an attempt to remedy this situation.

Using the logic that wards of the state deserve extra services to overcome their deprived, traumatic history, the federal government has authorized more child welfare monies to reimburse states for certain services and expenditures for abused children in foster care or other residential placement options (through AFDC foster care payments, $4176 million in the 1976 fiscal year) than to serve abused children who remain at home (through Title IV-B of the Social Security Act, $456.5 million in 1977). Such logic can be tragically turned on its head as states search for strategies to maximize federal reimbursement for serving populations with expensive problems. A state child welfare system can begin to place children inappropriately as a result of the financial reward that the federal government makes to the state government.

Increasingly, social service workers are represented in labor negotiations by public sector employee unions. Consequently, contract settlements have come to influence social policy in general and the child placement decision in particular. Because of the enormous growth in the number of protective services cases in many states, unions have bargained for more explicit and refined methods for measuring and limiting the caseloads of individual workers. Both parties to the negotiations, labor and management, recognize that some cases are more difficult and time-consuming than others, and so wish to award workers more credit for serving those cases. But, just as the rise of state or federal fiscal incentives cited above can have undesirable consequences, worker rewards, incentives, or credit for handling the most difficult cases can have unhappy results. Under the present labor contract covering child welfare workers in Massachusetts (Commonwealth of Massachusetts, 1977), a worker is required to carry no more than 180 "units" in his or her caseload. The definition and assignment of units is, in effect, a reward and incentive structure. Cases are defined as "very difficult" (higher reward) or "routine/moderately difficult" (lower reward); as a result the handling of cases varies (see Table 10.1).

A higher unit rate should increase the caseworker's sense of responsibility to the child in placement, but given the overburdened caseloads

TABLE 10.1: Unit system negotiated by union for Massachusetts child welfare workers

Intake (first month)		Ongoing Service (second month to two years)	
Type of Case	Units	Type of Case	Units
Individual or Child Only	4/case	Individual or Family	3/case
Family	6/case	Child in Placement	4.5/child
Voluntary Child Placement	7/case	Splitcase—Child in Placement Only	3/child
Court-Ordered Child Placement	9/case	Splitcase—Family of Placed Child Only	2/family
Children Suffering Serious A/N	12/family	Children Suffering Serious A/N	7/child, 3/family

of workers, they respond best to crisis and perceived risks. A child in placement is not perceived to be in immediate danger. Consequently, workers feel free to visit them less often than children-at-risk in their own homes. If a worker wishes to play it safe, and be handsomely rewarded for it at that, he may decide to place a child to make his own job a bit easier or more manageable.

COMMUNITY VALUES

In reaching a child placement decision in abuse/neglect cases, judges and social workers are perceptibly influenced by family life and child-rearing values of the community. Although juvenile judges today seem to be less ethnocentric than was common in earlier periods, some may still allow cultural characteristics of families and the marital status of the parents to color unduly their judgment. Other judges may not avail themselves of the support of an extended family to meet a family crisis that might avoid foster placement of the child. Perhaps more to the point, members of some communities may so ostracize a family relying on publicly provided social services that the family stands less of a chance of recouping and regaining custody of their child.

MEDIA INFLUENCE

Media publicity surrounding the deaths of abused children exerts a striking influence on decisions to separate a child from his family. Two recent cases in Massachusetts illustrate this point.

In 1974 a young boy named Walter G., who had been reported by

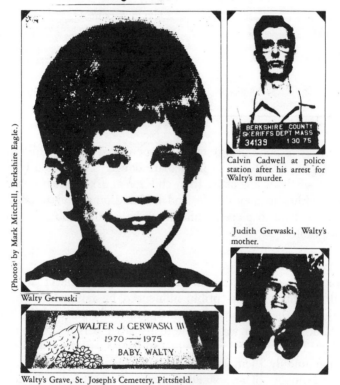

FOCUS

Editorials   46
Real Estate 48 to A52

Did Walty have to die?

(Photos) by Mark Mitchell, Berkshire Eagle.)

BERKSHIRE COUNTY
SHERIFFS DEPT MASS
34139   1 30 75

Calvin Cadwell at police station after his arrest for Walty's murder.

Judith Gerwaski, Walty's mother.

Walty Gerwaski

WALTER J. GERWASKI III
1970 — 1975
BABY WALTY

Walty's Grave, St. Joseph's Cemetery, Pittsfield.

These pictures, and an accompanying story, filled the front page of the *Boston Globe*'s "Focus" section, Sunday, May 7, 1978. The article directed public attention to the death of Walty G.

his school to public and private welfare authorities as an abused child, died when a series of warning signals were not acted upon. Extensive press and government postmortems identified a series of legal, policy, and programmatic impediments to action in this child's case. Statutory, policy, and program changes based largely on the findings from this case were proposed and some were enacted. A more sweeping mandatory child abuse reporting law, a state law requiring the court to appoint independent counsel for children in child abuse cases, and a clarification of public and private agency responsibilities in child abuse cases are all directly linked to the publicity surrounding Walter's death in the minds of the state's social workers, child welfare bureaucrats, judges, legislators, and press. In the spring of 1978, four years after Walter's death, a *Boston Globe* reporter wrote a scathing special follow-up report on the inadequacies of the state's protective service system to serve children like Walter. Ironically, the piece was written for the Sunday *Globe's* "living section." The article, which praised some of the progress made by the Commonwealth over the last four years, raised the possibility that other deaths like Walter's should be expected unless still further changes were forthcoming (*Boston Globe*, May 7, 1978).

Two weeks later, a two-year-old girl named Jennifer G. of Somerville, Massachusetts, died. Jennifer also had already been reported to child welfare authorities for suspected abuse and neglect and had even been temporarily removed from her home and placed in foster care. Over the objections of her foster mother, who reported the continued abuse of Jennifer by her natural parents during home visits, social workers returned Jennifer to her natural parents. She died a few months later. Upon learning of Jennifer's death, the state's child advocacy agency, the Office for Children, which had played a leading role in investigating Walter G.'s death, called for an investigation into the events surrounding Jennifer's death. A special five-member commission made a three-month-long intensive investigation, which led to widely publicized dismissals of two social worker staff members and two supervisors and administrators for professional negligence in the case (Office for Children, Child Abuse and Neglect Fact-finding Commission, 1978). The commission report also provided the impetus for two reforms. The first was a bill reorganizing child and family welfare services by separating them from the Department of Public Welfare and creating a new, independent Department of Social Services. This move had been proposed by the state's administration and liberal state legislators during the previous three legislative sessions but had failed each time since legislators feared a new Department would cost more money and create labor disputes. The second reform was a three-million-dollar increase in the Department of Public Welfare's protective service budget creating both a 24-hour hotline and emergency response system and three to six hundred protective day care slots for abused and neglected children.

Dozens of deaths of abused or neglected children had occurred in

Massachusetts between the tragic deaths of Walter and Jennifer. But only after a four-year follow-up by a journalist did a child abuse death next attract major media coverage and government inquiry. As a result of public and professional outrage at the workers' professional negligence, expressed primarily through news stories (for example, one worker had failed to report to the court a new bruise found on Jennifer's face during the period that the court was deciding whether to return the child permanently to her natural parents), protective services workers across the state began to take a safer course and remove children at risk from the home more frequently and more quickly. But children don't go to heaven when they're separated from their families because of alleged abuse and neglect: they go to the foster care system. Had the editors anticipated that their call for a prompt, effective action on child abuse reports would lead to premature, arbitrary separation of children from their families without consideration of alternatives, perhaps their news stories and editorials would have been worded differently. The media must learn to discipline itself to investigate not just the facts behind a tragedy but the likely consequence of the inevitable recommendations that follow such a tragedy.

DETERMINANTS OF THE INVOLUNTARY CHILD PLACEMENT DECISION

In his review of foster care practices in America, Robert Mnookin (1973, p. 607) concluded that "there is little systematic information about the circumstances that result in . . . placement over parental objections." Child placement decisions made by the state are embedded in a complex historical (Areen, 1975), legal-philosophical (Rodham, 1973), and sociopsychological (Goldstein, Freud, & Solnit, 1973) context that makes empirical study of the issue difficult.

One approach to investigating the factors that affect placement decisions has been the simulation study, in which judges are given case files to examine and asked to indicate the decision they would probably render if they were hearing the case. Phillips and his colleagues (Phillips, Shyne, Sherman, & Haring, 1971) have conducted a simulation study designed to explore the factors influencing a judge's decision to remove a child from home or to provide services to the family so that the parents could retain custody of the child. The agreement rate among three veteran judges reviewing the actual files of 94 children in this study was only 48 percent. Most importantly, in those cases where unanimous agreement on disposition was reached the judges' explanations for their decisions often did not refer to the same determining factors. Instead, each judge seemed to use his own unique value system. For example, even when judges agreed that the three-year-old physically abused daughter of an ambulatory schizophrenic mother and an unemployed alcoholic father should be placed out of the home by the courts, the judges selected different reasons for this decision, including age of the child, dangerousness of the injury, and chronicity of the parents' problems. Research with social workers has yielded similar results (Shinn, 1968).

Two large studies of foster children and their families—the Columbia University longitudinal study and the Gruber report for the Massachusetts Governor's Committee on Adoption and Foster Care—exemplify a different approach to the question. In those studies, investigators surveyed social workers who were responsible for foster children to ascertain the reasons for placing the children in foster care. Jenkins and Norman (1972) and Fanshel (1976) reported results from two different samples from the population of the Columbia study. Gruber (1973) has reported results from the Massachusetts study. Strikingly, four of the five most frequent reasons for separating children from their families were the same across all three samples. These reasons, in decreasing order of importance, were: mental illness of the person primarily responsible for the child's care; evidence of neglect or abuse; physical illness of the person responsible for the child's care; and evidence of abandonment or desertion. Together, these four reasons accounted for approximately 60 percent of the decisions to remove children in all three samples.

Both simulation studies and the foster care surveys suffer from two major limitations. First, they generally elicit from a decisionmaker only a single reason for placement, thus obscuring the fact that there may not be a single reason for a child placement decision (Mnookin, 1973). Second, in both simulation studies and surveys, there has been little consideration of many factors that may be more subtle, hidden antecedents to child placement (Fanshel, 1976). Crucial factors may include sociodemographic characteristics of the child and family such as race and family income. The way the case is handled by the health, social service, and legal institutions is also a factor (Gelles, 1975a). In reporting the percentage of different reasons for placing the children in foster care (Mnookin, 1973), the surveys also fail to identify the large majority of parents who voluntarily gave up their children for placement.

It is important to consider other potential sources of insight into child placement decisions, since systematic empirical research on the issue is so meager. A number of legal and policy analysts in the last few years have tentatively suggested some determinants of the contested placement decision. Schucter (1976), focusing on court handling of child abuse cases, identified three dimensions that appeared to differentiate among cases: severity of injury, family history, and reports and advice of professionals. Wald (1976, p. 11) has suggested that in the absence of specific guidelines for dispositional decisions and with vague investigatory reports by social service agencies as the court's only source of information on the family, "courts generally follow the investigator's recommendations, especially if the parent is not legally represented." Mnookin (1973), influenced by the Columbia study, concluded that the court removes children from their families because of inadequate parental supervision and guidance, the emotional illness of the mother, or child behavior problems.

The clinical folklore that has developed around child maltreatment cases in medical and social service settings forms another source of information. In the present study, the folklore on child removal seems to consist of five implicit hypotheses held by the service providers to explain why a child is removed by the courts. Service providers link each of the following factors to an increased chance of a child's being removed by the court: age (younger children); parental attitude (children with parents hostile to the medical and/or legal authorities); custody of the child prior to disposition (children placed in foster, group, or institutional care after hospitalization); reason for court petition (children suspected of being physically, rather than psychologically, abused); and race (minority children).

I examined the files of a small sample of contested court cases alleging child maltreatment to study the reasoning in decisions for child placement. The records contained four kinds of evidence: basic demographic information, hospital data, data from the welfare agency, and court data.

METHOD

Subjects. The sample was composed of 35 out of 36 families referred over a continuous 1½-year period from 1971–1973, by the Trauma X Team of Children's Hospital Medical Center in Boston to Juvenile Court on petitions alleging child maltreatment. At the end of the court proceedings, 12 families (35%) were separated and 22 families (62%) were reunited.[2]

These families represented about 20 percent of the child maltreatment cases handled by the Trauma X Team over the 1½-year period and 5 percent of the court petitions alleging child maltreatment filed in Massachusetts during that time. It is reasonable to suspect that in comparison

2. The records of one family were lost before they could be included in the study and the court had not reached a final decision in another case by the time of final data collection.

to a random sample of court-referred cases of child maltreatment, this sample contains a higher percentage of physically abused or endangered rather than emotionally neglected or abandoned children. Moreover, it is composed of cases that received a considerable amount of professional scrutiny in the process of referral from another part of the hospital to the Trauma X Team and from the Trauma X Team to court (see Trauma X Guidelines, Newberger, undated).

The 35 maltreated children ranged in age from a few months to over eleven years when the court petition was filed. But 30 (85%) of the children were under 5 years old: 11 (31%) were 0–6 months old, 11 (31%) were 6 months to 2 years old, and 8 (23%) were 2–5 years old. 19 (54%) of the children were boys, 16 (46%) were girls. And the major source of income for 17 (49%) of the families was AFDC and for 10 (29%) of the families was some form of parental employment. Finally, at the time the petition was filed, 6 (17%) of the mothers were age 20 or less, 16 (46%) of the mothers were 21–24 years old, and 13 (37%) were over 25 years old.

Thus, in comparison to Gil's 1970 national incidence study of physical child abuse, children in the study were younger in age, had younger mothers, were more likely to be black or Spanish-surnamed, and more likely to come from families reliant on Aid to Families with Dependent Children as the major source of income.[3]

Procedures. A family brought before a court on a petition alleging child maltreatment is subjected to greater invasions of privacy than most other American families. Ethical constraints should govern additional intrusions into the private life of the family for the purpose of collecting research information. Research on the involuntary child placement decision should use the most inobtrusive strategies and measures possible so that families before the court are not submitted to further unnecessary intrusion.

At present, the most inobtrusive strategy available is retrospective records research of cases that have already been decided. Evaluation researchers and social historians using quantitative analysis of institutional records have convincingly demonstrated the great scholarly value of records research, especially for studying phenomena that might otherwise prove inaccessible. In the case at hand, health, welfare, and court records

3. Gil's 1970 data rather than Gelles's 1978 data on characteristics of abusive families is used for comparison purposes in this paper because Gil employed a definition of abuse that was closer to the statutory definition under which children are reported in Massachusetts than was Gelles's more behavioral, scientific definition of physical violence.

TABLE 10.2: The relationship of predictor factor scores
to the child placement decision by the court ($N = 34$)

Factor Description	Standardized Discriminant Function Coefficient	Univariate F-test	p
1. Multiple problem, physical abuse	.71	3.57	.07
2. High positive agency involvement	−.73	3.73	.06
3. Low availability of legal representation	−.22	.29	—
4. High agency involvement with father	−.09	.10	—
5. Socially disadvantaged families	−.04	.03	—
6. Psychologically abusive or neglectful families	.35	.58	—
7. Rapid intervention	−.15	.09	—

are the single richest source of information on the child placement decision process. A summary of the specific procedures for the collection of
data from the records and their logical reduction and statistical analysis
is presented in Appendix B.

Results. Table 10.2 shows that two of seven possible factors were
associated with the courts' final child placement decision. The first factor
appears to describe multiproblem, physically abusive families with young
mothers and a history of instability due to drug or alcohol problems.
These families often lost their children to emergency foster care at the end
of hospitalization. The variables loading on the second factor appear to
indicate families that are relatively nontransient, that have a high degree
of positive involvement with child welfare agencies, and that are able to
sustain a relationship with the same social worker. Both of these factors
were at least twice as important as any other factor in predicting the final
decision. Although the predictive value of each of these factors considered
above did not reach statistical significance, the two factors considered
together were able to significantly predict the final outcome of a case.

Factors are a composite of weighted individual variables. Table 10.2
presents the weights of the individual variables that contribute to the two
factors associated with the court's child placement decision.

The data analysis methods employed contain the risk of obscuring the
impact of the important individual variables on the final placement decision. Therefore I also performed simple tests of association between each
of the 75 individual predictor variables in the final data set and the case
outcome variable. Table 10.3 presents the results of these tests.

TABLE 10.3: Individual variables contributing to the predictive factors
(N = 34)

Source of Information	Characteristics of Separated Families (Variables loading on Factor 1)		Characteristics of Reunited Families* (Variables loading on Factor 2)	
Demographic Data	Younger mothers	(.69)	Fewer recent family moves	(.43)
Hospital Records	Child diagnosed as physically abused	(.55)		
	Child placed in temporary foster care after hospitalization	(.67)		
Welfare Agency Records	Father psychiatrically evaluated	(.49)	Same social worker from investigation to follow-up	(.43)
			Social worker observes parent/child relationship	(.69)
Court Records	Family cited as unstable due to drug or alcohol abuse during hearings	(.70)	Judge orders family to establish contact with the welfare department	(.68)
	Family cited for multiple problems during hearings	(.54)	Parents cited for improved child care during hearings	(.64)
	Welfare representative present at first hearing	(.45)		

* For ease of interpretation, all variables are described so that they load positively on the factors. Loadings with absolute values of .4 or less are not reported. (Absolute values of factor loadings in parentheses.)

In keeping with the exploratory nature of this study, relationships with p-values $\leq$ .10 are reported. Only 9 of the 75 individual variables demonstrated a significant relationship with the court's final child placement decision (see Table 10.4). Since this figure is only slightly above the number of individual relationships expected to occur by chance, and since four of the five individual predictor variables most powerfully associated with the case outcome also loaded highly on the discriminating factors, the results of the chi-square analyses contribute very little to our understanding of the determinants of the involuntary child placement decision. Therefore, the following discussion will focus on interpretations of the discriminant analysis of the factor scores.

TABLE 10.4: The relationship of individual predictor variables to placement decision by the court

Variable	Value Associated with Placement	χ^2
Demographic		
*Number of recent family moves	More moves	p ≤ .02
		(N = 30)
Hospital		
Parental threat to remove child from hospital	No	p ≤ .07
(yes/no)		(N = 30)
*Person to whom child discharged from hospital	Foster care	p ≤ .02
(family/foster care)		(N = 30)
Welfare		
Any other report recommendations (yes/no)	No	p ≤ .001
		(N = 34)
Court		
Hospital lawyer present at arraignment (yes/no)	No	p ≤ .05
		(N = 34)
*Specific problem cited of unstable family due to	Yes	p ≤ .01
drugs or alcohol (yes/no)		(N = 34)
Number of family improvements cited	Less	p ≤ .09
	improvements	(N = 34)
*Improvement in parental care was cited during	No	p ≤ .002
hearings		(N = 34)
Improvement in family's contacts with counseling	No	p ≤ .05
agencies was cited during hearings (yes/no)		(N = 34)

* An asterisk denotes that the variable loads highly on a discriminating factor.

One word of caution is important. For descriptive purposes, the discussion is written about the high loading source variables of each of the discriminating factors and their possible relationships to the final case outcome. However, the source variables from the factor analysis must not be confused with individual predictor variables. The source variables are discussed only to make sense of the possible effects of the entire factor upon the child placement decision.

DISCUSSION

Interpretation of major findings. Despite the limits of the present study, a richer and more realistic picture of the factors associated with the involuntary child placement decision in contested court cases alleging child maltreatment has begun to emerge. A number of interrelated variables, representing a series of judgments made and recorded by the three gatekeeping institutions about the families, combine to create two major factors that correlate with the court's final disposition.

Using these two factors as guideposts, it is possible to sketch a picture of the different paths that the separated and reunited families take through the social and legal institutions. In the 35 cases reviewed for this study, the juvenile court more often permanently separated children from families that were previously identified by the hospital as physically abusive, by the welfare agency as having fathers in need of psychiatric evaluation, and by the court itself as multiproblemed and unstable due to drug or alcohol abuse. Typically, the mothers in these families were very young. Given the correlational nature of the data, it is not possible to determine whether any one of these events alone was necessary or sufficient to affect the final court decision, but it appears that this constellation of events did so.

The gatekeepers seem to consider this group of variables to be a series of clinically valid indicators of high risk to the child's health or welfare. This interpretation of Factor 1 variables as indicators of high risk is strengthened by the release practices of the hospital. Indeed, children from families with high Factor 1 scores were considered at such high risk of further harm that they were rarely returned to their families at the end of hospitalization but instead were placed in temporary foster care. In one sense, the court simply later ratified a decision first made by the hospital staff by making temporary foster care placement permanent.

The families of children who were returned by the court to their parents at the end of the proceedings followed a different path. First, unlike the separated families, these families usually regained the custody of their children following hospitalization. This fact may have in turn resulted in a number of other differences between the separated and re-united families. Perhaps because the children were known by the court to be potentially endangered, reunited families were instructed by the court early in the proceedings to establish contact with the welfare agency. Because these reunited families were less transient, they were able to sustain a relationship over time with the same social worker. This relationship, in turn, may have put these families in a position to demonstrate to the welfare worker, and through the worker's follow-up report to the court, that they were improving the care of their child(ren). The accumulation over the course of the court proceedings of this type of information (fewer family moves, more positive and stable casework contact, and documented improvements in child care) seems to have convinced the court that its intervention had lowered the risk of further serious harm to children in these families.

It is possible, however, to draw from these results a plausible interpretation of factors one and two that differ from "valid clinical indicators of high or low risk of harm to the child" interpretations. The labeling of families with terms such as "multiple problem," "history of drug or alcohol abuse," and "in need of psychiatric evaluation" may have an implicit purpose of identifying and controlling examples of deviance in the family that surpasses its explicit purpose of identifying the degree of risk of harm to the child. Similarly, children may be returned to families not because the risk of serious harm has been lowered by court intervention but because these families are responding to trouble as "normal" families would—they are cooperating with authorities and using the help provided. Moreover, "identifying the level of risk of harm to children," and "controlling the amount of deviance in families" are not mutually exclusive. Indeed, they may be part of the same task in the child protection field. But due to the legal and sociopolitical problems mentioned above, it is important to distinguish between these two possibilities as clearly as possible. While violation of parents' constitutional rights to the custody of their children and a family's right to autonomy, privacy, and cultural integrity may be justifiable to reduce the risk of further serious harm to a child, it is certainly much less justifiable to control nonharmful social deviance.

Given the correlational nature of this study and, as described below, the striking failure of the gatekeepers to collect important information on the impact of the alleged harm on the child's ongoing development and on the role of parental behavior and attitudes in creating and continuing maltreatment, it is presently impossible to distinguish between these two very different interpretations. As will be seen below, only a prospective study based upon a thorough reform of data collecting procedures during the involuntary child placement decision process holds much hope of making this critical distinction.

Relationship to previous research. Contrary to the assumptions of the research designs in the simulation studies and the foster care surveys, no single variable appeared to determine child placement. Instead, the decision seems more accurately to be described as a cumulative effect of gatekeeper and family interactions (Gelles, 1975a). Such a cumulative phenomenon may explain the failure of the simulation studies to identify common determinants of the placement decision even when unanimous agreement upon disposition was reached. Individual "reasons" are many and interrelated. Thus if one judge identifies the uncontrollable alcoholism of a parent as a prime determinant, while another judge focuses on the physical abusiveness to children, and a third judge notes the mother's immaturity, then all three judges, while seeming to operate within their own unique value system, could instead be describing three facets of the same family.

The results of this study lend support to several hypotheses advanced by clinicians and policy analysts (e.g., Mnookin, 1973; Schucter, 1976; Wald, 1976): First, the analysts and clinicians have emphasized the likelihood that each decision has multiple rather than single determinants. Second, the role of professional recommendations in the court's final decision, emphasized by both Schucter and Wald, is suggested by the present cases. The hospital recommendation of separation through temporary foster care or the child welfare worker's documentation of enhanced parental care through a follow-up report were contributors to the court decision and may have been of overriding importance in the eventual fate of each family. Third, Schucter's claim that the courts differentiate cases along the dimensions of (1) severity of injury and (2) family history of pathology find partial support in this study from the (1) physical abuse variable and (2) multiple problems, drug or alcohol abuse, and father's psychiatric evaluation variables of Factor 1. Both the policy analyses and clinical folklore have suggested that physical abuse of the child is more likely to result in the court's removal of the child than is neglect or psychological abuse. Policy analysts and clinicians are similarly in agreement that the custodian of the child at the end of their hospitalization (foster care versus parents) is an important predictor of eventual outcome. The results of the present study lend support to both hypotheses.

As important as the findings that did distinguish the separated and reunited families, are those that didn't, especially: the age of the child; the race of the child and parents; the family's source of income; the availability of legal representation for both child and parents; the child's behavior (as measured by referral for a psychiatric evaluation); and the parents' attitudes toward the helping professionals (as measured by the threat to remove the child from the hospital against medical advice).

These factors are frequently cited in the clinical and legal literature on child placement. Yet, because they didn't help distinguish separated and reunited families in this study, one can't immediately conclude that they don't influence the child placement decision.

For instance, the age, race, and income status of the child and parents may indirectly influence the placement decision by making the younger, black, and poorer families of the total population of maltreated children more likely to rely on the hospital rather than a private physician for medical care and more likely to be referred to a court to protect the endangered child. The comparison of the children in Gil's study and in our sample lends support to this suspicion (Gil, 1970).

Similarly, the paucity of social services available to help families after hospitalization, services limited almost exclusively to foster care for separated children, casework services for reunited parents (and almost nothing for the natural parents of separated children or for the children of reunited families) may place severe limits on the influence that the attorney can exert on the placement decision. This will continue to be the case unless the majority of attorneys representing abused or neglected children and their parents become more skilled at influencing the service delivery system informally, rather than trying to influence the court system formally (Mintzer & Casaly, 1977).

Two final factors, reported to be influential by clinicians and lawyers, highlight part of the dilemma of making sound child placement decisions. An index of the child's behavior (based only on whether the child was referred for psychiatric evaluation) and an index of the parents' attitudes toward helping professionals (based only on their threat to remove the child from the hospital against medical advice) were among the very few clear, concrete, and monitorable assessments of child development and behavior and parental attitude and behavior in each case record. The court renders one of the most complex, controversial decisions that a society can make about child and family life, yet it acts without sufficient specific information to make the decision properly. Why are the assessments of the child's behavior and development and the parents' attitudes and behavior necessary to make a sound child placement decision? This important question deserves close scrutiny and will be addressed below in the section on recommendations for future prospective research studies.

RECOMMENDATIONS FOR FUTURE RESEARCH

RETROSPECTIVE STUDIES

Because of the limits of records research to correlational, retrospective data, and the fact that the study was conducted on a small, urban, hospital-referred sample of Massachusetts court cases alleging child abuse, the results of the pilot study must be considered as primarily descriptive and hypothesis-generating. Given the importance of historical and jurisdictional variations in structural constraints described above, further retrospective records research should be performed with a larger sample of cases from other referral sources (especially: welfare agencies; law enforcement agencies; and family, neighbors, and friends), in a wider range of communities (including suburban and rural) under various child abuse reporting laws. A comparison between court-referred and noncourt-referred child abuse cases from the various referral sources should also be included in future research in order to better understand the influence of variables such as age and race. The factors identified in the present study as being important (physically abusive, multiproblem families; families with high agency involvement) have a certain face validity. Research with a larger, more heterogeneous sample would help establish confidence in the present findings that a few key variables may be sufficient to predict the outcome of court decision in contested child abuse cases.

PROSPECTIVE STUDIES AND REFORM OF THE DECISIONMAKING PROCESS

While retrospective records research studies may be the best place to begin studying the involuntary child placement decision, they are not the best place to finish. Only prospective studies can address the major unresolved questions about the nature and determinants of child placement: namely, does the decisionmaking process fundamentally identify indicators of high risk or label family deviance? and what are the true determinants of the "involuntary" placement, not simply the correlates?

In mounting prospective research studies to address these questions, one should be guided by the same ethical principle enunciated earlier—in order to safeguard families from risky, unnecessary intrusion, use the most unobtrusive strategy possible. This would involve the collection of case information through the official court decisionmaking process. To begin prospective studies of the nature and determinants of the "involuntary" placement requires nothing less than a reformation of how courts (and child welfare agencies) presently think about, collect, organize, and use information in their decisionmaking. Some of the most glaring limits as to how courts use information and a few recommendations to overcome those limits are described below.

Probably the major symptom of courts' difficulties with thinking about and using information in the involuntary child placement decisionmaking process is the length of time it takes for the court to reach a final decision. Because of the detrimental impact of uncertainty on the caretaker/child attachment, the length of time required to arrive at a final disposition is itself a major determinant of the quality of the decisionmaking process (Derdeyn, 1977b; Pike et al., 1977). For the families in the present study, the average length of time between the initial filing of the petition alleging child maltreatment and the judge's final decision was over two years. During that time, the judge continued the case nearly half-a-dozen times for periods of either three or six months, delaying the decision while hoping to gain a clearer understanding of the best disposition available. Most frequently, the case was continued because no new information about changes in the level of risk to the child in the home was developed to aid the judge in making a permanent decision about the child's placement. This was so in part because the caseloads of court and child welfare agency personnel place severe constraints on the amount of attention any one case receives, but also because baseline information was not systematically collected, presented before the court, and recorded from the beginning, on the following:

> the specific harms to the child that justified initial court intervention;
>
> the observable impact of the harm on the child's ongoing physical, social, and emotional development, and
>
> observable parental behaviors or environmental conditions which increased the risk of harm to the child.

The failure to collect and systematically organize this type of baseline information will affect the future course of the courts' intervention and decisionmaking process (Dukette, 1978). Without this information, parents were deprived of adequate notice about what concrete behaviors and conditions needed to be changed in the family in order to end court intervention and be reunited with their child; the child welfare agency was deprived of information about specific child, parent, and environmental problems on which to target services; and the judge was deprived of the baseline information and conceptual framework required to create a series of trials for the parents to discover whether the parents, with the help of the community services available, could reduce the risk of harm to the child to below the threshold level justifying continued state intervention and ultimately child removal.

In order to conduct this series of trials, clearly one needs "posttest" information as well as "baseline" information, especially:

> a comprehensive list of service goals (which function as a set of "hypotheses" about the ability of targeted services to address certain problems with the parent or environment and thus reduce the risk of harm to the child),
>
> a record of the impact of the services on the parental or environmental problems and on reducing the harm to the child, and
>
> a time frame (which would vary with the child's age) for making a final judgment on (a) the success of the parents and the state in reducing the risk of harm to the child to below the threshold level, and (b) consequently the child's permanent placement.

Each case, then, can be conceptualized as a clinical-judicial experiment on the success of services and court intervention to reduce abusive/neglectful behaviors and conditions of the family to below the threshold levels justifying state intervention and the removal of the child.

These six pieces of information are the basic elements required to conduct an unobtrusive, prospective study of the nature and determinants of the involuntary child placement process. They possess inherent legal, clinical, and research value and would be collected only through the official court decisionmaking process. Developing these six basic elements of information would both require and create changes in the nature of the judicial decisionmaking process concerning involuntary child placement. But the degree of clarity they would bring to judicial thinking, the ability to tease out risk-identifying and labeling activities, and to monitor the effects of interim judgments and actions on family functioning make it all worthwhile, because the chances are increased of protecting children at risk of serious harm without unnecessarily separating them from their families.

Appendix A

Final Set of 75 Variables Retained for Analysis

Demographic Variables

Subject's age
Number of siblings
*Subject's race (white/non-white)
Subject's birth order
*Subject's sex (male/female)
*Father in home (yes/no)
*Number of recent family moves (none/one/two or more)
*Any siblings at home not included in court petition (yes/no)
*Source of family income (self or spouse/welfare)

Mother's criminal history (yes/no or not mentioned)
Mother's age
*Child is from mother's previous relationship (yes/no or not mentioned)
Mother's employment history (mentioned/not mentioned)
Mother's race (white/non-white)
*Mother's age at first child (21 or less/22–24/25 or more)

Hospital Variables

*Admitting diagnosis (physical trauma/neglect or failure to thrive)
Duration of injury (chronic or repeated/single incident)

Person held responsible for injury (father/mother/other)
*Parental visits to hospital (yes/no or not mentioned)
*Number of children admitted

* An asterisk denotes that the variable was selected for the final factor analysis.

from same family (one/two or more)

*Person referring child to court (social worker/doctor or lawyer)

*Reason for hospital's welfare report to court (physical abuse/psychosocial)

Reason for hospital's welfare report to court (violent/ nonviolent)

*Length of hospitalization before court referral (less than 1 week/1–2 weeks/2 or more weeks)

*Parental threat to remove child from hospital (yes/no or not mentioned)

*Person(s) to whom child discharged from hospital (family/foster care)

Welfare Agency Variables

*Type of investigating agency (private/public)

Father consulted by social worker (yes/no or not mentioned)

Other family members consulted by social worker (yes/no or not mentioned)

Neighbor or friend consulted by social worker (yes/no or not mentioned)

Other public agency consulted by social worker (yes/no or not mentioned)

*Report preparation time

Report length

Total number of persons and agencies consulted in report preparation

*Report recommends welfare custody for child (yes/no)

*Report recommends therapy or counseling (yes/no)

Report recommends welfare casework with family (yes/no)

Any other report recommendations (yes/no)

*Social worker reports actually observing parent-child relations (yes/no)

Social worker reports observations made by family or friends (yes/no)

*Social worker reports clinical, diagnostic observations (yes/no)

Social worker reports knowledge of prior help seeking by parents (yes/no)

Social worker reports judgments of parent or child affect (yes/no)

*Follow-up investigator same as original investigator (yes/no)

Follow-up report recommends welfare custody of child (yes/no)

Any other recommendations in follow-up report (yes/no)

Psychiatric evaluation was made of subject (yes/no)

Psychiatric evaluation was made of mother (yes/no)

*Psychiatric evaluation was made of father (yes/no)

Psychiatric evaluations were made of any other persons (yes/no)

Court Variables

*Hospital lawyer present at arraignment (yes/no)

*Welfare representative present at arraignment (yes/no)

*Parents' lawyer present at arraignment (yes/no)

Mother present at arraignment (yes/no)

Father present at arraignment (yes/no)

Presiding judge (chief/rotating)

Counsel for parents appointed at arraignment (yes/no)

Number of problems cited at arraignment

*Number of court actions taken at arraignment

Time from arraignment to first hearing

Number of hearings held

*Number of problems cited at hearings

*Specific problem cited of unstable family due to drugs or alcohol (yes/no)

Specific problem cited that parents are incapacitated or ambivalent about child's return (yes/no)

Specific problem cited that parents are hostile and uncooperative (yes/no)

Specific problem cited that child's injury was severe or unexplained (yes/no)

*Number of court-ordered goals set during hearings

*Hearings resulted in court ordering psychiatric evaluation of parents or grandparents (yes/no)

*Hearing resulted in court ordering family contact with welfare agency (yes/no)

Hearings resulted in court ordering family contact with other counseling agencies (yes/no)

Hearings resulted in court ordering that family keep service appointments and visit children (yes/no)

*Improvement in parental care was cited during hearings (yes/no)

Improvement in family's contact with welfare agency was cited during hearings (yes/no)

Improvement in family's contact with counseling agencies was cited during hearings (yes/no)

Improvement in family's keeping appointments and visiting children was cited during hearings (yes/no)

Appendix B

The data collection and analysis procedures consisted of five stages. First, because the hospital, welfare, and court records of maltreated children had never been conceptualized and reviewed in quite this way before, every possible variable contained in the records was defined and coded, resulting in an initial set of over 400 variables (Howland, 1974). Second, this initial set was reduced to a final set of 76 variables (See Appendix A): 75 predictor variables and 1 case outcome variable (scored: child placed/child returned). This was accomplished by eliminating two types of variables that possessed little potential predictive value because they didn't vary enough among the families (defined as a variable for which at least 30 or 35 families had the same value; for example, place of residence scored: urban/suburban/rural); and those which were of questionable reliability (for example, father's psychiatric diagnosis). Third, 7 underlying patterns of relationships among the 75 predictor variables were discovered through a series of factor analyses. These underlying patterns of relationships, known as factors, made it possible to summarize most of the case information for each family, which was previously contained in the 75 predictor variables in 7 factor scores instead. Fourth, a discriminant analysis was performed on the 7 factor scores for each of the 34 families in order to statistically distinguish characteristics of separated families from those of reunited families. Fifth and finally, the individual relationship between each of the 75 predictor variables and the case outcome variable was studied through chi-square analysis to guard against any important influence on the court's child placement decision being obscured by the data summary techniques employed in the study.

V

SOCIALLY SANCTIONED
ABUSE

11

The Pariah Industry:
A Diary from Purgatory
and Other Places

Burton Blatt

In 1970, 64 percent of the approximately 186,000 people residing in state institutions for the mentally retarded were children under the age of 19 (Robinson & Robinson, 1976). Until recently, most of these children have remained in institutions well into their adult years, and the great majority have suffered abuse in the hands of the institution both as children and as adults. Consequently, to deal effectively with the problem of abused children in institutions for the mentally retarded we must first deal with the fundamental problem of abusive institutions.

For the above and other reasons, although this book is about children, this chapter is concerned with all people in institutions, whether children or adults. Because I have a point to make, I intentionally avoid the narrower concern. It is clear to me that if the general problem of institutional abuse is solved, the problem of institutional child abuse will be solved. It is clear that, if the future is any indication of the past, today's institutionalized children will inevitably become the next generation's institutionalized adults. Moreover, the recent shifts in state school populations toward more severely and multiply handicapped residents promise that, at least insofar as the mentally retarded are concerned, institutionalized children become institutionalized adults. From another point of view, there is justification for discussing all institutionalized people in a book on child abuse; at the root of much abuse is an assumption, pervasive if sometimes unconscious, that the mentally retarded of any age are less than fully human. Changing this attitude is critical to any reform. Moreover,

I am exceedingly grateful to Andrejs Ozolins of Syracuse University for his insightful suggestions during the development of this chapter.

recognizing that there exists the assumption that children are less than fully human is vital if the rights of all children who suffer in the society are to be improved. Things *can* be different if our attitudes about people change, and if such changes are reflected in different policies and practices. But for now, we must recognize that there is a decided trend toward placing the most severely handicapped in residential settings (Scheerenberger, 1976). At any point in time, 1 percent of the total population is sufficiently retarded to have been so identified; 10 percent of the identified group (or 1/10 of 1% of the total population) will at one time or another be placed in an institution or alternative residence (Blatt et al., 1977). However, those are gross estimates that "hide" the great discrepancies among the many published estimates of incidence and prevalence of mental retardation (Blatt et al., 1977).

This report is based on my last series of field visits to "the lower world" of institutions for the retarded. The idea of engaging in a round of field trips to homes for the mentally retarded took hold in the early winter of 1975. About a decade earlier, Fred Kaplan and I set out to visit five state institutions for the mentally retarded and found ourselves forcing, bluffing, or wheedling our way into hell holes. From our recorded observations, *Christmas in Purgatory* (Blatt & Kaplan, 1966) was published.

During the ensuing years, many laws and regulations were created to mitigate if not erase forever the mistreatment of institutional inmates. Many new programs were organized to provide more normalizing and humanizing institutional settings. New facilities were built. More people than ever before were trained to work with the disabled. Consumers and their advocates were welcomed to participate with policy and service delivery groups. Presidents of the United States, their Cabinet members, and various other federal, state, and local officials, as well as foundation heads and industrial leaders, ordinary citizens, and celebrities were made aware of the plight of institutional inmates. An impressive number of people pledged their personal and organizational commitments to a better if not complete solution of the problem. "Deinstitutionalization" became a rallying cry for many and became a priority of governmental agencies as well as of voluntary and scientific societies. People shouted polemics, hurled challenges, and made promises of all kinds: they promised not to forget, to achieve justice for those wronged, to create better institutions, to destroy institutions forever, to tame the wild beasts, to recreate our society so that people no longer would be made into wild beasts.

Ten years later, I felt it was time to intrude again, to visit the institutions we once described as bastilles, as dreaded places, as purgatory, as pandemonium. I also thought it was time to visit some of those places developed in more recent years to correct the abuses of the past. With Andrejs Ozolins and Joseph McNally, then students at Syracuse University, we visited fourteen residential centers in seven states. Our report of those experiences, *The Family Papers: A Return to Purgatory* (in press), described The Family, which has—whether wittingly or unwittingly, by deception or self-deception—succeeded in preventing thousands of mentally retarded people from participating in the entitlements of their citizenship. We discovered and documented what The Family has known for generations but has kept secret from the rest of the world. Who are The Family? It's all of those who work, or say they work, with the problems of retarded people in institutionalized settings. It's the supervisors, superintendents, and commissioners. It's the professional societies such as the American Association on Mental Deficiency and the Council for Exceptional Children.

In this chapter, I will attempt to explain what I found out during those visits and why I wanted to make them. Relying heavily on my diary of that period, I want to describe the forces that brought us together as collaborators, found us sponsorship, opened institutional doors for us, and all too often shut those doors when we asked the institutions to make good on their promises to permit publication of the pictures taken. Ten years ago, one could visit institutions only by stealth, or arm-twisting, or string-pulling. The only photographs we could get had to be taken with a concealed camera. Although the barricades of rules and restrictions are less formidable today, they still exist. Institutions are still hard to get into, and taking photographs in such places is still very difficult for anyone and next to impossible for most people. Once taken, The Family usually does everything it possibly can to prevent the publication of such pictures; everything has changed during the decade between Purgatory and today, but nothing is changed. Why? This chapter will explore some of the nearly infinite ways The Family has for keeping the lid on. Beyond The Family, it will examine such diverse factors as the economics of mental retardation, unionism, and the wish to avoid the fragile and mortal nature of mankind. Out of those conditions was born the Pariah Industry.

What does all of this have to do with child abuse? Not much if we think of every serious problem as isolated, and if we require one analysis to understand child abuse and still another to understand wife-beating. But what I've learned about institutional abuse has a great deal to do with my understanding of child abuse. If we think of the world as one, then there are infinite real connections of its parts. Prejudice is prejudice and abuse is abuse, wherever it exists and whomever it touches.

PURGATORY: 1965

On our original journey to Purgatory in 1965, we observed scenes of un-
mitigated horror and cruelty. The four institutions we visited, as well as
countless others across the nation, were a secret world of torment vigi-
lantly protected from intrusion and public scrutiny. While America busied
itself with the space race, flower children and the Super Bowl, here was a
world apart from it all, suspended in despair. Not just a few, but thousands of human beings spent their lives in conditions that would be de-
plorable for animals.

In many "dayrooms"—large rooms which in institutions presumably
serve the same function as the living room in your home—there was excre-
ment all over floors, walls, even ceilings. People were ill-clothed, and many
weren't clothed at all. The smell of filth was unbearable. The sound of
shouting, screaming, and moaning echoed in the tiled chambers. Care was
virtually nonexistent, and education was entirely nonexistent—although
these places were called "State Schools."

Even toward children, the heart of institutions was hardened. Without playthings, without friendship or stimulation from other human beings, institutionalized children were inexorably on the way to becoming
institutionalized adults.

There was nothing to redeem these places. In each of them there was,
of course, the occasional ray of hope, the rare person who treated residents with love and worked to help them. But no benefit to a few could
mitigate the betrayal of the many.

We also visited a fifth institution ten years ago that was quite different. The Seaside Regional Center in Connecticut showed what a difference could be made where genuine respect was accorded all human beings.

The budget was bigger, adequate to meet the residents' needs. But,
more important, Seaside was a place where the staff at all levels acted on
the belief that each person is valuable, capable of growth, deserving of
attention—and the residents responded in a way that justified this belief.
The experience of Seaside gave us courage to hope that the other institutions could be changed.

But we were wrong.

PURGATORY TODAY: FIELD NOTE EXCERPTS

In recent years, an enormous amount of money and energy has been invested in correcting abuses. To see what ten years and millions of dollars
had accomplished in the way of change, I decided to visit not only all of

"Return to purgatory." Photo by Joseph McNally.

the institutions represented in *Christmas in Purgatory*, but new experiments in the field, including modern institutions and alternatives to institutions.

Initially, my intention was to do this study by myself. *Christmas in Purgatory* had been done without a research budget, and I wanted to keep my faith that some important things can be learned without necessarily spending a lot of money. A small but full cup can be good.

Early in 1975, I started to implement my idea. I visited one large traditional institution, two of the newer regional center-type settings, and one community-based facility. At this point, The President's Committee on Mental Retardation contacted me. The Committee's Director, Fred Krause, felt I should apply for a grant to finish the work. By the time I had completed still another visit on my own, a grant from the President's Committee came through, and Andrejs Ozolins and Joseph McNally joined me in the study. For the visits to nine more facilities, for more than 3000 pictures taken, for the many hours of later work, discussion, and writing over a two-year period, the budget was $3300. For the three of us, an essential hypothesis of this examination was the belief that small can be better. And we wanted the conduct of the study itself to illustrate the relationship of smallness to fullness, of conservation to sufficiency. We wanted to examine what might be accomplished with limited resources.

A TRADITIONAL LARGE STATE INSTITUTION

Flying thousands of feet above the ground, I read a story in the *New York Times* about the institution I'm going to visit. The director has been transferred, the *Times* reports, to a new position while maintaining his previous salary of $42,000 a year. Another story stated that people are going to court to get the residents of the institution transferred to new facilities, back to their families, to foster homes, or to halfway houses, virtually anywhere so long as they are out of the institution. I knew that it costs $30,000 a year to keep each resident in the institution and I wondered if residents would maintain their "salaries" if transferred back to their homes. But the rules for mentally retarded people are different from the rules for their keepers. The *Times* carried no story on this difference. (Maybe it isn't fit to print.)

Back at this terrible place I've been trying to wipe from my memory. We trudged from building to building, classroom to classroom, living unit to dying unit, and I looked for the changes that ten years and a current budget of $70,000,000 have made in this institution.

Is it a difference that along the rows of toilets in full view of everyone there now appeared an occasional roll of toilet paper? A cynical member of our party remarked that this was the first time she had seen toilet paper here, that it was probably set out for our benefit. ("Not for our benefit to *use*," she explained, noticing my uneasiness, "but to *see*.") An occasional toilet now even had a seat, to insulate one from the cold of the porcelain. But hardly ever did a toilet offer *both* a seat and paper.

The buildings were the same as always. They were less crowded, less dirty, less foul-smelling, but the same. In Building 8, more people were wearing clothes, but not in a way that makes a difference. No inmate yet has clothes of his own; each day brings its chance at the grabbag, the common pool of garments. A person may draw a nice flannel shirt with buttons one day, but the next is apt to bring an old torn one. There may or may not be socks, or underwear; and the odds are good that, on any given day, the shoes will be the wrong size or have no laces or a brown shoe will be the mate to a white sneaker.

For most of the inmates there are still no activities, no recreation, no education, no deviation from purposeless routine. After ten years of prom-

"Purposeless routine." Photo by Andrejs Ozolins.

ises and resolutions, the people caught in this institution continue to be reduced to the same collection of head-bangers, shit-kickers, vomiters, sore-pickers, screechers, assaulters, sleepers, and weepers. And armed with their authoritative rings of keys is the same collection of attendants sitting or standing around, watching, chatting, drowsing. In a world of agony and chaos, the attendants are ready to swing into action should anything "unusual" happen. Otherwise, only seldom does one of them reach out and make contact with an inmate.

I had seen it all too many times before. A gust of clear fresh air rushed around us as the front door was unlocked for our escape from the terror inside. Suddenly the relief of regaining my freedom was shattered by a scream from above. "Goodbye, you fuckin' doctors!" A shirtless man, with a face twisted in anger, was waving his fist from a second story window. I smiled and waved to him. He waved back and, as anger gave way to a smile, he waved again, this time with open palm. He was in Building

191

8, a "custodial" dormitory for people the institution labeled "severely mentally retarded"—for people who label their keepers "you fuckin' doctors."

The tour took me through other dormitories, past rows and rows of beds where, now and then, a huddled figure with blanket drawn over his head was moaning, past naked people, or someone very small or very large, or someone who doesn't look different from you or me. Twisted and gnarled bodies are not to be found in this sea of beds—the special among the special are kept together in places reserved for them—the "crib cases" or "bed cases," and in due course my tour passed through these places too.

In the school building, even the teachers seem to have given in to the daze of institutional purposelessness that pervades the dormitories. "There is no progress here—most of the children regress." They speak calmly of what once might have made them angry, or what once might have fired their dedication. "If you complain to get changes or more support, it goes on your record as a mark against you."

The teachers speak about their lesson plans, their curriculum, their planning conferences on children. There is no planning, but there are plan books. There is no curriculum development, though there are plenty of curricula around. As for individual planning conferences, there is lots of talk, mostly complaining, about children. A fog of impotence hangs over the place, penetrated by only one clear understanding: "If you get too many marks on your record, you might lose your job. Jobs are hard to get these days."

Such helplessness in a place that had an average of $30,000 a year to spend for each resident was puzzling. Why aren't things better? My discussion of this with the supervisors gave me the one good feeling I had since the hot coffee on my morning flight from Syracuse. Those supervisors were human beings. They were worried and hurt. They did not know why things were the way they were. They knew the institution had a $70,000,000 budget and wondered why they couldn't equip a classroom adequately. They knew that the institution had been permitted to hire hundreds of additional staff and wondered why there were still only one or two attendants for large groups of residents. They knew that many specialized doctors and psychologists and other professionals had been made available for consultation and help, and they wondered why those supposed colleagues were so seldom seen, and when seen were so little help. "If you're puzzled," they asked, "how the hell do you think we feel?"

In seeing their confusion and concern, the idea came over me that, although there might be no hope for institutions, there was hope for the people. The supervisors lacked the vision or courage to put an end to institutionalization, but they had the humanity to recognize that de-institu-

"The institution school." Photo by Burton Blatt.

tionalization was the only decent answer to the horror in which they were implicated. They felt imprisoned and isolated as much as the residents. "I wish I could convince myself to speak out. I wish there were others who would speak out with me," they confided. "I wish we could go to their meetings and tell the administrators what they have done to the residents. And to us." It felt good to be convinced of their humanity. I only wish I could decide whether their anguish and good intentions excused their lack of courage.

A NEW SMALL STATE INSTITUTION

The day-long training session for this institution's staff featured several films on sex education. I did not stay to watch them, but I was tempted. They included one for "trainables," one for "educables," and one on "fertility regulation for persons with learning disabilities." I was curious about what the term "fertility regulation" would turn out to mean. Also an important lesson seemed to be implied by the fact that those who are mentally retarded were referred to as "trainables" and "educables," while those with learning disabilities were called "persons." But I doubted that would be the lesson under discussion, so I hurried off to my guided tour.

The institution was small (that is, for institutions), clean (as institutions go), more homelike than the traditional large places, and expensive almost beyond belief. The building, which when filled could hold about 140 residents, cost over $11,000,000, or almost $80,000 for each bed. The yearly cost of running the place with its 120 current residents was $8,000,000, or about $65,000 per resident. It was the most expensive program for retarded people I had ever seen, yet nothing particularly exceptional distinguished it.[1] The quality of life here was certainly above the average for institutions, but not all that different from many other such places one can find around the country. Throughout my tour, I could not take my mind off the costs. People sleeping in $80,000 "beds" and with "incomes" of $65,000 a year—and they were still institutionalized. They were still ostracized and isolated, killing time, their lives hopelessly and inevitably wasted. They had asked for bread and love, but they were given expensive stone and metal and hospitalization.

The more I saw, the more clearly I was driven to a harsh conclusion: People are not institutionalized for their good but for their money. Over and over, I find economics at the bottom of problems that well-meaning people have tried to treat as educational or philosophical or therapeutic. Most states finance institutions the same way people finance their homes, by mortgaging the property. To pay off the mortgage, the states count on the money to which mentally retarded people are entitled—most of it through social security payments. But such payments can be applied to construction debts only if those mentally retarded people occupy the buildings. Thus, if the people were moved from a fairly new institution to community accommodations, a serious problem would arise: Who would pay off the bond-holders?

Some time later when I made these points in a talk, using this new, small institution as an example, the director was irritated but inadvertently confirmed my argument. He pointed out that the institution was not full, that when it is eventually filled to capacity the *per capita* cost will fall from $65,000 to $40,000, maybe even as low as $30,000 a year. In finding fault with my presentation, he merely illustrated my point; the institution needs more inmates to defray and reduce the cost. For example, if only one person were left in the place, it would still have cost $11,000,000

1. In recent months I have been to an "institution" for the mentally retarded that budgets almost $90,000 a year per resident.

a year to have built it. In fact, if no one were left, it would still have cost $11,000,000 a year. The state committed itself to pay that cost no matter what. This is why the state simply cannot afford to evacuate institutions. If we challenge the institutional approach to problems like mental retardation, we threaten the solvency of the state in meeting its bond obligations, we endanger its economic structure by raising the specter of an unemployed army of civil servants who now work in institutions and, ultimately, we attack the stability of political organizations that rest on the continuation of present financial and employment patterns.

A NEW SMALL STATE REGIONAL PROGRAM

One alternative to large institutions is the "regional program," and I had the opportunity to visit one responsible for 730 individuals. All of the clients were in some form of residential community placement and were apparently well-served at an average annual cost of $8500 per client. I mainly visited families living in typical middle-class suburban or rural homes. One such family had two of their own children in addition to the three foster children placed by this program. Another couple, older and themselves the parents of a mentally retarded young man, had two teen-agers living with them as part of the regional program. These families and others I visited impressed me as good places: good for the clients and good for the families. It was a successful demonstration that a region can meet the special needs of mentally retarded people by using the resources that any community has: ordinary homes, ordinary people, with the guidance of some sensible and concerned professionals.

Of course, not everything was perfect. There were problems to be faced: concerns about foster parents who may be cheating, inadequate attention to the sexual development of foster children, and larger issues like government interference and red tape. However, the matter of dishonest foster parents, although serious, is not an argument against foster parent programs in general, any more than the fact of bad natural parents is an argument against procreation. Specific problems such as sex education are likely to be merely the same kinds of problems that all parents and children have. Perhaps it is only our lingering stereotype of retarded people that makes such matters appear especially difficult. In facing the sexual development of retarded children, we are self-conscious and awkward. With typical children we are unconscious and awkward.

But, while so much has been done in residential community placements to make life normal for retarded people, government regulations and impersonal bureaucratic decision-making seems relentless in making it abnormal. It does this in little but maddening ways like requiring institutional fire codes to be met in single-family homes or deciding inscrutably that a family happily getting along with three foster children must give one child up. But it also interferes in big, even more maddening ways. While this regional center was demonstrating that institutions are unnecessary, the state was constructing a brand new institution. While a superb community-based service was provided at a yearly average of $8500 per person, the residential program in the institution was projected to cost $35,000 per person. At a construction cost of $10,000,000, that state is demonstrating that no amount of new evidence that communities can take care of their own, and no amount of historical evidence that institutions are inevitably inhumane, can count against its determination to build monuments.

A COMMUNITY-BASED VOLUNTEER AGENCY PROGRAM

I have learned to distrust the pleasant trappings of new programs, the striking architecture or picturesque settings, and especially the promises that something different or good is happening. Yet, here was a facility that not only had the trappings, set in a beautiful valley at the foot of majestic mountains, but had actually kept the promise of being different. If there can be good institutions, this was one. But it was less a good institution than a day center.

At the core of the difference between this place and "real" institutions was the fact that the attractive new building was not the sum total of what was going on. In fact, it was a relatively small part, and the staff wore me out tramping all over town to group homes.

I visited young men and women, living independent lives in their own apartments, confronting the joys and vicissitudes of life with confidence and evident maturity. So many of my beliefs were reaffirmed and revitalized by these encounters with men and women, boys and girls, living in ordinary homes as ordinary people, which was in itself remarkable because they were people who might otherwise have been institutionalized.

The day center bears the unfortunate name of "normalization cottage," but I have never felt more at home outside my own home than at that cottage. I had dinner there with the children (those they called children really were children) and the house parents (who really behaved like parents). We stayed up half the night talking about the new world being created for people in this city. There was a lot that was pleasant to talk about. The Center is a fine new facility which cost $3,000,000 to build and serves 800 people each day. That's a bargain price these days, but even more importantly, the service delivered is helpful and purposeful, and that can't be said for institutions where the cost is ten times higher. The group homes created and supervised by the Center's staff are a still more impressive expression of human decency and kinship. There was a clearheadedness about the people here in facing the same problems that were faced by workers in the most horrifying of the big institutions—a clearheadedness that enabled them to meet the special needs of their clients rather than get caught up in the endless struggle to overcome the demands of the institution.

I had been invited to this center to give a lecture, but I found myself feeling awkward at being thanked for my talk. I was sure they couldn't possibly value what I had said as much as I valued what they had accomplished.

Conclusion

The field visits I have described were undertaken to examine what a decade of energetic reform had accomplished. I found institutions that were somewhat smaller in population, noticeably cleaner, less abusive. In a sense, I observed *ameliorated* abuse. Essentially, what progress has been made results from the degree to which institutions have become smaller but not essentially better. The primary question remains: Why do institutions exist even though they are not good for people? What follows may provide part of the answer to that vexing question.

Mental retardation is big business. The Rand Corporation reported several years ago that government agencies expend 2.8 billion dollars annually to serve mentally retarded youth (Kakalik, 1973). Mental health is big business. Governor Hugh Carey recommended a $924 million Department of Mental Hygiene budget for New York's 1977 fiscal year, "part of the Governor's 10.7 billion austerity budget" (*Mental Hygiene News*, January 30, 1976, p. 1). This recommended Mental Hygiene budget for 1977 may be contrasted with the $640.2 million appropriated in New York State for fiscal year 1973. Institutionalization is big business. The 1975 appropriation for the Willowbrook Developmental Center was approximately $62 million. This came to an annual expenditure of more than $20,000 per resident at Willowbrook and at virtually every other state institution in New York. Today, per capita expenditures at Willowbrook are nearly twice that amount. Even de-institutionalization is big business, from those who are engaged in trust-busting and monolith-wrecking to others who create and manage community alternatives. There is no way to avoid the plain fact that special education–mental health–mental retardation is big business. On almost any day, the *New York Times* includes front page stories, Sunday features, Sunday magazine cover stories, items in the news section, and items in the business section, each in some fundamental way related to the big business that is the Handicapped Industry (Blatt, 1976).

It is sacred business, too! Hardly anyone noticed that 1976 Presidential-candidate Ronald Reagan's ill-fated proposal to cut $90 billion from the federal budget avoided assault on allocations for the handicapped. Our pariahs have become holy Untouchables, for the most part segregated without the opportunity to lead normal lives, surrounded by government and philanthropic agents committed to protect to the last their right to be different, with that right to be backed by the dollars. In this modern era we insist on creating and maintaining certain problems, expending whatever outrageous resources are necessary to support them.

The handicapped are big business, but more like the game of Monopoly than the work of people who sell or buy or grow or invent. Like Monopoly, the Handicapped Business appears unreal, the money seems more like paper, and accomplishes little. The promises aren't really meant and few take them seriously. When Rockefeller, Carnegie, Mellon, and the rest of the robber barons made philanthropy big business, their efforts led not only to significant changes in the curricula of our schools but in the extent and manner of government aid to those in need. Prior to the turn of this century, most schools and all universities were uniformly devoted to the classics, the sciences, and the learned professions. Big business taught us that they could also be used to teach people how to do a job, how to earn a living, how to contribute to business, which one former President was wont to tell us is America's business. Big business also taught us how to organize our philanthropies to serve the people and, furthermore, how to organize the people—the State—to serve both business and philanthropy.

In America there is enough for everyone, for the rich and the poor, the healthy and the sick, the sound and the unsound, the philanthropic person and the business person. Let's look at some data.

In 1965, Governor Nelson Rockefeller embarked upon a five-year, $500 to $600 million mental hygiene construction program as part of a master plan for the mentally disabled. New York State approved 40 major projects at a construction cost of $320.3 million. The program included an additional $188 million for modernization of existing facilities, plus $100 million to help construct community mental health facilities. As of 1972, 23 of the original 40 major projects had been completed or were under construction; they exceeded cost estimates by 50 percent, or $94 million, a discrepancy that construction inflation is unable to account for. When the revised total plan was more or less implemented, 28 projects

"The institution is big business." Photo by Andrejs Ozolins.

had been completed at a cost of $343.5 million, $23 million over the original estimate for all 40 projects, and with but 48 percent of the original
number of beds planned (not an unmixed curse). When everything was
said, constructed, and explained, the 7500 beds that became the basic
products of the then governor Rockefeller's master plan cost the taxpayers
of New York State approximately $45,000 per bed for construction and
approximately 1½ to 2 times that amount additionally ($65,000 to $90,000)
to meet fund obligations, to pay off the banks, the foundations, and the
other bond holders who "own" those facilities.

A recently completed study by the New York State Department of
Mental Hygiene, unpublished but documented, disclosed that residents
in group homes for the so-called mentally retarded incurred expenditures
of $6700 per annum, while institutionalized residents required $34,000.
The data are difficult to believe, especially after visiting Camp Hill, or
L'Arche, or any number of normalized communities or homes, and then
contrasting those visits with observations in Willowbrook, Belchertown,
or even the spanking new Syracuse Developmental Center. "Segregation"
isn't the only issue. Willowbrook is segregated. But so is Camp Hill and,
in a sense, so is every village or community.

A recent report issued by the New York State Assembly Joint Committee to Study the Department of Mental Hygiene (1976) revealed that family care requires $7 a day and residential services for the mentally ill or mentally retarded cost from $50 to almost $90 a day. And, although family care and other community placements may incur additional educational and other treatment services, just as frequently such services may be available from existing city, county, or state programs.

There are fixed costs, some of gigantic dimensions, not accounted for in the above discussion: pension costs for personnel, government and other grants, various kinds of interest rates, costs that are so hidden that even the most penetrating search has yet to uncover them. The question that we return to again and again is why New York and other states continue to construct and support segregated places? Some answers include the following: unions—for example, the 65,000 union employees of the New York State Departments of Mental Health and Mental Retardation/ Developmental Disabilities increased by 10,000 in little more than three years—contractors, builders, architects, real estate entrepreneurs, and others anxious to be business associates of the most affluent purchaser of construction in any state, that is, the state itself.

In 1963, also at the behest of Governor Rockefeller, our legislature created the Health and Mental Hygiene Facilities and Improvement Fund, an organization that has had several name changes but has remained steadfast in its mission to execute the construction program of the Department of Mental Hygiene (New York State Legislative Review, 1973). Its first responsibilities involved the Fund in completing work on a $350,000,000 Mental Hygiene bond issue. However, since its January 1964 take-over date, HMHFIC (or you may use its newer name, the Facilities Development Corporation), has spent over one billion dollars on mental hygiene construction. Financing is arranged through the State Housing Agency, which issues bonds that are converted to the dollars necessary to construct our state schools and mental hospitals. Eventually, institutional and individual investors purchase these bonds because the income on them is tax-free. They provide the lender with a virtually fail-safe method to earn reasonable interest on his money. Standard and Poor & Moody have rated these bonds safe, even in the face of New York City's and New York State's various fiscal crises, because all income to mental hygiene facilities—income directly from patients or their families and income from federal or other third party sources, such as from Title 19 of the Social Security Act—is pledged to the Mental Hygiene Facilities Improvement Fund before other creditors are paid; the bond holders must be paid first, as in any good business.

The bond holders are happy, but we have a problem if we wish to free the retarded and others from institutional settings. How do we convert such segregated facilities to useful purposes? How can these thousands of people return to normal community life without the state bankrupting itself in attempts to meet bond obligations and other commitments to the business community? First, we must recognize the extent to which supposedly nonprofit philanthropic and helping agencies are entangled in the world of commerce. Second, we must interest other clientele in using the now-segregated facilities we have erroneously created for the handicapped, the aged, and other dependent groups. But we must *not* create new segregated programs and *not* involve devalued people in those conversions. Such usage would merely perpetuate past sins. To complete a conversion plan, as each facility is evacuated by mental patients, state school residents, and the aged, institutional program budgets would follow the clients to the community while new public agencies or private investors would pick up additional construction costs for the new tenants.

Let's stop the foolishness. We don't need long lists of recommendations. We don't need task forces, mission councils, or evaluation teams. The time is long past for such nonsense. We don't need joint accreditation commissions or coordinating groups. We need to empty the institutions. We need to convert the institutional model to a community model. The quicker we accomplish that goal the quicker we will be able to repair the damage done to generations and generations of so-called defectives. The quicker we convert the institution's monolith to diversified community support systems, the quicker will we forgive ourselves for what we have done to other human beings.

So far, I've said nothing about our research methodology, but we had one and we believe we adhered to it. I learned more at the Walter E. Fernald State School than at Boston University, more at the Willowbrook Developmental Center than at the New York Public Library, more at the Syracuse Developmental Center than at Syracuse University. I found more to study at the University, but I discovered more at the State School. Where does research end and reporting take over? Of those who believe this account, there will be some people who will mark it all down as journalism rather than as research. Research begins with definitions. We have definitions. It proceeds with the methodology. We designed a methodology. It requires precision in collecting data, in analyzing data, and in describing the settings and conditions. Here's where some readers may conclude we've failed. Where is the precision? There are those who assume that precision is enhanced with more knowledge, with the application of scientific principles and procedures. Quite the opposite actually occurs. The greater the knowledge, the more difficult it is to attain precision. For example, the Neanderthal was more certain—had more precision—in determining man from woman than some current leading experts. A hundred years ago, scholars in the field of mental retardation easily discriminated between the mentally retarded and the typical. Just 20 years ago, it was less difficult than today to determine who was blind; with the invention of high powered lenses, it became more difficult to discriminate between those who do see and those who don't. With transistorized amplification tools, those who were once deaf may now hear. With the advent of fenestration surgery, a deaf person may be cured. All of these advances have resulted in less precise and more ambiguous categorical designations than heretofore.

The definition of something is never removed from a social-psychological-clinical-political-economic milieu. Not even death or life are exceptions because today there is ambiguity even here. Possibly only pregnancy is an unambiguous condition. Conditions are metaphors and, therefore, can be understood only in terms of functional definitions and histories that bring perspective to these terms. When there was no more precise tool than an eyeball, as great or greater agreement was achieved by the eyeball than by the subsequent micrometer, and still later than by the electron microscope. Achieving precision requires agreement on definition and "satisfactory" reliability of measurement, and these are social and psychological as well as scientific components. Explicitly, the more one learns about a condition, the more ambiguous he may become. And, conversely, the less he knows, the more certain and reliable he can be. This confusion has led to the search for more precise definitions, and that objective has promoted the need for more precise instrumentation and scientific application to the solution of certain problems. Of course, we are not seeking a return to Neanderthal times, but a better understanding of what we are searching for and why. Furthermore, as we achieve agreement on a definition, the next step in a research program might well be to determine whether a micrometer, or the mind's eye, or a camera is needed to measure the mass. For this research, we concluded that cameras and naturalistic observations were the most precise research tools available for the examinations to be done.

Years ago, officials told us that we could not enter certain institutions because such intrusions would violate the privacy of the inmates. Was it invasion of "privacy," or was it "seclusion," or "suffering in mutual degradation" which was violated? What is privacy? What is concealment? What is designed to protect, and what is protected to merely serve oneself? That which is freedom to one beholder is tyranny to another. If we violated any privacy, it was the privacy of the caretakers that was violated. By definition, inmates have no privacy. The claim about such things as privacy, due process, equal protection, and equal opportunity for inmates is the talk of those who bear gifts that can be withdrawn rather than of those who would defend another's equality as a human being.

We saw institutions that provide services such as barbering that can be found easily and inexpensively in any ordinary town. We saw institutions with bizarre needs, such as one whose laundry processes 2.3 million pounds per year, yet the place remains dirty, and the people continue to look dirty. We saw institutions where the services may be defined by the kinds of workers the state employs and how the people look. Barbering is important. Dentistry appears to be less important. Laundry is very important. We saw institutions where there is a great deal of sitting around, or standing around, or lying about, each person alone. We saw dormitories and day rooms, each with many people, where no one can be alone but where everyone is alone. When there are "inviting" benches for a group to share, each selects his or her solitary table. Even in so-called normalized settings, where the "picture" is more pleasing to the eye, there remained little if anything to do. Mealtime was preceded by a waiting period. Post-mealtime by a waiting period. We saw dormitories built like bathrooms with beds. We saw old buildings, old corridors, old ideas. We also saw new buildings, new corridors, old ideas.

Years ago we embarked upon a study of five institutions for the mentally retarded. In the subsequent years, I have visited hundreds of other residential and day settings. Most recently, we focused our energies on fourteen residential centers located in seven states. Years ago, I visited Purgatory during the Christmas season. As I write this paper, people are welcoming Christmas again. What must I conclude? As Main Street changes, as your town changes, so too does Purgatory change. But as your town endures, so too has Purgatory endured. I had again spent Christmas in Purgatory.

12

Corporal Punishment in the Schools: Some Paradoxes, Some Facts, Some Possible Directions

Norma Deitch Feshbach

The case against the use of corporal punishment in schools has been made in so many contexts and affirmed by so many psychologists, educators, and lawyers (N. Feshbach, 1976, 1977; Gil, 1970; Reitman, 1977; Williams, 1975) that the tragedy of its continuation is a greater psychological puzzle than is the appraisal of its negative effects. It is a practice whose use and justification is characterized by considerable misinformation, inconsistency, and illogic. Its existence brings to mind a scene from *Alice in Wonderland* in which the testy Duchess admonishes Alice to speak roughly to her little boy, and beat him when he sneezes. The underlying humor in the Duchess' remark does not find its counterpart in the use of corporal punishment; its irrational component, however, is paralleled by the practice.

Ironically, there may be more inconsistencies and paradoxes than facts that identify corporal punishment in schools. Some of these paradoxes as well as the facts pertinent to this topic will be reviewed in this chapter. Recommendations for alternate discipline and possible directions will also be considered.

SOME PARADOXES

THE LESSONS THAT CORPORAL PUNISHMENT TEACHES

Corporal punishment is a highly prevalent practice in schools, yet it has not been demonstrated to be effective in training children. In fact,

The author wishes to thank Michael A. Hoffman for his critical reading of the manuscript.

the data suggest that punitive teaching strategies tend to depress academic performance as well as to have adverse effects on the personality development of the student. The research base for this assertion, like other data in this area, is frequently indirect and should be interpreted cautiously. Yet, there is growing evidence that student achievement is negatively correlated with the teacher's use of punitive behaviors (Bongiovanni, 1977; Rosenshein & Furst, 1971).

Many psychologists believe that one of the most negative and serious consequences of the practice of corporal punishment in schools is that it may actually teach children to be aggressive and use aggressive alternatives in solving problems and resolving conflicts. This inference is drawn on the basis of data from studies of childrearing practices, laboratory studies on punishment, and studies of school performance and behaviors. Basically, our knowledge of how parents actually raise children is very limited. Moreover, what is known indicates that parents who make frequent use of physical and psychological punishment in training their children, do so without full realization of the negative effects. In addition, many of the studies relevant to the effect of parental use of physical punishment reflect one or another methodological limitation. However, there is a surprising degree of consistency in the overall pattern of findings yielded by these studies; in general, they show that the degree of parental punitiveness is positively correlated with various forms of psychopathology, especially deliquency and aggressive acting-out behavior (Feshbach & Feshbach, 1971; McCord, McCord, & Howard, 1961). The positive relationship found in a large number of studies between parental use of physical punishment and aggressive, antisocial behavior in the child is especially revealing. The inhibiting potential of physical punishment appears to be outweighed by the frustration and modeling engendered by parental use of physical punishment.

The purpose of punishment is to reduce or eliminate the behavior that is being punished. Thus, in evaluating the effects of different modes of punishment and related disciplinary practices, an important criterion is the change that occurs in the punished response, a change that is rarely obtained by the use of corporal punishment in schools, since it is apparently the same children who tend to be swatted for the same school infractions.

The effects of educational discipline are not limited to an isolated prohibited response. Teachers and educators function as models, as sources of emotional security, as socializers and protectors. Because of the close relationship between child and teacher, the effect of certain types of punishment, especially corporal punishment, extends beyond the unacceptable behavior to nondeviant behaviors, to the child's self-system, and may foster unintended and undesired side effects. Consequently, in assessing certain practices such as punishment and discipline, it is necessary to go beyond the intended change in behavior and assess other areas of the child's personality that may have been differentially affected by the use of a particular mode of punishment. A child who is hit for not standing in line properly, for chewing gum, or for being sassy not only becomes motivated by fear to avoid these behaviors, but also learns that aggression is appropriate under certain circumstances; namely when one is disappointed or frustrated by others. The situation is a complex one, with many parameters influencing the child's response to the punishment administered for his infraction. However, an essential point is that the effects of a specific mode of punishment or discipline technique occur within the context of a larger interpersonal response system and may have broad consequences.

The evidence from laboratory studies with children on the use of punishment other than physical pain indicates that punishment fails to communicate the appropriate response to the child. Moreover, the evidence calls into question the effect of punishment as a suppressor of the undesired behavior (Parke, 1970). The suppression of an undesired behavior through punishment requires the right combination of a number of parameters including timing, intensity, consistency, and the affectional relationship between the child and the punitive agent. Although corporal punishment was not employed in these latter studies, its effectiveness should be dependent upon the same parameters as other modes of punishment. Neither a teacher hitting a child in anger at the moment of the crime nor a dispassionate vice-principal swatting the child several hours after an infraction satisfies the conditions that enhance the effectiveness of corporal punishment as a deterrent to future unacceptable behavior.

CORPORAL PUNISHMENT IN SCHOOLS AND DISCRIMINATION IN SCHOOLS

The use of corporal punishment in schools is frequently discriminatory in nature. The data in this area indicate that such punishment is more often directed toward minority group members and dramatically more often to males than females. Until recently, specific data relating to this issue were very sparse. In a survey carried out for the California State Assembly in 1973 it was found that 31 percent of children who were recipients of corporal punishment were minority children (California State Assembly Report, 1973).

More recent information on this issue was obtained in conjunction with a survey carried out by the Office for Civil Rights of the Department of Health, Education and Welfare. The data obtained from school administrators in 116 schools from the states of Pennsylvania, Maryland, West Virginia, Virginia, and Delaware were analyzed in terms of the use of corporal punishment by race (Glackman, Martin, Hyman, McDowell, Berv, & Spino, 1978). Overall, black students received a higher proportion (14.4%) of corporal punishment than did white peers (8.1%); but females of minority groups (1.2%) other than blacks (3.5%) received a slightly lower proportion of punishment than white females (1.4%).

The data revealed very clearly that minority children, particularly males, are corporally punished far more than their white peers, sometimes at a ratio of 4 to 1. Further, the analysis of changes from elementary to secondary school reflects that while the punishment rate for whites drops as they reach secondary school, the same decrease is not observed for minority males or black females. It does drop for females of minority groups other than black. The implications of the findings are not totally clear. Are teachers more prone to use physical punishment toward minorities? Do children of different ethnic backgrounds behave more inappropriately? Also, the data base itself is full of omissions. Nevertheless, while it is wise not to over-interpret the data, the findings are compelling and support clinical observation and newspaper reports.

The frequent claim that the use of corporal punishment in schools also reflects sex discrimination appears to be borne out from this same study. The interpretation regarding the basis for males' greater propensity for being the object of the swat is not clear from the data. However, the difference or discrimination in boys versus girls being the target is evident.

CORPORAL PUNISHMENT: CAPABILITY AND CULPABILITY

A frequent justification for the legal sanctioning of corporal punishment is that teachers and other educational personnel require it for self-protection. Violence in the schools is increasing and this factor deters school districts from abolishing regulations permitting the practice of corporal punishment. There is considerable irony in this type of rationale because corporal punishment is often injudiciously applied to the very young, or the intellectually limited, or the emotionally disturbed child. Incidents of children as young as age two being badly beaten while attending day care centers appear in newspaper accounts across the country (Maurer, 1978). Similarly, the use of aversive procedures, including the use of corporal punishment in the education of emotionally disturbed and behaviorally disordered children and youth, has been on the increase and has raised considerable concern in the professional and academic communities (Rutherford & Neil, 1978; Zigler, 1979).

Moreover, experiences with abolishing legal sanctions for its practice have not led to wholesale outbreak of undisciplined behaviors. Preliminary findings of a study examining the changes in disciplinary problems following the elimination of corporal punishment in 59 school districts reveal only one school district reporting an apparent increase in problems due to the elimination of corporal punishment. Fifteen districts reported no changes, 12 districts did not have the information, and 2 districts reported a decrease in problems (Farley, Kruetter, Russell, Blackwell, Finkelstein, & Hyman, 1978).

The task of implementing effective discipline with individuals who because of age, ability, or other factors have limited intellectual skills is not an easy one. But the ethics involved in the use of might against the least mighty of our society is a serious issue.

Society's responsibility for the protection of children and the handicapped is an almost universally recognized need (N. Feshbach, 1978; Rogers & Wrightsman, 1978). The rationale of this need is derived from the acknowledgement of children's vulnerability due to their immature developmental status. The practice of corporal punishment by a parent surrogate and by other significant socializing adults who interact with children in the context of child care centers and other educational institutions should be incompatible with the recognition of the special vulnerability of children.

The fact that educational and child centers are the only public institutions in the United States, including the military, prisons, and detention stations, in which corporal punishment can be a prescribed discipline practice is one of the more extraordinary paradoxes inherent in the use of corporal punishment in the schools. If an individual commits a crime and is committed to an institution, legal sanctions protect him from corporal punishment. But if a child commits an infraction in an educational context of an institution for the mentally retarded or emotionally handicapped, there are only a few states where he or she is protected from corporal punishment. The particular irony lies not merely in the fact that objects of corporal punishment in the schools are children rather than criminals, but most especially in the fact that educational institutions sustain the practice.

CORPORAL PUNISHMENT AND CHILD ABUSE

Perhaps the most overwhelming paradox presented by the legal existence of corporal punishment in education institutions is the fact that it coexists with a national policy approved and funded by Congress dedicated to the eradication of child abuse. The implementation of the Child Abuse Prevention Act (1973), which stimulated a national campaign to end child abuse, led to legislation at the state level requiring educators and other professionals who interact with children to report parents who abuse their children.

At the same time, 46 of the 50 states have other state laws that sanction the physical punishment of children by educators, a practice that, incidentally, is considered by many individuals as an institutional form of child abuse (N. Feshbach, 1976, 1977; Friedman, 1976; Gil, 1970; Reitman, 1977; Williams, 1975). The individual state laws read differently, reflecting variations in the administration of punishment, the context in which it takes place, and sometimes the circumstances that permit and justify its use (Wood & Lakin, 1978). Rarely do the legal statutes that define concretely the categories of "misbehavior" and legitimize corporal punishment detail the extent of the specific discipline practice. There is wide latitude in the states' laws with regard to the specifics of the practice.

On the basis of existing laws and practices, the judicial system allows courts to remove a child from its parents for the very same abuse that educators have the license to carry out. Many educators carry insurance policies that sometimes provide coverage of over a quarter of a million dollars for a single offense committed against a child.

CORPORAL PUNISHMENT AND *In Loco Parentis*

Corporal punishment in the schools is a key issue in the current debate over children's rights. This issue, like most others in children's rights, raises the question of the balance of rights (N. Feshbach, 1978; Feshbach & Feshbach, 1978b). Does the extension or deprivation of a right or responsibility of one segment of a society affect or infringe upon the rights and responsibilities of another segment in that society? This question is especially relevant to the use of corporal punishment in the schools. Here we have the possibility of children's rights conflicting with teacher rights (e.g., the child's need or right not to be the object of physical abuse versus the teacher's right or role to maintain authority and manage a classroom); the child's right versus the parents' right (e.g., a child's freedom to choose not to receive discipline in the form of physical punishment versus the parents' decision to grant permission to the school to exercise this type of control). Moreover, the issue of corporal punishment in schools raises the question of possible conflict between parents' and family's rights versus the rights and roles of educators—the latter representing the state's rights. For example, parents may not consent to give the school permission to administer physical discipline to their child—a right or privilege that the school assumes. Incongruously, the state, in assuming this right, may, under the guise of *in loco parentis*, be preempting an important individual or family right.

The doctrine of *in loco parentis*, enunciated in the eighteenth century, is one of the legal justifications for extending disciplinary responsibilities to educators. Essentially, a parent may delegate part of his parental authority, during his life, to the tutor or schoolmaster of his child, who is then *in loco parentis*, and has such a portion of the power of the parent, viz., that of restraint and correction, as may be necessary for the fulfillment of the role for which he is employed. Thus a parent surrogate, such as a teacher, is given the right to deal with a child or youth as the parent would in the same situation, including the use of reasonable corporal punishment.

However, the application of the concept of *in loco parentis* may go too far. The teacher's right to punish a child physically for an infraction frequently supercedes parental wishes. For example, in one well known Supreme Court case, *Baker v. Owen* (1975), teachers' prerogatives regarding physical punishment were interpreted to be the more important. In this case the Supreme Court let stand a lower court ruling that North Carolina school authorities had the right to use corporal punishment on a sixth grade boy despite his mother's written note forbidding them to do so. This ruling supported the rights of school authorities to use moderate corporal punishment in disciplining children. Thus the basis for the original sanctioning of regulations such as corporal punishment in schools, the delegation of parental authority to a surrogate, is reinforced by a Supreme Court decision supporting the surrogate's authority in contrast to the parent's. The paradox here lies in the conflict between a ruling that supports a particular practice and the philosophy or justification behind the practice.

CORPORAL PUNISHMENT AND ASSUMPTIONS ABOUT CHILDREN

The accepted practice of corporal punishment in our schools contrasts not only with legislation against child abuse but with other contemporary efforts on behalf of children; for example, the activities of professionals and government groups regarding children's participation in research. These professionals are asking questions regarding the freedom and competence of all individuals, including children, to make choices regarding various types of physical and psychological treatment (Frankel, 1978; Ferguson, 1978). The principles at work in the formulation of a rationale for informed consent and privacy for children's research participation are based on assumptions that contrast sharply with the assumptions that permit the use of corporal punishment in schools. Two of the assumptions underlying the recommendations of the National Commission for the Protection of Human Subjects are first, a consideration of the child as a person, not a chattel of his parents, the state, or any other institution of the society; and, secondly, the recognition that parental consent is a necessary but not a sufficient condition for children's participation in research. These principles impart a dignity to the conception of the child that differs markedly from those implicit in the use of corporal punishment.

A joint statement on the use of corporal punishment released a number of years ago by the National Conference on Corporal Punishment, ACLU, the American Orthopsychiatric Association, and the National Education Association's Task Force on Corporal Punishment illustrates this latter position:

> The use of physical violence on school children is an affront to democratic values and infringement of individual rights. It is a degrading, dehumanizing and counter-productive approach to the maintenance of discipline in the classroom and should be outlawed from educational institutions as it has already been outlawed from other institutions in American society. (Reitman, Follman, & Ladd, 1972, p. 36)

SOME FACTS

One of the major ironies with regard to corporal punishment in the schools is the discrepancy between the prevalence of the practice and the knowledge base regarding its effects. Very little accurate information exists. The general issue of children's rights evokes strong reactions from individuals in our society and the specific issue of corporal punishment seems particularly provocative and personal. Perhaps this emotional component is partially responsible for the myths that surround this topic, the lack of available information, and the denial of the extent of its use, as well as the denial of the many physical dangers that sometimes ensue from the practice, including brain damage (Friedman, 1976).

STATES RIGHTS

Some preliminary data in regard to the use and extent of corporal punishment in schools are available. Approximately 80 percent of the public schools in the United States permit the practice of corporal punishment in schools. Three states have statutes that prohibit the use of corporal punishment. New Jersey was the first state to ban the practice, although the language used in the specific statute regarding its use has varied over the years (New Jersey Revised Statutes, 18A; 6–1). Maine is the latest state to prohibit corporal punishment. The regulations in both New Jersey and Maine prohibit the use of corporal punishment but allow for a reasonable degree of force to be used when a need arises for control (Maine Laws, 17 AMRSA; 106; sut.; 2.). The wording of the statute in

Massachusetts, the third state that has passed legislation forbidding corporal punishment, is less qualified. It reads, "The power of the school committee or any teacher to maintain discipline upon school property shall not include the right to inflict corporal punishment" (Annotated Laws of Massachusetts, 71:376).

There are a variety of laws and rules governing corporal punishment in other states, including bans (not laws) prohibiting its use (e.g., Hawaii); regulations sanctioning its use but allowing for parental discretion (e.g., California); regulations pertaining to its use as justification of reasonable force (e.g., Arizona); regulations that assign local districts the responsibility for approval and regulation (e.g., Arkansas); and regulations that prohibit local districts from having the authority to forbid its use (e.g., Nevada, North Carolina) (Wood & Lakin, 1978).

Although estimates indicate that six percent of the students in the United States have been recipients of physical punishment during a given year (Glackman et al., 1978), frequencies of occurrence vary from state to state. As the following table reflects, corporal punishment is a low prob-

TABLE 12.1: Estimates of frequency of pupils receiving formal corporal punishment by states

< 1%	> 1% < 2%	> 2% < 5%	> 5%
Massachusetts	Michigan	Kansas	North Carolina
New Jersey	Alaska	Idaho	South Carolina
Rhode Island	Washington	Wyoming	New Mexico
Hawaii	Oregon	Delaware	Ohio
New Hampshire	Pennsylvania	Arizona	Kentucky
Maine	Virginia	Louisiana	Alabama
Minnesota		Nevada	Tennessee
North Dakota		Illinois	Texas
New York		Indiana	Arkansas
Wisconsin		Missouri	Mississippi
South Dakota		West Virginia	Oklahoma
Vermont			Georgia
Connecticut			Florida
Utah			
Nebraska			
Maryland			
Iowa			
California			
Montana			
Colorado			

Source: U.S. Office for Civil Rights, 1976

ability occurrence in twenty states. However, the estimated percentage of pupils receiving corporal punishment can go as high as 12 percent within a particular state and more than a dozen states have records ranging from 5 percent to 12 percent. The region of the country in which corporal punishment is practiced the most appears to be the southeast. Two of the most significant court cases challenging the legality of corporal punishment in schools have stemmed from abuses occurring in Southern states (*Baker v. Owen*, 1975; *Ingraham v. Wright*, 1977).

THE INGRAHAM V. WRIGHT CASE

The 1977 ruling by the Supreme Court in the *Ingraham v. Wright* case dealt a very severe blow to the cause of the abolition of corporal punishment in schools. The ruling seemed incongruous in view of the strength of the evidence against the defendant, the school principal, Willie J. Wright. In 1970 a junior high school student in Florida named James Ingraham was slow in responding to his teacher's instruction. He was taken to the principal's office and pinioned on a table by two assistant principals, while the principal beat the boy more than 20 times with a two-foot-long wood paddle. The beating was so severe that the boy suffered a hematoma requiring medical attention that kept him out of school for 11 days. A classmate was also paddled several times for minor infractions.

The United States Supreme Court, in considering the constitutionality of these punishments, held that punishments administered to these and other students at the junior high school in question did not violate the cruel and unusual punishment clause of the Eighth Amendment to the United States Constitution. The court also held that the due process clause of the Fourteenth Amendment to the United States Constitution does not require notification of charges and an informal hearing prior to the infliction of corporal punishment. The United States Supreme Court in consenting to review the case had limited themselves to two issues: whether the cruel and unusual punishment clause of the Eighth Amendment applied to the administration of discipline through severe corporal punishment inflicted by public school teachers and administrators upon public school children, and whether infliction of severe corporal punishment upon public school students without notice of the charges for which punishment is to be inflicted and an opportunity to be heard violate the due process clause of the Fourteenth Amendment. The court refused to review the following question presented by the petitioners: was the infliction of severe corporal punishment upon public school students arbitrary, capricious, and unrelated to achieving a legitimate educational purpose and therefore in violation of the due process clause of the Fourteenth Amendment?

The decision was a split one, five-to-four, with Judge Powell presenting the majority opinion and analysis. In April 1977, the children at Drew Junior High School in Dade County, Florida, lost. And so did the individuals from significant and relevant professional groups such as the American Psychological Association and the National Education Association, who had filed briefs on behalf of the student petitioners.

CORPORAL PUNISHMENT AND SCHOOL INFRACTIONS

What are some of the other infractions, aside from a slow response to a teacher's instruction, that make one eligible for corporal punishment? They vary, and include a diversity of behaviors. The following is a list of behaviors that in some states and in some contexts make a student eligible for corporal punishment: failure to do homework or other assignments, truancy, congregating in halls and lavatories, smoking on school grounds, impertinence, tardiness, teasing, not paying attention, using profane or obscene language, cheating, vandalism, stealing, chewing gum, sailing paper airplanes, failing to say "sir," wearing sloppy clothing, striking classmates, throwing a kickball at a time other than a designated play period (this latter behavior being the behavior in question in the North Carolina Supreme Court's *Baker v. Owen* case, 1975).

As is evident from the above roster, some of the behaviors seem more critical than others. Some of the infractions are more a matter of manners than morals; some infractions are in the interpersonal sphere and more serious. The imbalance between the severity of the infraction and the severity of the punishment as well as the lack of differentiation between types of infractions eliciting corporal punishment are not likely to convey the fundamentals of justice necessary for the development of moral judgment (Kohlberg, 1969).

THE IMPLEMENT AND THE IMPLEMENTERS OF CORPORAL PUNISHMENT

The most frequent implement in the administration of corporal punishment is a paddle. The specific criteria surrounding the attributes of the paddle are very clear. In general, the specification is that paddles be not less than 13 inches nor more than 24 inches long; that they vary between 2 and 3 inches wide; and the designated thickness be between one-fourth and three-fourths of an inch. The final requirement is that the paddle be made of hard wood. The specification as to whether the paddle should be solid or latticed was difficult to ascertain. While being swatted with a paddle is the most prevalent form of physical punishment, such punishments as the forced eating of cigarettes and the standing at attention for long periods of time can also be included in the broader category of corporal punishment.

Who administers the corporal punishment? Data from a recent study (Hyman, Bongiovanni, Friedman, & McDowell, 1977) indicate that while the classroom teacher is the most frequent administrator of corporal punishment, vice-principals often have the privilege. Again, it should be pointed out that this data is preliminary and at best an estimate. A shroud of secrecy surrounds the use of corporal punishment in the schools, and the difficulty of obtaining systematic information regarding its use is legendary.

In general, it is safe to say that there has been no effort by school systems to evaluate the use of corporal punishment and to determine whether it fosters or meets any of its objectives, which allegedly are to restrain the child, to inculcate obedience, to correct, to punish, to control misbehavior, and to promote the welfare of the child.

OTHER COUNTRIES, OTHER PRACTICES

Other countries have been more successful in eliminating corporal punishment in schools. The practice has been abolished in Austria, Belgium, China, Cyprus, Czechoslavakia, Denmark, Ecuador, Finland, France, Germany (corporal punishment was temporarily reestablished during the Nazi regime), Holland, Hungary, Iceland, Israel, Italy, Japan, Jordan, Luxembourg, Mauritius, Norway, Phillipines, Poland, Portugal, Qatar, Rumania, Sweden, Switzerland, and the U.S.S.R. (Reitman, Follman, & Ladd, 1972).

Countries in which corporal punishment is still officially sanctioned in schools are Australia, Barbados, Canada, Erie, New Zealand, South Africa, Swaziland, Trinidad and Tobago, the United Kingdom, and most of the United States. Of note is the fact that Britain and the Republic of Ireland are the only countries in all of Europe in which corporal punishment is allowed. Similarly, the major difference between the countries which have and have not eliminated corporal punishment is the history of British colonial influence in the country.

SOME POSSIBLE DIRECTIONS

A MATRIX OF FACTORS

What then are the values, assumptions, traditions, and problems that exist in our society that support and reinforce the perpetration of this vestigial custom?

Gil (1970) and Williams (1975) have argued that corporal punishment in the schools is an expression of violence against the children of our societies, and indeed corporal punishment may be one manifestation of violence deeply rooted in our society. From this perspective it may be viewed as a fraternal twin to the more general problem of child abuse. Moreover, the sanction of corporal punishment in our schools probably reflects our culture's conceptualization of the child as a creature with low status, inherently antisocial, in need of strong, even repressive, tactics, and requiring discipline based on fear, especially fear of physical punishment.

Probably the issue of power, and an unwillingness of educational administrators to relinquish power and control, represents a significant obstacle to change (N. Feshbach, 1976). Out of what is undoubtedly a complex matrix of interlocking variables that have engendered and sustained corporal punishment, there appear to be several related factors that may contribute to the resistance of its elimination. From our perspective, two critical factors that must be recognized, researched, and resolved before corporal punishment in the schools will be eliminated are the presence of teacher stress and the absence of a functional theory of discipline or its corollary, classroom management.

TEACHER STRESS

A number of investigators have pointed to the potential role of stress, personal and ecological, as a mediating factor in the manifestation of a wide array of punitive parental practices ranging from verbal criticism to more severe and harmful abusive displays (N. Feshbach, 1973; Dohrenwend & Dohrenwend, 1974). In a recent study we asked 25 practicing teachers and 26 student teachers to list and rank the ten sources of stress they experienced as classroom teachers (N. Feshbach & Campbell, 1978). A comparison of the findings yielded by the responses of these two groups indicated some similarities and some important differences. Experienced teachers reported interactions with children as the most frequent source of stress. While children's behavior and discipline are also a major source of stress for the student teacher, concern over teaching competence and performance is the primary source of stress for this group.

The findings from this preliminary study resemble those reported by previous investigators (Fuller, 1969; Olander & Farrell, 1970) and are also highly congruent with the findings of a recent study carried out with the membership of the Chicago Teacher's Union (1978). The findings of this latter study are especially revealing both in regard to the sources of teacher stress and to the extensiveness of this problem.

Of the 10 most highly attributed sources of stress in a 36-item, rank-ordered sources-of-stress inventory, seven fall within categories referring to job-related administrative and managerial tensions and three fall within the disruptive children category. Of note is the distortion of interpretation made by the presenting of the findings. For example, in a report in the publication *Chicago Union Teacher* (Chicago Teacher's Union, 1978), the theme of student violence and discipline is extracted as the major cluster of importance.

The import of these studies is that while student misbehavior contributes to teacher stress, there are many other factors that make the professional role and tasks of the teachers so difficult. The advent of teacher accountability, desegregation, mainstreaming, and other educational changes have placed additional educational, housekeeping, and recordkeeping responsibilities on the shoulders of our classroom teachers. The current public school has become a focus of pressure and stress for its teachers who are beset by administrative demands, parental expectations, and their own internal professional standards. Perhaps the most painful aspect of the situation is the fact that the vagaries of student performance give teachers fewer opportunities to experience a sense of competence. Given these circumstances, it is not unreasonable to suggest that the increased interest of many teachers in the use of corporal punishment may be a displaced expression of overwhelming problems confronting them.

Unfortunately, it is only too easy to focus upon the child rather than upon the more powerful groups and forces that operate in the educational complex. The unprecedented demand by the United Teachers' Union of Los Angeles (UTLA) in a contract negotiation with the Los Angeles School Board—that the prohibition against corporal punishment, a prohibition for which so many had struggled for so long, be revoked—illustrates this tendency.

Apart from the incongruity of including swatting kids in the same category as salary increments and important work and fringe benefits, the use of corporal punishment in the schools does not achieve the goals that the teachers are seeking—a reduction of pressure and stress, and an improvement of discipline and classroom management. Elsewhere we have suggested a number of specific recommendations that might reduce, and help teachers deal with, stress in schools (Feshbach & Campbell, 1978). The list includes administrative and staffing recommendations, changes in preservice training, the expansion of on-site or in-service training, training in stress and management skills, and the broadening of a social support system. The development of effective discipline strategies for dealing with student misbehavior and other disruptive classroom problems is also required.

TOWARD A THEORY OF DISCIPLINE

To be opposed to corporal punishment in schools does not imply opposition to the use of discipline or mean the denial of a need for a repertoire of effective discipline techniques. In an earlier paper, we have suggested that sanctions employed for disciplinary purposes be intrinsically connected to the source or determinant of the infraction or the misbehavior itself (Feshbach & Feshbach, 1973). From this perspective we have distinguished four major categories of determinants of infractions which can be linked to different discipline strategies: (1) inadequate ego controls, (2) misappraisals, (3) objectionable habits, and (4) cognitively mediated objectionable behavior.

Inadequate Ego Controls. The young child, especially, performs actions on impulse and commits infractions because (s)he lacks self-control mechanisms. Verbal admonitions with age-appropriate explanations are useful here. The parent or teacher when explaining, "No, don't play with the radio; it may break and you won't be able to listen to it," is providing the child with a verbal structure that the child can repeat and use to help regulate his/her behavior. Changing the environment and removing objects that evoke undesired behaviors is also a useful approach but may not, of course, always be feasible. In general, the parent's or teacher's tactic here is to prevent the impulsive action from occurring, as well as providing the child with verbal explanations and other responses that will facilitate the development of self-control.

Misappraisals. Children frequently fail to carry out a chore or they commit some other infraction because of ambiguous communications regarding what is expected of them and regarding the consequences of failure to conform to expectations. "Ignorance of the law" may be an inadequate excuse in the courtroom, but it is very germane in the home and school. Adults who rear and train children need to make clear the behaviors that are approved, those that are disapproved, and the nature of the contingent punishment. In considering possible "punishments," L. Kohlberg's (1969) distinction between retributive and distributive justice is very useful. Retributively based punishments are retaliatory in nature and bear little relationship to the infraction. Distributively based punishments are restorative in nature and are intrinsically related to the infraction. Swatting a child who has been aggressive to a peer is an example of retributive punishment. Requiring the child to aid or make an adjustment to the injured child is an example of distributive punishment. Loss of a privilege that is contingent upon positive social behaviors is another example of distributive punishment. Distributive punishments generally entail not only a loss of some privilege and the expenditure of time and effort but also participation in an approved behavior.

Objectionable Habits. If a child's misbehavior is an instance of a persistent, specific, habitual mode of behavior, then the teacher's best strategy is to ignore the behavior and to elicit and reinforce a desired response in the presence of the stimuli that evoke the disapproved response. Rather than punishing a child for moving about restlessly, the teacher should reward the child when he or she is sitting engrossed in an academic task. Sometimes, a habitual behavior may be so disruptive that the teacher may have to exercise immediate control through punishment. However, the principle of distributive punishment should apply here.

Cognitively Mediated Objectionable Behaviors. These behaviors are not due to lack of control, to poor habit, or to misinformation, but are carried out by the child with forethought, challenge, and awareness of the consequences of the misbehavior. It is to this kind of situation that the principle of distributive punishment best applies. This procedure should be effective unless there are other complicating factors involved. If the behavior persists, increasing the level of punishment is not likely to be effective and may well be counterproductive. Under these circumstances, the teacher may need to seek outside guidance and help. Sometimes training procedures that enhance more positive social behaviors can be introduced.

Our field study on Empathy Training (N. Feshbach, 1979), carried out in the Los Angeles City schools, in which children are being trained in empathic skills for the purpose of regulating aggressive behavior and promoting positive social behavior, is an example of the kind of training strategy that relates to the fourth category of determinants. The child who is empathic is more able to perceive events from the perspective of others and to share affective experiences (N. Feshbach, 1978). Because of these properties—the ability to experience the other's pain as well as pleasure and the capacity to understand a situation in terms of the other's frame of reference—an empathic child is less likely to use aggressive solutions in conflict situations and more likely to engage in prosocial behaviors than a child who is not empathic (Feshbach & Feshbach, 1969; Hoffman, 1975).

This presentation of alternatives is intended to be illustrative rather than complete. The propositions offered here require empirical study, validation, and refinement. However, this appears to be a more productive course to pursue than approaches that focus on obedience derived from rigid role definitions, enforced by the use of physical punishments. Although behavior *in situ* does not neatly align itself in accordance with our conceptual categories and many misbehaviors will stem from mixtures of these determinants, we considered each of the categories separately for purposes of analysis.

ALTERNATIVES

The preceding discussion regarding discipline was intended to provide a theoretical basis for the enunciation of basic training procedures and practices to be used with children in educational contexts. More specific strategies and alternatives to recommend in lieu of resort to physical punishment include parent conferences, counseling, preventive problem committees, crisis information centers, core teams, in-service training, teacher consultation, detention, chores, responsibility programs, special education services, expulsion, behavior modification, discussion, court referrals, rehabilitation, and lectures.

A central clearinghouse of information is the Center for Corporal Punishment and Alternatives in the Schools (Dr. Irwin Hyman, Director, 833 Ritter Hall South, Department of School Psychology, Temple University, Philadelphia, Pa. 19122). It collects and analyzes data on corporal punishment, keeps copies of laws and proposed laws on the subject and conducts research on ways in which teachers can keep order without engaging in acts of battery. The Center also sponsors workshops and clinics for the development and training of effective and alternative discipline practices. Of note, also, is the *Last Resort* newsletter of the Committee to End Violence Against the Next Generation (EVAN-G), edited by Adah Maurer, in Berkeley, California. The newsletter features up-to-date information regarding the status of efforts to abolish corporal punishment as well as suggestions to combat its negative effects.

POSSIBLE RESEARCH DIRECTIONS

The successful abolition of corporal punishment will probably require diverse efforts in multiple contexts. The struggle for its elimination will have to occur simultaneously at the legislative, the professional, and the research levels. However, some of the additional research useful to the advocate must also be relevant to the needs of the staff in the public schools.

An analysis of articles on corporal punishment and discipline practices directed toward school principals and school boards during the seventies (Feshbach & Hoffman, 1978) suggests that the restrictions of court rulings and increased disruption in the schools are the two main concerns of administrators in the determination of disciplinary methods. It appears that principals are most interested in learning about the efficiency of short-term alternative disciplinary techniques. Comparative studies that show reductions in disruptiveness (e.g., vandalism) obtained through less abusive means than corporal punishment would be most influential with this audience. It would seem that discussion of the long-range impact of alternate methods would be relevant only if it dealt adequately with the issue of immediate behavior control.

The studies of corporal punishment and discipline directed toward teachers also reflect their interest in the area of classroom control. Research evaluating the direct and indirect effects of all classroom control strategies, including corporal punishment, would help teachers. The study of sociological forces within the school and community that press teachers, especially new teachers, to practice corporal punishment would help us understand basic attitudes underlying the use of corporal punishment and the way these attitudes change.

The collection of data on the form and scope of corporal punishment as it is now used in the schools might do a great deal to reduce community support for the practice. Comparison of the use of corporal punishment in the home and in the school could also be beneficial. The assumption in the community that the nature and effect of corporal punishment in the home and in the classroom are identical does not seem to be capable of passing close empirical inspection.

The justification of corporal punishment as an admittedly damaging but "necessary" evil could be challenged by further psychological research. Comparison of the discipline levels across schools differing in their employment of corporal punishment would aid in determining the merits of harsher practices. Examination of the grades, future employment, and general satisfaction of the students in different punishment settings should temper the belief that corporal punishment is a realistic method for achieving control whose benefits outweigh its costs.

GOOD WILL TOWARD CHILDREN

In July 1979, a new law went into effect in Sweden that explicitly forbids parents to beat or humiliate their children (Commission on Children's Rights, 1978). This new provision has been introduced into the Parenthood and Guardianship Code and will be administered by a Civil rather than a Criminal Court. Essentially, the provision states that children may not be punished by means of blows, beatings, boxing the ears, and other similar means, and that children may not, for any other reason or cause, be subjected to acts of physical or mental coercion. It is still too early to assess the success of the new law, its effects, or its special problems. Moreover, it is clearly a statute about which many Swedes have conflicting feelings. Considerable education in alternative discipline practices will be required before it can be effectively implemented. Yet it represents a clear, bold acknowledgement of the value to be placed on children and their development, and of the destructive potential of physical punishment. If a country can deem it unhealthy for parents to physically punish their children, it is not unrealistic to work toward the elimination of legal sanctions that permit educators to physically punish children.

VI

THE CULTURAL CONTEXT

I wish to acknowledge the collaboration of Jane Wilson in editing the chapters contained in this section.—George Gerbner

13

What We Were Up Against:
Media Views of
Parents and Children

Peter O. Almond

The Carnegie Council on Children spent over five years considering the condition of children in the United States. In addition, the Council, supported by Carnegie Corporation of New York, devoted considerable time and effort to disseminating the findings. Its first report appeared as *All Our Children: The American Family Under Pressure*, a book that engendered a modest share of reviews, editorials, and press coverage (Keniston et al., 1977).

That the Council would receive mass media attention and that its subject, children and families, would similarly get consideration was not always so certain. Children aren't considered "hot topics" for the media, not unless children figure in a scandalous or heart-rending story or in some shocking data and statistics. As a children's television producer put it after visiting forty-two corporations in search of funding for a public TV series on child development, "They just don't *care* about children." Despite these obstacles, the Council's report did get some coverage, in both the general press and more specialized periodicals. The Passaic, New Jersey Sunday *Herald-News*, for example, headlined the AP wire story, STUDY: CHILDREN OUT OF CONTROL. *All Our Children* was featured reading in a Louisiana library; there were talk show appearances including the *Today Show*; and on the night of the report's release, there was even a story on the CBS evening news.

Toward what end, and with what hopes did the Council undertake a general public affairs/dissemination effort? And, in fact, what was the Council saying? A scholarly journal published a review that concluded:

The Carnegie Council on Children has performed a service by lending its name and weight to the call for a more just economic system in the interests of families and especially of children. As a multidisciplinary product, that awkward animal known as a commission report, it is both readable and more coherent than most. But I live in a country that has yet to implement the 1930 Children's Charter, a virtual Bill of Rights for children. I would have welcomed a bit less vision from the Carnegie Council and more concrete proposals on how to go about the difficult task of making even a piece of that vision a reality. (Zigler, 1978)

Another seasoned policymaker commented, "That Carnegie report you worked on was really a dud. . . ." He was saying we did not need all that time and money to be told that the system has to change or that some "watered-down" income redistribution should take place.

In all these cases, the observers found similar shortcomings with *All Our Children:* it was neither tough nor precise—and it was old news. But was it? The Council attempted to identify and refute a collection of myths that contaminate the public's perception of children and families. The media cling to these myths; they are familiar, convenient, easily adapted to conventional formats of news and entertainment. In short, myth is easier to report than the more subtle and complicated reality documented in *All Our Children.* The policymakers were aware of the myths and familiar with their distortions and inaccuracies. But like the public and the press, they too were hungry for "news" and concrete action agendas.

When Americans look at children, the Council argued, think about them, teach them, or plan policies and programs for them, we usually neglect half the picture. Americans are enormously perceptive about individual children and their individual problems, but we are far less understanding of the broad economic and social forces that influence and circumscribe the range of choices parents are able to make for their children.

The function of parents is changing drastically. At a time when parents' expectations for children are rising, their ability to affect their children's lives is shrinking. Business, government, and schools are among the forces that exert great influences on the physical, mental, and emotional growth of children with little or no regard for parental wishes.

Parents are the world's outstanding experts on the needs and reactions of their own children, but they now bear the responsibility of coordinating the efforts of teachers, doctors, and TV producers, all of whom deal with a specified aspect of their child. Parents should retain the power to influence these forces; however, a parent today often is like a conductor trying to lead an orchestra when all the musicians are sitting with their backs turned and everyone is playing from a different score. When a parent's efforts fail, he or she is usually blamed.

Families are also changing. They are shrinking in size and changing in shape. There is an unfortunate tendency to mistake these signs of change for signs of collapse. Articles such as "The American Family in Trouble," "Can the American Family Survive?" "Is the Family Dead?" "The Calamitous Decline of the American Family," "The Family out of Favor," and "Do Americans Suddenly Hate Kids?" reflect not only a national anxiety over changes that are taking place, but in some cases take on an accusatory tone that seems to view changes in today's family as short-term and selfish aberrations. The fact is that mom is no more going to return full time to the kitchen than television is going to vacate the livingroom.

For the first time in history more than half of all schoolage children have working mothers; 40 percent of all children will spend some portion of their childhoods in single-parent families; almost one million mothers with no legal marriage partner will keep their babies and establish their own households each year. Because of these changes, children are being nurtured in a variety of new family forms. For the sake of the children, these families should be recognized, supported, and encouraged. Instead, Americans tend to do the opposite: They consider the parents in these families to be at fault and in need of reform.

OUTMODED MYTHS

Casting blame and offering advice spring from the assumption that the problems of individuals can be solved by changing the individuals. This implies a second assumption as well: that families are free-standing, independent, and autonomous units, relatively insulated from social pressures. If a family proves less than independent—if it is visibly needy or if its members seek help—then it is by definition not an "adequate" family. Adequate families, the assumptions runs, are self-sufficient and free from outside pressures.

These two assumptions form the core of an American myth—the myth of personal self-sufficiency. With deep roots in the nation's history, this myth has blocked Americans' ability to see the powerful social and economic forces that have *always* influenced parents and families. In fact, today's parents are not abdicating their roles, they are being dethroned. The myth of Equal Opportunity also distorts our vision. For too long we have believed that the United States is a society that rewards hard work and talent with success, and that personal qualities largely determine the position individuals ultimately attain as adults.

The fact is, an individual's ultimate position on the social ladder is more often determined by his departure point than by his or her personal industry and talent; the rule is not inexorable, but the odds favor children born with prosperity, power, and prestige. Playing the game by these rules not only relegates one child in four to poverty and neglect, it also subtly teaches him to blame himself for his failure.

These myths, deeply rooted in history, have been compounded by the explosion of technology. In many people's minds, the "ideal" American family is still the Dick and Jane family—father breadwinner, mother housewife, two children (and probably Spot the dog and Puff the cat). In fact, of course, that image now applies to only about one out of every sixteen families.

This is a development that many people find deeply unsettling. Yet our new forms of families remain real families. The bonds of love and care that engage an adult with a child—and the child with an adult—are as strong in the many new kinds of families as the love and care of parents and children was in the past. Single-parent families, families with two earners, so-called chosen families can be perfectly good families. But unfortunately, our American mythology—to say nothing of policy—has yet to catch up to that fact.

Moreover, it is hard not to feel anxious as a parent when today's transformed families are still expected to be in charge of their own destinies, at a time when they increasingly share childrearing with scores of other forces and influences. Television, of course, is a flickering blue babysitter for between two and four hours a day, but parents have only a puny voice, if any, with the networks and program producers and advertisers who wield this massive influence on their children. The marketing and production decisions of food companies that routinely add more than 3000 chemicals to the food children eat are decisions largely outside most parents' ability to change. And though so far only a few people see this next connection, one of the most profound influences of all on children is the economic system.

"What do you do for a living?" is the most important question in America today. Children know this. And children, like it or not, assume a massive share of their own identity from their parents' occupations and socioeconomic status.

Families, in short, share their responsibility with scores of outside forces. Yet our national mythology insists that they do not; that families are the self-sufficient "building blocks of society." This insistence on national myth compounds the uncertainties of parents, who often are struggling with guilt in addition to their other problems.

Given these circumstances—this topography of national myth—the Carnegie Council concluded that until family policy addresses the social and economic factors that contribute so massively to family problems, social programs will remain directed at healing wounds, not preventing them. To put it another way, it is time for Americans to start holding the social and economic institutions of our society just as accountable for their influence on family life as we have traditionally held parents.

The Council's policy recommendations attempted to reflect these concerns. They called for broad social reforms to strengthen parents' authority in raising their offspring. The Council specifically recommended: (1) Reducing unemployment for at least one parent in every family where there is a child so that in such families the unemployment rate is no more than 1 or 1½ percent; this means reducing the general unemployment rate to no more than 5 percent. (2) A backup system of family financial supports, perhaps achieved by reforming both current tax and welfare policies to include a "credit tax" paid for by a redistribution of income at graduated rates from the top 25 to 30 percent of the income distribution. (3) An end to job discrimination, including barriers and ceilings, that limit employment for members of minority groups and women. (4) More flexible working conditions, including "flexitime" hours, upgraded part-time jobs, expanded and protected childrearing leaves for both mothers and fathers, and methods of protecting the benefits and seniority of parents who take leaves of absence for child care. (5) A series of measures to ensure that family services are available to families at all income levels. Such services would include medical care, homemaker services, and good child care. (6) A program of national health insurance supplemented by preventive public health measures. This would, of course, require a substantial revision of the fee-for-service model of medical care. (7) More parent involvement in all family services, including participation in community boards and councils with real authority to plan services and set priorities. (8) Family maintenance services for those cases in which legal intervention is needed. Failing that, we endorse fuller rights for children in foster families, and especially their rights after a fixed time to be placed in a permanent substitute family.

These recommendations could become a reality in ten years if the country started to act on them now. The first step is for parents to see their job in a new way. Too often parents look to themselves rather than society for the cause of their family problems. They ask how to change the victims of our society rather than how to change the forces that victimize.

Traditionally we have thought of childhood and politics as totally separated. It is important for parents to realize that in addition to being private nurturers, they must become public advocates for children's interests. Those interests, obviously, must be interpreted far more broadly than they have been. Persuading parents and children's advocates to see the needs and rights of children in social terms is an exercise in consciousness raising. Children's issues are not "kiddie" issues—they are issues of social justice and the wider social welfare of the nation.

Aided by support from Carnegie Corporation, the Council attempted to convey its perspective to mass institutions such as the press and an array of public and private policy institutions whose activities bear on children. Success might best be measured by the degree of continuing awareness media and policy institutions show as children and families continue their changing essential roles.

14

Portraying Abuse:
Network Censors' Round Table

Donn H. O'Brien
Alfred R. Schneider
Herminio Traviesas

At a conference in November 1978, executives in charge of broadcast standards from the three major television networks discussed their industry's role in portraying the problem of child abuse. Their exchange concentrated on the policies that networks have evolved for handling controversial social issues in drama and situation comedy, as well as in documentary format. These network censors suggested possible roles for experts and policymakers concerned with the future direction of television programming about child abuse.

DONN H. O'BRIEN (CBS)

How does a medium that devours 18 hours or more of written material each day develop prosocial themes? Well, for many years television didn't, except for news reports and sporadic documentaries. Prosocial subject matter is fairly new in television; it entered the medium through made-for-television movies. In 1970, producer Norman Lear convinced CBS that controversial subject matter could be the basis of popular situation comedies. Lear's *All in the Family* has proved this many times and broke ground for dramas and comedies involving rape, alcoholism, and teenage pregnancy. Now many weekly situation comedies bravely deal with real life themes.

HERMINIO TRAVIESAS (NBC)

When reviewing the more than 2500 outlines and scripts considered each year, NBC uses its own code of broadcast standards, plus the code of

The following statements are based on a transcript of remarks at the conference on child abuse held in Philadelphia on November 20 and 21, 1978.

the National Association of Broadcasters. These program standards represent what is and what is not acceptable to *most* viewers, and are based on the millions of letters and phone calls, both of praise and complaint, received over the years, as well as the comments of the managers of local affiliated stations. Editors from the network's Broadcast Standards Department apply these guidelines at every step in the production process, from scriptwriting and preliminary screenings up to the moment of broadcast. Some problems must be referred to the network's senior executives.

ALFRED R. SCHNEIDER (ABC)

One broadcast standard requires that an entertainment program be strictly expository in dealing with controversial issues. The program may enlighten, inform, and even present a point of view, but it cannot take an advocacy position.

Another key standard requires that we avoid sensationalizing or misrepresenting a problem. This is a difficult consideration when the topic itself may be inherently sensational. In the case of child abuse, portrayals of stress, violence, and sexuality are sometimes necessary for a truthful representation, plot development, and character delineation. But how does one accurately portray an ugly incident of abuse, showing its causes and effects, without overstating physical violence?

TRAVIESAS

The NBC guideline on violence illustrates the dilemma any network faces in trying to present programming on child abuse. The guideline states that:

> NBC recognizes its responsibility to the public with respect to the depiction of violence—the intentional infliction of physical harm by one person upon another. In all cases, such depictions must be necessary to the development of theme, plot or characterization. They may not be used to stimulate the audience or to invite imitation. Violence may not be shown or offered as an acceptable solution to human problems.
>
> Scenes showing excessive gore, pain or physical suffering are not permitted. Scenes depicting abnormal or morbid acts of violence or the use of cruel and unusual weapons are not permitted. Scenes containing extensive and detailed instructions in the use of harmful devices and weapons or describing techniques for the commission of crime or the evasion of apprehension will be avoided.
>
> *Exceptional care must be taken in stories where children are victims of, or are threatened by, acts of violence.*
>
> These considerations also apply to advertising and promotion material.

Audiences are sensitive to television's depiction of violence, particularly to stories in which women and children are the victims of violent abuse. Therefore, we often refrain from showing horrors, even when we know them to be factual. Great care is taken to use sound effects, makeup, and camera angles in a way that avoids excessive violence. Since 1971, several of our prime-time series have used these techniques in depicting the problem of child abuse.

SCHNEIDER

Family, a prime-time series on ABC, tackled the issue of child abuse a few years ago. The series' main characters, Doug and Kate Lawrence, discover that a promising young attorney in Doug's firm is mistreating his son. After an unsuccessful attempt to deal directly with the parents, Doug and Kate reluctantly go to the police. Even then, the parents continue to deny abusing the child until Kate persuades the mother to cooperate with the police and the father to get help.

Although this segment focused on the psychological rather than physical abuse, the network was still concerned that the child's bruises not be unduly vivid, and that the legal process be depicted accurately. It also seemed necessary to portray the ambivalence of the Lawrences, but without implying that their ultimate decision to go to the police was too difficult or in any way inappropriate.

TRAVIESAS

Portrayal of child abuse becomes doubly difficult when it involves sexual misuse as well. In 1977, NBC presented *Sybil*, a movie based on a true story about a woman with multiple personalities. *Sybil* presented an especially sensitive problem for the network because Sybil's cure resulted from her discovery that she had been sexually abused as an infant.

We worked to ensure that this revelation was not too shocking for the audience, and the sexual attack was never actually portrayed. The show won prestigious awards, but many viewers wrote to complain that the network had exercised bad judgment in presenting a "disgusting" story. Such negative reaction from a segment of the public does not stop a network from presenting stories that deal with controversial social issues, but it does motivate us to develop better ways of presenting realistic stories.

O'BRIEN

Mike Wallace reported on child abuse for a *60 Minutes* segment, "Mommy, Why Me?" As Wallace acknowledged, this report was triggered by a letter from Parents Anonymous, at a time when the organization was having financial difficulties. The raft of mail and telegrams that followed the program helped the organization to secure funds and to continue its work.

60 MINUTES: "MOMMY, WHY ME?"

Wallace	"Mommy, Why Me?" is a story about child abuse. A few months back a letter came to us and told us about an outfit called Parent's Anonymous, an outfit that tries to help mothers and fathers who maltreat their children physically, emotionally. We had known about child abuse, but we didn't know about Parent's Anonymous.
Mom	I said, you know something, right now I hate her so bad and I can't stand that kid so bad. This is a horrible thing for a mother to say. It is so bad that I could very easily go in there and kill her.
Wallace	The pity is that Lonnie loves her daughter, Stephanie. And the fact is that Lonnie is no different from countless other parents whose rage explodes into physical violence.
Mom	Well, certain times it's not very hard to hit her at all. It's the anger. I mean, when you're with a kid 24 hours a day, sometimes I just can't handle her. You know, I can't even handle my own feelings sometimes, let alone her too. Sometimes, if I am in a real super angry point, I will go into her bedroom and I'll keep hitting her. It's not just the stopping point. In fact, my husband has come in and literally said, "Honey, back off," when he sees me get angry. She looks up at me and just has the most pathetic sad-looking face on a kid. You know, "Why, momma, why me? Why are you doing this to me? What did I do to hurt you?"
Another Mom	He'd come to the table like any typical kid and he'd spill his milk. Well, I'd take him and hit him about ten or fifteen times, but I wouldn't remember if I'd hit him ten times or five times except, you know, he'd have great big welts on him.
Wallace	You mean really hard.

Another Oh yeah. I have hit him hard enough to break my hand.
Mom Took it out on Perry really bad and he'd have marks on
him.
I'd constantly beat that poor child till it was unbelievable, and the school didn't say anything, and I wanted
help but I didn't know where to turn, and this was my
way of saying help, and nobody heard me.

Wallace Tell me something, Perry, what would you tell the kids at
school or the teachers or the neighbors when they saw
bruises on you?

Perry I'd say that I did that while I was playing.

Wallace You'd never tell on your mother.

Perry Uh, uh.

Wallace Why?

Perry Because I was afraid she'd get put in jail.

Wallace Here's what we're talking about. A child malnourished by
parent. A child stabbed by a parent. A child burned by
parent. Actual cases investigated by the Abused Child
Unit of the Los Angeles Police Department. One of the
few such units in the United States.
New York City doesn't have one.
Chicago doesn't have one.
When the evidence is clear-cut the first thing to do is
protect the child.
Take him out of the home.
Usually into public care facilities or a foster home.
Everyone of these youngsters has been evicted. Yet they
may have to face abuse again; unless the courts deem the
parents totally unfit, these children will soon go home.

Lady And it's senseless. When you've abused a kid it's like extended self-destruction. Get that rottenness in me.

Wallace It was her older daughter, she said, who finally stopped her from actually killing Faith. Jolly Kay said she desperately wanted help but she could find none.

Then one day while talking to a social worker, she wondered if she might benefit from sharing her experiences with other mothers in the same boat. From that tiny beginning in 1969, PA has mushroomed now to almost 600 chapters nationwide.

Secretary Good Morning, Parent's Anonymous. This is the national office.

Mom You pick up that phone and say if that kid says one more word I'm gonna tear him apart.

Secretary Are you sure everything's alright now?

Mom I don't know how many times because of that 24-hour toll-free number parents have called us from Florida, New York, Maine, all over and that free phone call saved that family, and saved that child, saved that child from another incident.

Wallace Why does an abusing mother do it?

Mom It's safe.

Wallace What?

Mom It's safe.
Child abuse is safe.
See, if I get angry at you—you know, maybe you're the local bill collector—if I get angry at you and I belt you, you might belt me back.
But if I hit my kid, my kid's not gonna divorce me; they're not gonna cast me out, they're not gonna cut me out of their will, they're not gonna take me to court for slander, libel or verbal assault, or anything like that. So a kid makes a safe target.

HELP DESTROY
A FAMILY TRADITION.

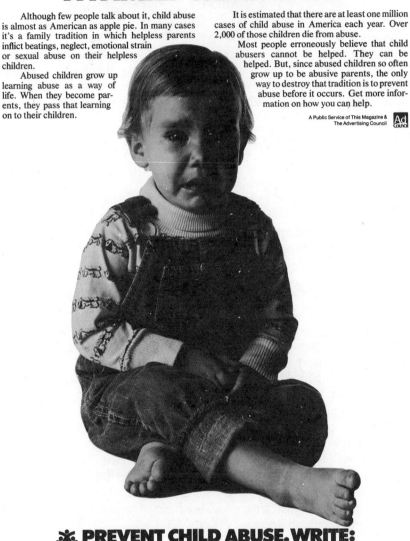

Although few people talk about it, child abuse is almost as American as apple pie. In many cases it's a family tradition in which helpless parents inflict beatings, neglect, emotional strain or sexual abuse on their helpless children.

Abused children grow up learning abuse as a way of life. When they become parents, they pass that learning on to their children.

It is estimated that there are at least one million cases of child abuse in America each year. Over 2,000 of those children die from abuse.

Most people erroneously believe that child abusers cannot be helped. They can be helped. But, since abused children so often grow up to be abusive parents, the only way to destroy that tradition is to prevent abuse before it occurs. Get more information on how you can help.

A Public Service of This Magazine &
The Advertising Council

PREVENT CHILD ABUSE. WRITE:
National Committee for Prevention of Child Abuse, Box 2866, Chicago, Ill. 60690.

One example of a series of Public Service Announcements on child abuse developed by the Advertising Council and the National Committee for the Prevention of Child Abuse.

SCHNEIDER

Network coverage of child abuse is complemented by that of affiliated stations, where the problem can be addressed at a local level. For example, in 1972 Geraldo Rivera of WABC-TV, New York, brought national attention to the problems of the institutionalized mentally retarded with *Willowbrook: The Last Great Disgrace*. The Detroit station WXYZ-TV produced a series of public affairs shows on sexual exploitation of children following the murders of several children by an apparent sexual deviant. These programs were supplemented by a series of public service announcements (PSAs) warning: "Kids, don't go with strangers."

TRAVIESAS

Authorities and professional groups with expert knowledge of social problems seem to have overlooked public service announcements as a method for alerting the public to problems such as child abuse. As of 1978 NBC had received only one series of PSAs on child abuse, "Child Abuse Prevention," which was produced by the Advertising Council (as are most PSAs) and sponsored by the National Committee for the Prevention of Child Abuse.

O'BRIEN

How can we have more shows and films depicting our social ills? Foremost in the minds of the executives who make programming decisions is the number of people who watch any one program. The audience for two recent programs—"Mary Jane Harper Cried Last Night" and the *60 Minutes* segment "Mommy, Why Me?"—was so great that both programs were rebroadcast. These success stories encourage network executives to develop exciting and informative material. The prospects are more than encouraging.

SCHNEIDER

Scholars, physicians, and other professionals concerned about child abuse can aid the networks in two ways. First, by acting as sources of factual, authoritative, and objective material. Second, by helping with the task facing the dramatist, writer, and producer of presenting relevant problems without propagandizing for any one solution.

15

Children and Power on Television: The Other Side of the Picture

George Gerbner

Popular stories and images depicting children cultivate certain assumptions about and behaviors toward them. Today television is the "wholesale" supplier of such stories to most people. Television is the mainstream of mass-produced culture that provides the broadest common bases for collective action and interaction in industrial societies.

Despite the widespread imagery of the troublesome—and troubled—child from Dennis the Menace to the young girls in the *Exorcist* and *Born Innocent*, and many others in the press, movies, and television, there is no reason to suspect that television incites violence specifically against children. Its stories and images tend to cultivate conventional values and norms that abhor rather than condone child abuse. Among these norms, however, are also conventional assumptions about people and power. The way television fits children and adolescents into its dramatic world of power can be seen to provide the other and more hidden side of its valuation of them. This chapter, then, describes our research* as a basis for some conclusions about the role of television in supporting a social scenario within which the more problematic as well as the more benign aspects of our treatment of children find their niche.

INDICATORS OF TV CONTENT

An examination of the Vanderbilt Television News Archives for 8 years showed little attention of any kind paid to children and youth. An aver-

* Collaborating in this research were Larry Gross and Nancy Signorielli. Thanks for assistance also go to Jack Daly, Debra Giffen, Mark Gonzales, Heather Harr-Mazer, Susan Luciano, Geoffrey Stevens, Kendall Whitehouse, and Wendy Wolfenson.

age of 63 stories a year mention children and youth on the network evening news. Less than 6 percent of that, or only 3 stories a year, deal with child abuse. With only the most dramatic and sensational exceptions, child abuse is even less newsworthy on the air than in the press.

An analysis of *TV Guide* plot synopses for 7½ years revealed similarly few programs, or about one a month on all of television, that involved any mention of abandonment, neglect, hurt, or abuse of children. A third of these were repeat telecasts. Of course, there are few programs depicting children at all, and most of them appear as situation comedies or children's cartoons.

A more systematic analysis of the world of television drama was based on ten years of monitoring and related studies, in which we noted the incidence of victimized children and adolescents in over 10 percent of network programs.

Cultural Indicators is an ongoing project that relates televised images and messages to conceptions of social reality held by viewers, and to action related to those conceptions. At the time of this writing, the Cultural Indicators data bank consists of reliably coded observations of over 1500 network prime time and weekend daytime programs, and nearly 15,000 dramatic characters representing all speaking parts in those programs, and many surveys of adult and young viewers (see Gerbner et al., 1979).

The World of Television Drama

Television entered the American home in the 1950s. Within 30 years it has saturated the land and is an active presence in 98 percent of its homes for an average of 44 hours a week. A new era has begun.

Nielsen reports that the typical viewer lives with television about 30 hours a week. Children and their parents watch more, their grandparents the most, and teenage girls the least (but still over 23 hours a week).

Viewing for most people is a ritual performed with little selectivity or deviation. Children spend, on the average, over 6500 hours in the world of television before entering school. Even during the school years, time spent with television equals or exceeds time spent in school. Our own research shows that the generation born after television is significantly more imbued with the television view of the world than the generation born before television.

Television is now our common and constant learning environment. Drama is its most vivid and popular curriculum. In one week, the typical evening (8–11 P.M.) viewer of a single network station will encounter about 300 dramatic characters playing speaking roles. (That is in drama alone, not counting commercials, news, game or talk shows, documentaries, or, of course, other viewing times.) Of these, 217 are males, 80 females, and 3 are animals or robots of no clear gender. The racial composition of this typical slice of the world of prime time dramatic television is 262 whites, 35 members of other races, and 3 whose race is hard to tell.

The children of the typical family will meet another 137 dramatic characters in speaking parts during weekend daytime hours. Gender and race in weekend daytime (clearly identifiable for only two-thirds of these—mostly cartoon—characters), are about the same as in prime time.

Overall, the world of television is three-fourths American, three-fourths between 30 and 60 (compared to one-third of the real population), and three-fourths male.

Clearly the world of television is not like the real world. Its demography reflects its purposes: to produce audiences for advertisers. Looking at it through the prism of age reveals a population curve that, unlike the real world, but much like the curve of consumer spending, bulges in the middle years of life. That makes children and the elderly relatively neglected, old people virtually invisible, and the portrayals of these and other minorities, as well as of women, sensitive barometers of the dramatic equities of life.

CHILDREN IN THE WORLD OF TELEVISION

As we can see in Table 15.1, one out of every five Americans (18.3%) is a child under 10 years of age. But in prime time, only one out of every 60 characters (1.9%) is a child under 10 years of age. Even in weekend day-

TABLE 15.1: Age distribution of the American population and the population of characters in television drama

	Totals	1–9	10–19	20–29	30–64	65+
Census	100% 203,208*	18.3	19.7	14.5	37.6	9.9
World of TV	14,973	1.9	12.2	18.5	65.0	2.2
Males	11,074	1.7	10.5	14.4	71.4	2.0
Females	3,883	2.5	17.0	30.3	47.2	2.9
Prime Time	11,505	1.7	7.9	20.5	67.7	2.3
Males	8,387	1.4	6.7	15.7	74.1	2.1
Females	3,111	2.3	11.2	33.4	50.5	2.7
Weekend Daytime	3,468	2.9	26.6	12.1	56.3	2.1
Males	2,687	2.5	22.6	10.5	62.9	1.6
Females	772	3.6	40.5	18.0	33.9	3.9

*Note: The actual population figures are based on the 1970 U.S. Census. The television population figures are based on the Cultural Indicators archive of character in network television drama 1969 through 1978.

time children's territory, the young viewer will find only 1 out of every 34 speaking parts (2.9%) belonging to a child under 10.

Another fifth (19.7%) of the American population is between ages 10 and 20. This group has more dramatic and romantic potential and thus more substantial representation on television. Although prime time teens number less than 8 percent of the total prime time population, weekend daytime teens are actually overrepresented. Girls under 20 make up nearly half of the entire female population on weekend daytime programs.

On the whole, then, the world of television drama is nine-tenths white, three-fourths male, and virtually devoid of young children but more hospitable to teens. Girls dramatically increase in visibility as they reach maturity. A closer look will show how this visibility is distributed.

In order to take that closer look at a fairly sizable group of characters, we shall examine the combined category of children and adolescents.[1] Our typical viewer finds 22 children and adolescents playing speaking roles in an average week's prime time programs. Of these, 4 (18%) are nonwhite and 8 (36%) are girls, which makes this the most racially and sexually balanced of all prime time age categories. However, 7 of the 8 females are white. Thus 39% of all white youngsters are girls, but only 25 percent of all nonwhite youngsters are girls.

The viewer of a typical weekend's daytime television finds 20 youngsters playing speaking parts. Of these, 5 (25%) are nonwhites and 6 (30%) are girls. Here 5 of the 6 females are white. Therefore, on children's television 33 percent of all white youngsters are girls, but only 20 percent of black youngsters are girls. Children find the same lopsided cast populating their (mostly cartoon) programs as those of prime time. Overall, the world of television ignores children, underplays adolescents in prime time, shows a more interracial cast of youngsters than of other age groups, and casts more white females and black males as children and adolescents than as members of other age groups.

The class structure of age portrayals shows more children and adolescents, especially nonwhites, coming from lower socioeconomic backgrounds than do members of other age groups. Seven percent of prime time white youngsters are "lower class." (There is practically no observable class structure on children's television.) Fully one-third of all nonwhite youngsters are "lower class." Both are the highest percentage of "lower-class" characters in any age group of the respective dramatic character populations.

1. The combined child-adolescent category is slightly different in numbers (although not in proportions) from the "Under 20" category. The youngsters analyzed as children and adolescents excluded married and other "young adult" roles, and all those who could not be reliably classified for sex or race.

PERSONALITY TRAITS

Analysts' judgments of personality traits for each dramatic character were recorded on bipolar adjective scales. Mean ratings were obtained for each age group. These ratings show young adults as the most attractive, and settled adults as the most smart and efficient characters in prime time television drama. Children and adolescents stand out only in being less powerful and less violent than adults.

In weekend daytime programs, children and adolescents equal young adults in being attractive, smart, and efficient but still rate less powerful and less violent. Young boys are generally rated less fair than young girls. Young girls are more favorably presented, but lose favor as they become adolescents. The adolescent girl in prime time is very attractive but less happy than the younger girl, and less warm and smart and fair than adolescent boys or younger siblings.

Children are not the favored people of television. They are shown as relatively weak, poor, and vulnerable. Prime time is not a happy time for young boys or for adolescents of either sex. Young boys and older girls are likely to mean trouble.

The nature of that trouble is implicit in patterns of conflict. Where males outnumber females 4 to 1, much of the action revolves around predatory sex, money, and power. Crime and violence are symbolic demonstrations of norms and rules of the game of power.

The population of the world of television provides the backdrop against which the action unfolds. Television presents young people as they become dramatically and socially useful for it. The representation of women is concentrated in the sexually most available age brackets, largely in the late teens and early twenties. Children and adolescents, as a group, are more sexually balanced, racially mixed, and "lower class" than any other age group on television. White girls and black boys weigh heavily in the balance. The troubles they bring are of different kinds.

VIOLENCE AS DEMONSTRATION OF POWER

In the world of television, two-thirds of all major characters are involved in violence. This rate has remained within ten percentage points of that proportion for at least ten years.

In prime time, the rate of involvement goes down to 56 percent of major characters. In weekend daytime children's programs, by far the most violent part of television, it goes up to 80 percent. Men are more likely to get involved than women, and adults are more likely to get involved than children, although about half of all women and children are still involved in violence.

In an act of violence, as we defined it, one party compels another to act against his or her will on pain of injury or death. The other falls victim to that act. Involvement implies risk; a character's chances of being a perpetrator or victim indicates fate and degree of vulnerability.

For example, 46 percent of all major characters in network television drama commit violence and 55 percent suffer it (with 64% being involved in both ways). A ratio of risks can be obtained by relating the number of victims to the number of aggressors. Thus the overall risk ratio is 6 : 5, meaning that for every 12 victims there are 10 violents, or there are 20 percent more victims than violents in the world of television. The ratio for women and nonwhites is 13 : 10. The ratio for nonwhite women is 18 : 10. So, if and when involved, women and nonwhites are more vulnerable to victimization compared to their inflicting violence than are white males.

Now let us examine the risks encountered by children in the world of television. The overall victimization ratio of children and adolescents is 16 : 10, the highest of all age groups. The reason is the frequency of victimization among boys. Over 6 out of 10 boys are involved in violence; their victimization ratio is 17 : 10, which is the highest of all male groups. "Only" half of all girls are involved in violence; their victimization ratio is 13 : 10, which is average for women.

A closer look at victimization by race and age shows interesting differences. Nonwhite girls are less visible but more vulnerable than the whites. White girls, especially visible in adolescence, are relatively safe. That safety, however, turns to vulnerability in young adulthood. With a victimization ratio of 18 : 10 for all young women and 25 : 10 for nonwhite young women, the older girls are even more vulnerable than the younger boys.

As measured by the violent-victim ratio, the pecking order of the world of television has mostly whites and adult males on top. At the bottom are women—old, nonwhite, young, and lower-class, in that order. Next in line, and the lowest ranking male character in the pecking order, is the young boy.

The structure of power in the world of television drama thus affects boys and girls differently. Young boys are the most underrepresented, the most racially mixed, and the most badly battered. Young girls start out underrepresented but become more numerous, more desirable, less happy, and much more vulnerable as they mature (as if to prepare them for the fear and insecurity young women exhibit in our viewer studies).

Conceptions of Reality

Victimization is but the tip of the iceberg of relative devaluation and neglect. The pattern we found is part of the general context of mass entertainment as socialization primarily from an adult majority, male-oriented consumer point of view.

The results of our research on viewer conceptions show strong and stable associations between patterns of network dramatic content and conceptions of social reality. Heavy viewers tend to respond to many questions more in terms of the world of television than do light viewers in the same demographic groups. We have found that television cultivates an exaggerated sense of danger and mistrust in heavy viewers compared to similar groups of light viewers. When asked about chances of encountering violence, about the percentage of men employed in law enforcement and crime detection, and about the percentage of crimes that are violent, significantly more heavy viewers than light viewers respond in terms more characteristic of the television world than of the real world. Mistrust is also reflected in responses suggesting that heavy viewers believe that most people just look out for themselves, take advantage of others, and cannot be trusted. When samples of junior high school students were asked, "How often is it all right to hit someone if you are mad at them?" a significantly higher proportion of heavy than of light viewers answered, "Almost always."

Our results reflect the fact that heavy viewing is associated with greater apprehension of walking alone at night in the city in general and even in one's own neighborhood. Heavy viewers also overestimate the proportion of people involved in violence and the number of criminals, compared with similar groups of light viewers.

Television viewing appears to be associated not only with heightened perceptions of danger but also the tendency to act to protect themselves. Far more heavy than light viewers of police and crime programs report that they "bought a dog for purposes of protection," "put new locks on the windows and doors for purposes of protection," and "kept a gun for purposes of protection." Schoolchildren who watch more television are also more likely to exhibit violence-related fears;[2] to believe that the police frequently use force; and to assert that the average policeman will often shoot fleeing suspects. Finally, children and adolescents who watch more television are more likely to mistrust people and believe that others "mostly just look out for themselves." These findings support the conclu-

2. From a survey conducted for the Foundation for Child Development (New York) by Nicholas Zill in 1976. (Available from the FCD.)

sion that one correlate of television viewing is a heightened and unequal sense of danger and risk in a mean and selfish world.

RESPONSIBILITIES OF TELEVISION AND OF CITIZENS

The responsibilities of television are as large as its freedom of action is limited. The Constitutional prohibition against legislation abridging freedom of speech or of the press turns out to shield not so much the public interest as the right of corporate owners to serve the limited interests of their clients, the advertisers. Any program policy that does not strive for maximum audience ratings at minimum cost to provide the best buy for the advertising dollar is beyond the scope of serious consideration for inclusion in the regular daily or weekly television fare.

Within those limits, the contribution of television is twofold. On the one hand, many excellent programs and public service announcements do their best to provide information and inspiration for controlling child abuse. On the other hand, the aggregate and long-range configurations of the daily dramatic ritual may undercut these efforts at enlightenment.

Television is an integral part and chief cultural arm of the industrial establishment of society. Its principal function is to help introduce members of society to their places and their roles in the social order. It is paid to assemble large audiences and tell them stories that sell styles of life, people, products, and services at a profit. Other stories do not sell so well to those who underwrite their production, the sponsors, and do not, therefore, become a significant part of the symbolic environment in which people learn who they are and how things work.

The stories shown in the dramatic world of television need not present credible accounts of what things *are* in order to perform the more critical function of demonstrating how things really *work*. In fact, illumination of the invisible relationships and dynamics of life has always been the principal function of drama and fiction. That function is best performed when the "facts" can be invented so as to lend themselves to compelling demonstrations of the "natural" and seemingly inexorable social order.

In a world of such demonstrations, casting has a message of its own. Large real-life populations that are virtually invisible in the world of popular fiction and drama are set up for neglect, abuse, and eventual annihilation. (The absence of the very old from the world of television hides the stockpiling of millions of old people in human warehouses where they languish and die out of sight and out of mind.) With children, the underlying picture is more mixed but, on balance, not much more reassuring.

On the surface, program by program, most of television reflects and conveys decent, if safe and selective, values of conventional middle-class urban and even urbane liberal morality. This is called entertainment. It animates most of the industry's institutional representatives. Understandably, they become defensive and angry when confronted with the results of deeper and less familiar but more systematic and critical analysis. Like other industries that have been found to produce defective, unsafe, and even deadly products or by-products when they thought they were just serving an appreciative and lucrative market, television has a vested interest in confusing, avoiding, or dismissing the implications of independent and critical research.

In cultural production, even more than in the tobacco, pharmaceutical, automobile, airplane, nuclear energy and other industries, the confusions and evasions can be quite prolonged. What the cultural industries discharge into the climate of common consciousness is not some clearly identifiable and measurable pollutant, but rather it discharges the environment itself, including most of the norms, standards, and definitions by which its quality is supposed to be measured. As the Scottish patriot Andrew Fletcher once said, "If a man were permitted to write all the ballads he need not care who makes the laws of the nation." The right and freedom to produce a self-serving common symbolic world confers the power to interpret it by the same standards that govern its production in the first place.

Nevertheless, attention will have to be paid to independent critical research, at least by citizens and their organizations, as distinct from cultural consumers and their suppliers, as the human cost of enduring social problems rises in relation to the benefits derived from concealing or perpetuating them. This analysis considers the usual preoccupation with plot as part of the artifact of entertaining rationalization and distraction. We concentrate on associations of casting, social typing, and fate. These associations seem to be remarkably stable from year to year; they are rooted in well-established group relationships.

The casting, as we have seen, tells its story by proportions and omissions. Every single plot may be plausible and well motivated, yet the total context can still be functionally distorted.

The low visibility of children in the world of television is part of such functional distortion of reality. It also helps to hide, but not necessarily limit, the other functions. These have to do with children's and young women's high rate of victimization, and the further association of victimization with age, sex, class, and race. Disproportionate preoccupation with even sympathetically presented or "accidental" victims in an underrepresented population, relative to exhibiting their own share of numbers and exercise of power, diminishes and degrades that group.

The notion that ours is a "youth oriented society" may be a slogan of little substance. Consumers of personal products, and characters in commercials and dramas that sell them, are the most numerous in the early middle years of life. But the orientation is more toward markets and power than youth. Children and adolescents lose out on all counts.

The underlying aggregate structure of the world of dramatic television counters its overtly righteous messages. Children take on the characteristics of a social minority with less than their share of attention, values, and resources, and consequently diminished life chances. What some define as abuse may simply play out roles implicit in that dramatic context.

The need is for action toward creating a culture, and television system, that can afford to address itself to the nation's future, its children. That would require a broadening of the resource base for mainstream television through whatever mechanism is most effective to give the creative talents of television's professionals the time and money they need to break the constraints that now bind them to markets that use but have little use for children. Citizens, writers, actors, and producers must work toward a system of popular storytelling whose culture-power cannot devalue and hurt children any more.

16

Covering Abuse:
Content and Policy

Gaining Access
Tom Wilkinson

On the night of October 21, 1975, most of Washington's major television stations broadcast a film clip in which one Glenda Abbey tearfully appealed to the community for help in the search for her missing four-year-old son Shawn. She spoke in a broken voice of how much she missed him, how much she loved him, how much she needed him. It was a compelling news report and struck sympathetic chords in the community.

The next night, October 22, Glenda Abbey and her boyfriend, 23-year-old Michael Leonard, were arrested by police and charged with murder—specifically with tying a 33-pound concrete block to Shawn's 40-pound body and throwing him off a bridge into the Potomac River. In later court hearings, it was revealed that Leonard regularly beat Shawn for such things as refusing to eat his dinner and mispronouncing the word "bathtub."

That story captured the essence of child abuse, and it got wide play in the Washington media. It was news.

In 1975, according to statistics for the Washington area, there were 3270 cases of child abuse reported to authorities. There were not 3270 stories about child abuse in the *Washington Post*. The paper's library, in fact, records only ten such articles in the *Post*, two of which were letters to the editor. Is it true that all the rest weren't news? Probably not.

In 1977, the *Post* improved. The library clips show that the paper published fifty child abuse stories that year—five times as many as in

Tom Wilkinson is Metro Editor for the *Washington Post*.

1975. Eleven stories were two and three paragraph "shorts" from places like Peoria and Walla Walla, detailing especially gruesome child abuse cases. These shorts are commonly called "fillers" because they are used to fill small, odd-sized holes in the newspaper. Major stories they are not.

Eleven other stories covered administrative matters—bills introduced, agencies formed or disbanded, a mayor's committee reports on the problem. One story was a regional agency report, one a Jack Anderson column, and another was a local columnist's piece; three appeared opposite the editorial page and two others ran in the Sunday essay section. The rest, approximately ten stories, reported local incidents of child abuse.

Does the *Washington Post* cover child abuse on a systematic basis; do we accord it the same kind of coverage we give to politics, Congress, fashion, or recipes?

The answer is no.

Should we? Or should any newspaper?

According to published reports, five million children in 1977 were shot, stabbed, kicked, beaten, or bitten by their parents. The press should probably cover that behavior in a systematic fashion, but the odds are it won't.

There are several reasons why. First, the *Washington Post*, like other large media outlets, receives approximately one million words every day from its local, national, and foreign correspondents, from wire services and news agencies, from freelance writers, and from other institutions. The newspaper has the capacity to publish about 100,000 words—or 10 percent of the information received. Competition for space is fierce.

Second, child abuse does not fall squarely into a specific area of reporting. Is it part of the police beat, medicine, sociology, or government? Child abuse probably falls within all four beats, and because it does it falls through the cracks. The *Post* doesn't have a child abuse reporter per se, and I doubt that any major newspaper does.

Third, child abuse cases often come to family court, where they disappear from public view. Two things prevent the press from covering family court—us and them. Judges don't let reporters in the courtroom and the *Post*, at least, has a general policy of not publishing the names of juveniles involved in crimes. There have been exceptions to this rule, but I suspect that in child abuse cases judges would be inclined to keep the courtrooms closed. Moreover, there is a danger in exposing an immature juvenile to the unusual pressures of publicity, particularly if that juvenile is the victim of the crime instead of its perpetrator. In short, the press is out of the ballgame when it comes to covering child abuse through the family courts.

Finally, newspapers could put more effort into covering hospital emergency rooms, where incidents of abuse often first come to light. However, an accusation of child abuse based on the judgment of a doctor or nurse in an emergency room presents grave legal problems for any newspaper. It is also not sound journalism. Despite popular misconceptions to the contrary, journalists do believe in verifying information; to publish such accusations without proper verification violates several of the *Post*'s rules. Furthermore, it is my understanding that many physicians suffer from tunnel vision, treating the injury without inquiring about its cause and, hence, missing cases of child abuse.

Given the constraints facing any newspaper, how can press coverage of child abuse be increased—and improved?

The issue here is access, perhaps the most vexing question faced by the media. Theoretically, everyone has equal access to the press. Like so many theories, this one doesn't correspond to reality. The simple fact is that access is the province of those who know how to get it.

A newspaper is only as good as its sources. Reporters and editors depend on people in other walks of life to provide information, guidance, and verification; in short, to be sources. Become a source—although you may not be meeting reporters in shadowy, underground garages, as a recent movie would have you believe.

Notice the bylines on newspaper stories. In addition to boosting the reporter's ego, the byline indicates who is covering a specific topic or general area. Large papers have medical writers; almost all papers have police and government reporters. Call those reporters and introduce yourself. If you have a story idea or some information, tell the reporter. If you don't, tell the reporter that you will call again when you do. Repeat this with editors. Find out who they are, call them up, and tell them who you are.

Start to consider what you know as a professional in terms of newspaper stories. Is the information something the public ought to know? Will it help to solve a problem? Sources don't have to write the story, they merely provide information. Sources may not even approve of the published story, but the source has overcome the biggest hurdle: gaining access to the media.

An example should illustrate my points. I recently had a 30-minute telephone conversation with a staff member of the Child Protection Center at Children's Hospital in Washington, D.C. The Center is four years old and the *Post* probably covered its opening in 1974. The Center now employs 30 persons. In 1974 they handled 150 cases of child abuse; in 1978 they handled 600. That's probably a story.

The Child Protection Center recently created an eight-person team to investigate sexual abuse of children. The team conducted a survey. That's probably a story.

The Center is trying to cope with its increased case load despite cutbacks in social services mandated by tighter governmental budgets. That's probably a story.

According to the staff, one of the most significant problems they face is the psychological inhibition most people have about accusing someone of child abuse. That's probably a story.

In order to overcome the ignorance and psychological blocks that prevent medical personnel from recognizing an incident of child abuse and then reporting it, the Child Protection Center sent traveling teams to all the emergency rooms in metropolitan Washington, D.C. for education sessions. That's probably a story—or at least it could have been one at the time the classes were underway.

In short, I learned of five possible stories during one half-hour conversation.

Newspaper editors are interested in specific facts, general trends, new directions. The *Washington Post* won't cover every individual case of child abuse, because that's not news. But professionals who deal daily with the problem of abuse can build conduits and provide illumination. Learn to *talk* to the press. What happens next, that's news.

Responsibility to Sources
Margaret Osmer

Television has impact—for those who watch it and for those who produce it. Power brings responsibility. The broadcast journalist who attempts to cover a complex and potentially exploitable social problem must balance several—and at times conflicting—factors to ensure that the power of the medium is used to clarify rather than distort. For example, in covering as sensitive a subject as child abuse, the reporter deals first with the abuser and the abused: two vulnerable people whose lives will be affected by the temporary attention and exposure of the media.

I covered such a story in 1970. The young woman I interviewed was

Margaret Osmer has worked for ABC news as a broadcast journalist, and is currently Director of Programs for the Council on Foreign Relations.

a participant in C. Henry Kempe and Ray Helfer's program for abusive parents at The Denver University Hospital. Twenty-one years old and the mother of four children, she was herself a child, who had neither the time to enjoy her youth nor the maturity to cope with her children.

The dilemma facing any television reporter became apparent after discussions with the mother and her counselors. Television needed the mother to give its coverage the necessary impact, or the human dimension of first-hand experience. But what of the impact of television on the mother? It was obvious that she was enjoying the attention from the film crew, myself, and the counselor; the idea of being on television was a dream beyond dreams. And yet, it also meant coming to terms, publicly, with the shame, guilt, and confusion of her brutality toward her children.

After still more discussion, we all agreed that the benefits outweighed the risks. The young mother convinced herself that her appearance might help someone else; if even one other mother in a similar situation were to restrain herself from abusing her children, it would be worth the appearance.

The mother was candid and effective in her interview—poignant, remorseful, and persuasive. Her performance was a major factor in the success of the presentation, first with the television audience and later with the many professionals who saw it at medical schools across the country.

But upon checking back with the hospital in Denver, I discovered that the young mother had experienced a relapse after the program was aired. Granted, it was not *ultimately* serious, but the sudden withdrawal of our attention combined with the public replay of her confessions and some people's critical reactions were too much of a strain. Fortunately, she had ample professional support.

The point is clear, however: television should not crash into people's lives just to get a vivid picture. Because of its impact, television has a responsibility to alert the audience to pervasive problems that are perpetuated by public ignorance, fear, and social stigma. We must sensitize. We must *not* sensationalize.

The more vivid the picture, the more stark the sound, the greater the impact: any good electronic journalist will reach for that, but not without measuring the merit against the cost. If television is to shake the public's sensibilities with the horrors of a problem like child abuse, it must also offer solutions to the problem, even if they are in their most experimental stages.

Time is critical in this regard. First, the reporter needs enough air time to present the subject properly. Second, the story must be broadcast at a time when the people who ought to see it will see it. Finally, a sense of social timing is essential. Just as some types of entertainment shows will sell one year and not the next, so too with news stories; audiences are not static in their responsiveness to social issues. At the time I did the documentary on child abuse, for instance, I was appalled at the extent of sexual abuse of children. I wanted to report what I had learned. However, after discussing it with my peers and my superiors, it was clear to me that this subject was too sensitive. Child abuse per se was hard enough for them to accept; incest, to the extent I had been informed it existed, was beyond their comprehension.

That has changed.

The breaking news story is generally an unsatisfactory format for covering a sensitive issue such as child abuse. There is time only to recount the facts of who did what to whom; facts that anger viewers without enlightening them. That is why I believe issues of this kind are best handled in a magazine or full documentary piece. If this is impossible, a "follow-up" piece can be useful. Too often hard news is hit and run—and has to be because of the constraints of time and format. However, good journalism will take the hard news story one step further, reporting not only what happened, but how to avoid or correct such a problem in the future.

This is not to say that electronic journalists should preach or reform. The ideal role for any reporter is that of objective observer. But information on what to do in a crisis *is* news and is worth communicating.

Television is a glamorous medium and runs the risk of lending a glamorous gloss to a grim and ugly subject such as child abuse. It is necessary to strike a balance. Viewers are lost if a problem is presented as too stark and severe. On the other hand, a sympathetic portrayal of the child abuser allows viewers to excuse their own abusive behavior.

Television can and should play a role in dealing with social problems. But just as treatment of child abuse by physicians and social scientists must be constantly reevaluated in the light of new findings, so too must television's approach to such issues.

Television is a means of communication, not an end in itself; it can be as effective as we make it. We in television news are not the social conscience of the nation, but we can endeavor to keep the public alert to problems in our society and the progress made in solving them.

Magazine Coverage
Nancy Signorielli

Stephan Pfohl (1977, pp. 310–323), in a lengthy discussion of the origin and development of the modern concept of child abuse, noted that the media's role in the

> proliferation of the idea of abuse . . . cannot be underestimated.
> . . . What was publicized was not some amorphous set of muggings but a "syndrome." Titles such as "Cry rises from beaten babies" (*Life*, June 1963), "Parents who beat children" (*Saturday Evening Post*, October 1962). "The shocking price of parental anger" (*Good Housekeeping*, March 1964), and "Terror-struck children" (*New Republic*, May 1964) were all buttressed by an awe of scientific objectivity. The problem had become "real" in the imaginations of professionals and laymen alike. It was rediscovered visually by ABC's "Ben Casey," NBC's "Dr. Kildare," and CBS's "The Nurses," as well as in several other television scripts and documentaries. (Paulsen, 1967b, pp. 488–89)

Policy agendas recently issued by a number of government and social welfare agencies have recognized the mass media as important tools for promoting public awareness of child abuse (National Center on Child Abuse and Neglect, 1976; Social and Rehabilitation Services, 1977). Media coverage is also regarded as a way to encourage the public to report cases of child abuse (Gil & Noble, 1967).

The public itself has acknowledged the media's importance as sources of information about abuse. Gil and Noble's (1967) study, conducted by The National Opinion Research Center, found that 72 percent of the respondents obtained knowledge about the general problem of child abuse from newspapers and 56.2 percent from radio and television. In short, the mass media were the primary sources of information.

Although scholars, policymakers, and the public acknowledge the importance of the media, virtually nothing is known about the type of coverage afforded to child abuse. This study attempts to fill that gap by analyzing coverage of child abuse and child-related violence in popular periodicals. The research included a survey of *Readers' Guide to Periodi-*

Written with the assistance of Heather Harr-Mazer.

cal Literature and a detailed content analysis of a sample of magazine articles about child abuse. By using editions of *Readers' Guide* from March 1972 to April 1978 we located all articles relating to child abuse that were published in popular periodicals. Articles were included if they dealt with the physical or mental injury of children, sexual abuse, negligent treatment, or maltreatment of a child under the age of 18. Articles falling under the topic headings of Child Abuse (or Cruelty to Children), Child Molesting, Civil Rights—Children, Corporal Punishment, Malnutrition—U.S., and Murder (children only) were included.

These article descriptions and titles were coded for topic heading, magazine, type of magazine, publication date, presence of visuals, and number of pages. The titles were also coded for the presence of twelve themes: Physical Abuse, Neglect, Sexual Abuse, Murder, Pornography, Boys, Girls, Law, Therapy, Preventive Measures, Education, and Government Activities.

To supplement the survey, 50 magazine articles relating to child abuse were subjected to a detailed content analysis. The articles included were all listed in the *Readers' Guide* under the headings of "child abuse" or "cruelty to children."[1]

These stories were coded for an extensive list of content items and then analyzed using simple distributional techniques (cross-tabulations).[2] In addition, each article was coded on a 5-point sensationalism scale (1 = not sensational; 5 = very sensational) to determine whether or not the article dealt with child abuse in a sensational manner.[3]

1. In the 1976–1977 edition of *Readers' Guide*, the category "child abuse" replaced "cruelty to children."
2. Stories were coded by two independent coders on an extensive recording instrument. The data were subjected to a reliability analysis by calculating agreement coefficients for all content items. Content items were included in the analysis if they met the following reliability criteria—an item was accepted unconditionally when its agreement coefficient was .800 or higher and accepted conditionally (i.e., caution was exercised when interpreting the findings) when the coefficient was between .600 and .800. The data used for the analysis were a random selection of one of the two independent codings of each article.
3. For this analysis, sensationalism was defined as: "The exploitation of marginally relevant personal or gory details in order to attract attention to the article."
    Coders were also instructed to consider the following things when rating each article for sensationalism: whether or not

a. the article had an "emotional, tear-jerker" tone;
b. the article put undue emphasis upon personal and domestic details;
c. the article dwelt upon personal cases rather than discussing the broad issues;
d. the article discussed gory details of violence rather than just mentioning that violence occurred;
e. the article contained a lot of adjectives, especially "color" adjectives.

TABLE 16.1: Articles relating to child abuse
and child welfare by year

	N	%
Total	242	100.0
1971	2	0.8
1972	20	8.3
1973	29	12.0
1974	41	16.9
1975	31	12.8
1976	29	12.0
1977	63	26.0
1978*	27	11.2

* Through April 25, 1978

GENERAL SURVEY OF "READERS' GUIDE"

The survey of *Readers' Guide* uncovered 242 articles published in 54 different magazines. Table 16.1 reveals that press coverage of child abuse has increased considerably since 1971. Also, if the 1978 coverage maintains its present pace of 27 articles published in the first four months alone, 1978 will lead all other years in coverage of child abuse.

Which kinds of magazines cover child abuse?

Grouping the 54 periodicals by readership shows that the largest percentage of articles related to child abuse were found in women's magazines, while other types of publications—such as news and business, essay, education, and popular science—covered the topic less often but in roughly equal amounts (see Table 16.2).

In addition to child abuse, these articles focused on the abandonment or kidnapping of children, sexual abuse, institutional care, general child welfare, the law, and parent-child or family relationships.

TABLE 16.2: Articles relating to child abuse by magazine type

	N	%
Total	242	100.0
Women (e.g., *Ladies' Home Journal, Good Housekeeping, Vogue*)	71	29.3
Essay (e.g., *Nation, Saturday Review*)	43	17.8
News and business (e.g., *Time, Forbes*)	39	16.1
Education (e.g., *PTA, Child Today*)	37	15.3
Popular science (e.g., *Scientific American, Science News*)	35	14.5
Special interest	10	4.1
Religion	7	2.9

Table 16.3: Appearance of child abuse topics by magazine type

	Total		News-Essay-Business		Women's		Other	
	N	%	N	%	N	%	N	%
Total	242	100.0	82	100.0	71	100.0	89	100.0
Physical abuse	51	21.1	20	24.4	10	14.1	21	23.6
Law	27	11.2	12	14.6	7	10.0	8	9.0
School	24	9.9	6	7.3	6	8.5	12	13.5
Prevention	23	9.5	2	2.4	11	15.5	10	11.2
Sexual abuse	23	9.5	7	8.5	13	18.3	3	3.4
Neglect	21	8.7	4	4.9	7	10.0	10	11.2
Therapy	20	8.3	2	2.4	8	11.3	10	11.2
Government action	18	7.4	9	11.0	1	1.4	8	9.0
Killing	13	5.4	6	7.3	3	4.2	4	4.5
Pornography	8	3.3	2	2.4	4	5.6	2	2.2

Story titles were used as an indication of the whole article's theme or general topic. Table 16.3 shows physical abuse to be the most prevalent topic, appearing in 21.1 percent of the story titles. "Law" ranked second, appearing in 11.2 percent of the titles, with schools and education, child abuse prevention, and sexual abuse also appearing frequently.

Table 16.4 presents the prevalent title themes found in three different types of magazines—news, business, and essay periodicals; women's periodicals; and education, religion, science and special interest magazines. Physical abuse was the dominant title theme in magazines for general audiences and for more educated readers. Law and government action were also important themes for these two types of periodicals. Physical abuse also dominated the titles in women's magazines, with special em-

TABLE 16.4: Distribution of articles and sensationalism score by magazine type, 1971–1978

	N	%	Sensationalism Score	
			$\overline{X}$	s
Total	50	100.0	2.2	1.42
Education	12	24.0	1.7	1.23
Women	12	24.0	3.7	1.15
News and business	8	16.0	2.5	1.60
Essay	7	14.0	1.9	1.22
Popular science	6	12.0	1.2	0.41
Religion	5	10.0	1.6	0.55
Special interest	0	0.0	0.0	0.00

phasis given to sexual abuse and methods for preventing child abuse. Therapy was also an important theme.

The survey suggests that child abuse has become more newsworthy since 1971, but it is still regarded as a woman's issue and restricted to incidents of physical abuse.

CONTENT ANALYSIS OF CHILD ABUSE ARTICLES

Definitions of child abuse are often controversial. Indeed, some have argued that developing an adequate definition of child abuse is one of the most urgent tasks facing scholars, policymakers, and social service professionals who are attempting to prevent and treat child abuse (Zigler, this volume).

This study did not impose its own definition of child abuse on the sample of articles. Rather, it accepted the definition of *Readers' Guide* as an indication of how abuse was popularly defined, or generally understood, by most people, at least in the 1970s. In one sense, the content analysis identifies the specific features of that definition.

Sensationalism is an issue of considerable concern to professionals trying to correct the problem of child abuse, and for good reason: the media often cover the topic sensationally, as this study shows.

Although child advocates may argue that sensational coverage distorts and exploits a serious problem—perhaps doing more harm than good—sensationalism solves several *editorial* problems; that is, it can be the response of reporters and editors trying to fulfill the responsibility to cover serious social issues, while continuing to turn a profit. Sensationalism permits an important but unpleasant topic to be covered in such a way that it still captures the readers' attention—and sells magazines.

Table 16.4 presents the distribution of the articles by magazine type and also reports the sensationalism score for each type.[4] Almost one-quarter of the articles were published in women's magazines, with another 25 percent appearing in education periodicals. News and business and essay publications were the next most important sources for articles specifically related to child abuse. Women's magazine articles were the most sensational; "quite sensational," in fact, with a score of 3.7 out of a possible 5.0. News-business periodicals were somewhat sensational, rated at 2.5, while articles in popular science periodicals, such as *Scientific American*, were rated as the least sensational, with a score of 1.2.

4. Although child abuse is covered most often by women's magazines, it is not necessarily covered by women. In those articles where the sex of the author could be identified (56%), female writers (54%) were only slightly more prevalent than male writers (46%), and both were equally sensational (1.0 and 1.5 respectively).

TABLE 16.5: Presence of general themes and sensationalism scores in child abuse article titles

| | Appearance of Theme | | Sensationalism Score | | | | |
| | | | Theme Appears | | Theme Does Not Appear | | Significance |
	N	%	$\bar{X}$	s	$\bar{X}$	s	Level
Physical abuse	10	20.0	2.4	1.65	2.2	1.38	ns
Neglect	5	10.0	1.8	1.79	2.3	1.39	ns
Sexual abuse	8	16.0	3.5	1.20	2.0	1.34	F = 8.64 p = .005
Fatal abuse	1	2.0	1.0	0.00	2.3	1.43	ns
Pornography	7	14.0	3.4	1.27	2.0	1.36	F = 6.30 p = .016
Law	2	4.0	4.0	0.00	2.2	1.40	ns
Therapy	9	18.0	1.4	1.01	2.4	1.45	ns
Prevention of child abuse	7	14.0	2.1	1.68	2.3	1.40	ns
Schools—Education	4	8.0	1.0	0.00	2.3	1.43	ns
Government action	2	4.0	1.0	0.00	2.3	1.43	ns

Physical abuse was the theme most frequently highlighted in the articles' titles, although these same articles were not especially sensational. Instead, the highest sensationalism scores were given to stories whose titles emphasized sexual abuse or child pornography (Table 16.5).

Table 16.6 reveals that child abuse means *physical* abuse, at least for the authors and readers of the articles in this sample. Physical abuse, especially the beating of a child, was the type of abuse covered most often, with 86 percent of the stories mentioning some type of physical abuse and more than three-quarters reporting the beating of an individual child. Child neglect was also an important topic, mentioned in 76 percent of the articles. However, neglect was usually treated in general terms; only 12 percent of the stories reported lack of clothing, 14 percent cited malnutrition, and 18 percent mentioned leaving young children by themselves. Sexual abuse and mental-emotional neglect were discussed in more than half of the articles, although sensationalism scores for all the topics but incest were quite low. Different genres of periodical—news-business magazines; women's magazines; and education, religious, scientific, and special interest periodicals—did *not* differ in the types of child abuse related topics they covered (Table 16.6).

Many of the articles suggested ways to reduce child abuse. The "criminal" solution—i.e., reporting cases of abuse to police and/or the possible prosecution of child abusers—was often mentioned but usually not advocated. Three-quarters of the stories focused on preventive steps,

TABLE 16.6: Type of child abuse in popular periodicals focusing upon different audiences or subjects

	News-Essay-Business		Women's		Other		Total	
	N	%	N	%	N	%	N	%
Total	15	100.0	12	100.0	23	100.0	50	100.0
Physical Abuse	12	80.0	10	83.3	21	91.3	43	86.0
Beating	12	80.0	9	75.0	17	73.9	38	76.0
Burning	5	33.3	5	41.7	9	39.1	19	38.0
Broken bones	6	40.0	5	41.7	6	26.1	17	34.0
Killing	12	80.0	7	58.3	11	47.8	30	60.0
Confining child	2	13.3	2	16.7	3	13.0	7	14.0
Sexual Abuse	8	53.3	6	50.0	13	56.5	28	56.0
Rape	3	20.0	3	25.0	2	8.7	8	16.0
Incest	3	20.0	4	33.3	1	4.3	8	16.0
Mental-Emotional Neglect	10	66.7	8	66.7	11	47.8	29	58.0
Coldness, apathy	2	13.3	5	41.7	6	26.1	13	26.0
Nagging	4	26.7	4	33.3	7	30.4	15	30.0
Neglect	11	73.3	8	66.7	19	82.6	38	76.0
Of clothing	1	6.7	0	0.0	5	21.7	6	12.0
Malnutrition	2	13.3	0	0.0	5	21.7	7	14.0
Health	3	20.0	0	0.0	7	30.4	10	20.0
Leaving child alone	2	13.3	2	16.7	5	21.7	9	18.0

such as methods of intervention designed to isolate and understand situations that can precipitate abuse and/or those people who might be more susceptible to inflicting abuse. Other solutions included specific government and privately sponsored programs as well as training for medical personnel in isolating and combating abuse.

Myth and fact combine to form a popular conception of child abuse. More than half of the articles sampled emphasized as a *fact* the theory that an abused child is likely to become an abusing parent. Moreover, almost half of the stories noted that anyone can be a child abuser, while almost four out of ten articles reported that child abuse is increasing.

If the authors of these stories were often anonymous, at least in terms of their sex, the subjects of the articles were equally anonymous. For the most part, the articles offered very little information about child abusers. Although parents are often cited as abusers, their race and socioeconomic status is not reported: When an abuser's sex is mentioned at all, abusers are evenly divided between males or females, with most of these articles focusing simultaneously on pairs of male and female abusers. An abuser's sex is even less likely to be mentioned if the articles deal with sexual abuse.

Articles reporting an abuser's sex or socioeconomic status are rated as somewhat or quite sensational. Those citing parents as abusers are also more sensational than others.

The victims of abuse are almost as anonymous as the abusers. Race and socioeconomic status are rarely reported; however, articles that do mention these demographic characteristics are more sensational than those that do not. The victim's age and sex are noted in almost 60 percent of the articles. Although adolescents are rarely mentioned as victims, the articles about them tend to be somewhat sensational. Articles also discuss male victims less than female or both male and female victims, but when male victims are mentioned, the article tends to be rated as more sensational.

Victims rarely react to their abuse, although those articles which report that a victim struck back or became emotionally upset tend to be more sensational. In only 4 of the 50 articles sampled did a victim consider reporting or actually report an incident of abuse to authorities. These findings are consistent with the claim of reporters and editors that unless a case has been brought to court, the age, sex, race, and other details about the victim and abuser are deliberately omitted to avoid legal suits for the publication.

In conclusion, the research shows that over the past eight years, a fairly large number of popular magazines have covered child abuse. Moreover, the number of published articles, while small, has been increasing. In fact, 1978, the last year studied, should stand out as the year in which the largest number of child abuse articles will have been published.

Of the many different types of popular periodicals, women's magazines contain more—and these more sensational—articles about child abuse than other types of periodicals. Women's magazines are also more likely to suggest ways for readers to correct or to prevent child abuse.

The fact that women's magazines lead all others in covering child abuse reinforces the notion that women have principal responsibility for children in our society. It is surprising, however, that these articles are rated as the most sensational. One can only speculate and hope that writers and editors are using sensationalism constructively; to attract readers and increase awareness of a serious problem.

News and business magazines, as well as popular science periodicals, covered child abuse less often and less sensationally. As a result, men, as well as women who do not read women's magazines, are less exposed to the problem. Moreover, because these articles tend to be less sensational, they may attract fewer readers than their counterparts in women's magazines.

Most of the articles analyzed here focused on physical abuse, especially the beating of children. However, these same articles were rated as significantly less sensational than articles that did not cover physical abuse. Neglect—physical as well as emotional and mental—was also given fairly extensive and unsensational coverage. The topics that appeared less frequently in child abuse stories were sexual abuse and child pornography, and when these topics did appear, the articles were rated as significantly more sensational. Articles focusing upon incest were rated as the most sensational of all child abuse stories.

Government programs to combat child abuse were more likely to be mentioned in news and business magazines, while women's magazines focused more often on private problems. This may be due to the fact that news and business magazines cover government regularly. Information about prevention and treatment methods was covered equally well by news, business, and women's magazines.

Although most authors discussed the issue of prosecuting child abusers, the majority felt that treatment and prevention—that is, isolating situations that could lead to child abuse and finding ways to prevent abuse before it began—were the most effective methods for solving the problem.

Finally, it is interesting to note that articles very rarely mentioned the race and/or socioeconomic status of abusers or victims. The anonymity of abusers and victims may allow readers to disassociate themselves from the problem; to assume that one's own friends, neighbors, and family are not involved. Thus, these articles may actually serve to reinforce the notion that child abuse is "out there" and that it "does not and cannot happen here" despite the fact that research shows child abuse to be widespread.

Responsibility for the Subject

John Mack Carter

I have no real knowledge of child abuse. I was not an abused child. I have never abused a child. And, until recently, I believed that I had never *seen* an abused child.

My ignorance would be unremarkable except for the fact that first, child abuse has reached epidemic proportions in America, and second, that I am editor-in-chief of *Good Housekeeping*, a major national publication that is pleased to call itself "the magazine America lives by." Child abuse is an important feature of American family life. As the editor of a national magazine that covers family life, I should be more informed; but I'm not. And even more to the point, my ignorance is not unusual, it is typical.

I began to attack my particular ignorance as an editor might: I asked my assistants at *Good Housekeeping* to do some research. By the time they were through, I'd collected several shopping bags filled with books and brochures, documents, and dissertations.

I joined *Good Housekeeping* in 1974; several members of the editorial staff have been there much longer. I asked them if the magazine had published any stories on child abuse and what the readers' response had been. Naome Lewis, senior fiction editor, recalled the publication of a story by Pearl S. Buck that drew thousands of letters. Entitled "Matthew, Mark, Luke and John," it told the truthful, poignant story of four Korean orphans of war who suffered hardship and deprivation.

"But the heaviest heartbreak mail came in when we printed the story of the baby in the frying pan," Naome said.

"The baby in the frying pan?" I said. "You mean an actual story of a human baby fried in a pan? How could anyone publish such a terrible story?"

"*Good Housekeeping* did," replied Naome, "in 1970. We published it under the original book title *No Language But a Cry*. Written by Richard D'Ambrosio, it was the story of an 18-month-old baby fried in a pan by her parents, after suffering almost every day of her life. The child was mute until she was 14, disfigured sickeningly and little more than inert matter until a band of nuns and a sympathetic psychiatrist came along, unlocked her lips, salved her psyche and had her disfigurement helped by cosmetic surgery. Our mail was mammoth on that one. Readers were outraged by her story, but praised us for printing it."

"But was the outrage sustained?" I asked. "Were other children helped because *Good Housekeeping* published the story?"

Naome and the other veteran editors looked blank. The general supposition was that *some* readers contributed *some* public service for abused children thereafter, but this could not be documented. Our consensus was that reader arousal does not necessarily result in action.

What a fine thing for an editor to admit! For, like the most avid advertising copywriters, editors strive to present material that not only captures the imagination but also prompts action.

Returning to the shopping bags in my office, I found that they contained dozens of documents and publications from government agencies, national commissions, foundations, and other parts of the public sector that work—or seem to work—at developing solutions to the problem of child abuse. The literature contained material that was moving, shocking—and frustrating because it confronted me with my ignorance. For example, I didn't know that federal agencies were in the process of developing standards for programs and projects designed to prevent the problems of child abuse and neglect.

The shopping bags also contained material from the private sector. One booklet appeared more at home at *Good Housekeeping* than the privileged information from the scholarly institutes. This was a report from the General Mills American Family Forum of May 1978. The theme of that conference was cheering: "Mental Health—An All-Family Goal." In the list of general recommendations, the following sentence stood alone looking important: "The needs of children must be better served." The full summary was a resourceful and sincere attempt to identify the dangers threatening family life today. But it did not mention America's "throw-away" children.

The shopping bags contained more reports of private-sector activities: open hearings on the consequences to children of a mother's return to the work force, transcripts of well-planned conferences that studied the effects of divorce on children. But the children referred to in these reports are not abused: Confused? Yes. Disheartened? Yes. Unhappy? Yes. But they are rarely abused.

There seemed a "niceness" about many of these conferences, held sincerely by corporations and public-service organizations. This "niceness" is not surprising when you remember that the buzzword of the late 1970s is "happy." Happy news is everywhere. A traveler can click on the television and find "happy news teams" laughing and joking with each other in cities across the country. A newspaper called the *National Enquirer* sells over five million copies each week by giving the public the bright side of reality. The *National Star* sells three million copies each week doing the same thing in color. *People* magazine sells more than two million copies a week on the principles of "I'm okay—you're okay" and "being famous is fun."

Nice people want happy news. But are any "nice" middle-class Americans taking practical steps to recycle broken children into mended adults?

Again the shopping bags hold answers. The "nice" members of the Association of Junior Leagues are working hard to prevent child abuse. The General Federation of Women's Clubs is more sensitive to the problem. And the sparkling, wholesome Future Homemakers of America are up to their healthy young armpits in the trash barrels that contain the battered babies of today's society.

As the editor of a magazine that reaches almost 20 million "nice" people in this country, I have many enviable opportunities—and a serious responsibility.

VII

DEVELOPING A SOCIAL POLICY

17

Knowledge Transfer
and the Policy Process

Nicholas Hobbs

KNOWLEDGE AND POWER

Francis Bacon, a contemporary of Shakespeare, is credited with first observing that "knowledge is power." But in his day that brave phrase, so pleasing to scholars, reflected reality only at the margins of action. What mattered then, and for three centuries after, were land, population, troops, and tradition. Apart from the personal inspiration of charismatic leaders, all power was derived from these ancient sources.

With the Industrial Revolution, the source of power changed from control of land and people to the control of the means of production of material goods, as Karl Marx pointed out and as British imperialism demonstrated. The Allies won World War II partly on the basis of America's tremendous productive capacity and performance. But the War was decisively won—and might well have been lost—on the basis of knowledge. For the first time in history Bacon's aphorism ceased to be a mild metaphor and became a powerful truth. When Stalin asked at Malta how many divisions the Pope had, he asked an outmoded question.

The crucial questions today in assessing the power of any nation are how many libraries and laboratories does it have, how many scholars and scientists, how many post-docs, how many technicians and mechanics, how many scholarly and scientific journals and knowledge networks, how many programs to train future scholars and scientists and technicians—

This work was made possible by grants from the Foundation for Child Development, the Needmor Fund, the Carnegie Corporation, and the National Institute of Mental Health, as well as by funds from Vanderbilt University. The views are those of the author.

and how good are all of these? I speak here only of power, not of wisdom or worth. If you want to know how great a nation is, how strong, how wise as to its future, how worthy in the present, ask these questions about knowledge, but also ask: How well does it care for its most vulnerable people, especially its children?

But if knowledge is to be utilized in the service of children it has to be communicated to policymakers at appropriate times and in understandable and usable form. This essay explores how knowledge can be transferred in the process of formulating and executing policy.

SOURCES OF KNOWLEDGE FOR POLICY PURPOSES

If we should adopt the prevention of child neglect and abuse as a national purpose to which we are seriously committed, where would we turn for the knowledge necessary to succeed in the enterprise? From what institution would policymakers derive instruction to launch a powerful attack on the problem? Knowledge relevant to public policies is produced by a number of institutions in our country. The problem is that none of these arrangements seem to work very well in the transfer of knowledge in the service of public policy formulation. I propose to comment briefly on some of the strengths and weaknesses in the knowledge-generation and knowledge-transfer function as now exercised in our society.

National commissions, committees, and task forces are a favored mechanism for mobilizing knowledge and judgment about major public issues, especially when there is a base of knowledge or experience for the groups to build upon. The commission mechanism has several attractive features: it can enlist the services of distinguished and competent authorities at little or no cost; it can give a relatively quick response to some complex problem when competent judgment and counsel are most needed; and it can often engage public interest, for a while at least. But there are many problems with the commission approach, among which I would mention the difficulty of engaging the full attention of very busy people; the difficulty of recruiting a capable staff for a short-term endeavor; the temptation to use commissions to delay or avoid making difficult decisions; the tendency for representatives of constituents to trade off advantages, thus producing a political least-common-denominator effect; and the dispersal of intellectual capital when the commission's work is completed. Not the least of the disadvantages of this method of knowledge-transfer is that people in the United States appear to pay much less attention to commissions than people in other countries do.

It may be that the parliamentary form of government enhances the possibility that commission reports will be given serious attention; in countries so governed (England, Sweden, France, Canada, for example), it is customary to appoint members of the government to important commissions, sometimes to the chair. In our country, commissions seem to be most effective when they are identified with authority and are instruments in the exercise of political power, for better or worse. For example, the Joint Commission on Mental Health of Children, which was legislated by the Congress but sponsored by professional groups, was notoriously ineffectual, while Mr. Kennedy's President's Panel on Mental Retardation was extraordinarily influential. Its recommendations led to the establishment of the National Institute of Child Health and Human Development, a dozen mental retardation research centers, a score of university-related clinical facilities, and a continuing presidential committee concerned with mental retardation. The two illustrations are, of course, insufficient to support a conclusion about what makes commissions effective in the United States; they may serve, however, to raise the level of a hunch to the dignity of an hypothesis.

In-house policy research groups have potential for becoming an effective instrument for the transfer of knowledge in the service of policy. They have emerged in government only since World War II, and their long-term effectiveness has not yet been fully demonstrated. Some research shows that decisionmakers believe in such groups but do not pay much attention to their recommendations (National Research Council, 1975). Their work in budget analysis, for example, may be more highly valued than their analysis of policy options. The groups are much a part of the political establishment and may be less independent, as well as more transient, than might be desirable. Their work is not ordinarily available for peer review. Finally, many major federal bureaus, and most state governments, have no in-house resources for policy study.

The Congressional Budget Office may in time reverse earlier pessimistic conclusions about in-house policy groups. The office appears to be successfully establishing in the Congress its authority to examine policy as well as to analyze budgets. It may be more permanent, and less affected by political changes, than other offices responsible for policy studies. It has shown a disposition to open communication, in some matters at least, thus gaining the advantage of external review of its work.

The endowed policy study groups, such as the Brookings Institution, and the enduring, not-for-profit research organizations, such as the Urban Institute, have been major contributors to the shaping of public policies, some over a long period of time. They are sufficiently well-funded (and well-led) to attract and hold first-class minds, and they are an important national resource in the knowledge-transfer business. They have an important tradition of independent publication. However, such institutes do tend to drift toward the dominant discipline represented (usually economics) at the expense of their interdisciplinary potential, and they make only modest contributions to identifying and training new talent for policy studies. Institute staff members with experience in universities sometimes remark on the muting of collegiality, the inadequacy of library resources, and the absence of students who can challenge the adequacy of one's scholarship and the clarity of one's thought.

The independent, entrepreneurial research organizations that ring Washington and cluster about major centers of higher education, like Boston and Palo-Alto, began to flourish during the Johnson, Nixon, and Ford presidencies and have become a major source of knowledge and counsel for federal bureaus. They have a number of attractive characteristics. They are highly flexible; they keep overhead costs low by expanding and contracting in response to available work; they provide a quick turnaround; and they know that to stay in business they have to produce an acceptable product on schedule. Officers of federal agencies are appropriately annoyed by the inability of some university-based investigators to take deadlines seriously; the private research groups do not make that mistake. But these organizations have their limitations, too, and their limitations tend to be the mirror image of their strengths.

The entrepreneurial research groups (as well as some universities) are highly dependent on the "R.F.P.," which is federalese for "request for proposal," a mechanism that surely must reach some new height of absurdity in man's search for knowledge if not for wisdom. It may be a good device for buying paper clips, soap, and ammunition, but not ideas. In the RFP game, bureau officers have been known to let it be understood what outcomes are expected, and it is not too much to surmise that the product is influenced by these wishes. Universities are not exempt from these pressures, but at least their survival is not as dependent on the good will of bureaucrats as are the entrepreneurial shops. The policy enterprise would probably benefit greatly from a policy review—at arm's length by a truly disinterested body—of the RFP mechanism, especially with respect to the production and utilization of knowledge.

Before examining the university as a source of knowledge to inform policy, I should like to mention and pay homage to a neglected agent of knowledge-transfer: the honest broker. I refer to the Edward Ziglers of the world, to the Wilbur Cohens, the Urie Bronfenbrenners, the Robert Cooks, the Elizabeth Boggses, the James Gallaghers—those benchless Barney Baruchs for children and families—and the Julius Richmonds—

before he moved to the other end of the bench. Full of knowledge, experienced in the ways of government, working without material compensation, independent, and deeply caring, they are a major national resource in the service of wise policies in the area of our concern. May their tribe increase! But even their mode of operation has limitations. The relationships are personal and necessarily private, not secret yet not open to public scrutiny without destroying their great value, nor are they systematically available to all policymakers. Honest brokers will always be needed, but their efforts must be supplemented by other formal arrangements for the transfer of knowledge in the policy process, of which the research university might become one of the most valuable.

The University as a Source of Knowledge

Only in our leading research universities can one find resources to address the complex, interrelated, and wide-ranging knowledge requirements of policies affecting families and children: the range of essential disciplines, adequate libraries and computers, collegial access to national and international networks of scholars, competence to train new generations of investigators and knowledge-transfer specialists, and a strong tradition of public service.

Our success in knowledge utilization in technological endeavors, such as agriculture, space exploration, high-science medicine, and communications, is nothing short of dazzling. But our failure to use knowledge to provide families and children adequate nourishment, to make available to them safe and decent living spaces, to keep them healthy, to prevent neglect and abuse, and to nurture a mutual commitment to community is so great as to constitute an ever-present threat to the stability and productivity of the social order. Richard Nelson (1977) calls this "the moon and the ghetto problem." If we can put a man on the moon, why can't we eliminate the ghetto, or juvenile delinquency, or child abuse and neglect? One powerful reason is that the knowledge base for solving complex people-problems is not yet in place. Providing such knowledge through basic research and scholarship is one of the major functions of the research university. Another powerful factor in the moon-ghetto paradox is that it is not at all clear that we *want* to solve many of the people-problems in our society. But more of that later.

To address public policy related to the problems of people, including the problem of child neglect and abuse, requires knowledge from many disciplines—from biology, psychology, sociology, medicine, law, political science, economics, history, education, social work, the humanities, and others. Furthermore, the knowledge must be integrated across disciplines and then translated into simple and usable forms. Scientists and scholars are not notably good at this sort of thing. They first have to learn to talk with each other across disciplines, to learn not only new vocabularies, which is relatively easy, but also to understand diverse and idiosyncratic modes of thought and methods of problem-solving, which is extraordinarily difficult. Occasionally in our Center for the Study of Families and Children, at Vanderbilt University, when communication seems inexplicably to break down, someone points out that we "sound like Hindemith," and we back up to get through the difficult passages with a freshened sensitivity to disciplinary styles and casts of mind.

Universities will have to change before they can provide a congenial habitat for serious scholars who want to do policy work. Policy studies require modes of enquiry at variance with customary academic patterns of work. The classical research university prizes individual scholarship most, and values less highly that work involving the pooling of talents, even if the product is similar to that produced by individual endeavor. In the social sciences especially (so central to policy studies), the departments encourage empirical, quantitative studies, testing a specific hypothesis related to some contemporary theory. Outside of history and the humanities, studies that synthesize knowledge are acceptable but not admired, and their perceived value is diminished proportionately by the number of contributors involved. It is interesting that some of the most exciting, policy-relevant work on the family today is being done by social historians, who successfully combine quantitative, analytic, and synthesizing methods. But young, untenured social science professors who stray into policy studies may do so only at jeopardy to their careers.

When we started our Center for the Study of Families and Children, we sought the counsel of highly respected people who had had experience both in universities and in government. Their advice, strongly given and subsequently followed, was that we should *not* undertake a program of empirical research addressed to particular issues in family life and child development in the established pattern of academic research, which had been precisely our original intention. What we should do, our advisors said, was to undertake a program designed to integrate and synthesize the vast amount of empirical work that has already been done, and to interpret that work so that policymakers could use the knowledge in addressing major policy issues affecting families and children. The objective should be to make usable what is already known. Their position, you will understand, in no way diminishes the importance of empirical studies; indeed, it emphasizes their importance, because knowledge synthesis would be impossible without empirical research to synthesize. There is no way even to get started on the analytic and integrative process without a substantial foundation of empirical work. Our advisors simply identified a neglected function that must be performed to make knowledge usable in the policy process, and we are trying to learn how to follow their advice.

After two years of effort we think we may have worked out one way to approach the task of synthesizing and interpreting knowledge in the service of policies affecting families and children. The process, involving five steps, is simple, rational, and straightforward (in description at least, if not in execution). The steps involve: (1) a definition of the problem in the light of a thorough analysis of what is known about it; (2) an analysis of current policies bearing on the policy issue being studied; (3) a synthesis of steps one and two and the identification of major policy options; (4) the analysis of the advantages and disadvantages of these options; and (5) the development of implementation and evaluation plans for preferred options. In step four, options are analyzed with respect to values served, costs, demographic constraints, ethical implications, public acceptability, political feasibility, unexpected consequences, and ease of implementation. In practice, of course, the process is not linear or sequential; there is much looping back and leaping ahead. Knowledge gaps have to be recognized and either bridged sturdily or the project modified or abandoned. Values have to be made explicit, a neglected step in much policy analysis. And finally, all the parts must be put together as an intelligible whole and communicated in many levels of detail and styles of presentation for various users, including a summary in a half-dozen pages of simple and direct English for policymakers who value knowledge in the policy process but who do not have time to do what we think policy analysts should do for them.

We are now one year into a three-year project to apply this analytic and integrative schema to the problem of child care and parent education. My colleagues and I are finding it the most demanding intellectual task we have ever undertaken, and it will surely be among the most rewarding if we can bring it off successfully.

VALUES IN THE POLICY PROCESS

It is commonplace in policy analysis to emphasize costs and benefits, a calculus appropriate to the origins of policy analysis in the defense department and in the discipline of economics. Costs are always important and must be weighed, but as we have debated public policies affecting families and children, issues of value emerge as the dominant concern, and cost-benefit analysis recedes to the level of a technical procedure of routine significance only. What people care about are the values served by public policy. Yet procedures for value analysis have not yet been developed. Seldom if ever does a commission or a policy study group make explicit the value assumptions underlying its recommendations; indeed, there appears to be little awareness of the central role values inevitably play in family policies. Most analysts are content to endorse values harmonious with their private intuitions, and do not bother either to make these clear or to lay out the values served by various policy options. We are trying to learn how to make value analysis a central element in policy analysis.

There is no gainsaying the fact that the problem of supporting families in order that families can nurture children well is a difficult one, loaded with value questions. It is difficult to differentiate in advance between help that does indeed strengthen families and help that is an unwarranted and weakening intrusion into family life. In the face of such formidable complexities, procedural solutions to problems become more attractive than substantive solutions. Commission reports, legislative proposals, and the works of individual authors addressing public policies involving family life and child development have, in recent years, settled with great frequency on recommendations that avoid confrontation with value questions, thus escaping the need to be precise about objectives, to make a prediction, or to take a stand about desirable and undesirable outcomes of any policy.

The list of procedural solutions to policy issues is long: due process, decentralization, income supports, vouchers, mediating structures, individual educational plans, parent participation, local control, staff-child ratios, and so on and so on. I have no objection to any of these procedural solutions when appropriately used to achieve some stated objective. What I object to is that the procedural solution is often considered to be the complete solution, and it helps policy analysts, policymakers, and citizens alike to evade the question of objectives or goals that *should* be sought. Sooner or later we have to take a position on what kind of society we regard as a good society, on what is a good family, a good education, a good outcome of childrearing. Both goals and procedures for achieving goals should be value explicit.

I am mindful of the fact that knowledge transfer itself is a procedural solution to the grave problems of our society, which is perhaps one reason why policy analysis is so popular, why policy study centers are popping up all over. It seems to me that a substantial knowledge-transfer capability is essential to improving the quality of public decisions about policies. And it seems equally clear that knowledge-transfer operations, no matter how well executed, are not enough. Somewhere between the laboratory and the library, on the one hand, and the legislature and ballot box on the other, policy analyst or policymaker, or both, must decide what the goals are, must choose between the better and the worse outcome, and let his position be known. Otherwise, the knowledge-transfer business will be a sterile if not destructive enterprise. Legislation itself may well have to be vague about values in order to gain the support of constituencies with diverse values, as every seasoned politician knows. But this is a part of the political process, a process best served, we argue, by prior policy studies that are explicit about the value consequences of choosing one course over another.

THE LIAISON FUNCTION

The knowledge-transfer operation will be successful only if we can devise new ways to facilitate communication between the generators of knowledge and the users of knowledge in the formulation of public policies. Scholars and scientists in universities and even in independent policy research institutes are generally content to study a problem, speculate on the policy implications of their work, publish a report, and move on to the next problem. From this point on, there is much in the knowledge-transfer process that is haphazard, and the waste is great. A serious address to the problem will require the development of formal arrangements to ensure intercommunication between scholars and scientists, on the one hand, and policymakers, on the other, at every stage in the process of knowledge generation and application, with universities playing a central but not exclusive role.

Lawrence Lynn (1975) comments on "the uncertain connection" between knowledge and policy, and Caplan, Nathan, Morrison, and Stambaugh (1975) speak of "two communities," noting that "social scientists and policy makers operate in separate worlds with different and often conflicting values, and different languages." I would add "different time frames." Weiss (1978) believes the gap between social science research and policy is exaggerated but observes "there is obvious room for improvement. The prevailing expectations for use of social science knowledge and research are much higher than reported use." Rein and White (1977a) ask: "But along with the growth of research, which is often mandated by the legislation that institutes new social policies, there has grown a chronic sense of frustration, among both those who carry out the research and those who commission it. The feeling is that research does not really serve to guide policy, or is misused, or lies on a shelf unused. Has the contribution of research to action been oversold?" Writing elsewhere (1977b) they observe: "But the policy-research alliance is an uneasy marriage, posing deep dilemmas that threaten continually to erode the responsibility and credibility of each partner in the match, the researcher and the policymaker alike." Discussing the use of research, Boggs (1976) points out that "both in Congress and in the executive branches, there are identifiable communication networks, but there are several interfaces at which considerable loss of signal as well as distortion can take place." These observations raise a number of important questions about the transfer of knowledge in the policy process: Is the basic research worthy of trust? Is available knowledge analyzed, evaluated, and integrated in ways useful to the policymaker? Or does failure, or limited success, derive from faulty communication between the producers and the users of knowledge?

In our Center, we are interested in discovering ways to reduce uncertainty in linking knowledge to policy, without compromising the objectivity of the university. Discovery is the right word, for we do not yet know how to go about the task and we do not find many good models to emulate. An obvious first step is to budget for the function and assign responsibility for it. Thus we have created a Liaison Division and staffed it with people who aspire to be "policy liaison specialists" (Dokecki, 1977). The function of the Division is to help bridge the gap by keeping policy researchers and policymakers in continuous communication at every stage of a policy analysis and synthesis study—from the stage of defining the problem and designing the study through carrying out the study (with needed midcourse corrections) to sharing outcomes in face-to-face communication. Thus far the main means of communication has been a series of seminars and informal breakfasts and luncheons with parents, service providers, state and federal officers, legislators and legislative staff members, and media representatives. The meetings have been instructive to us and seem to be of value to policy people, who find it challenging to be brought into a problem-solving effort early. They also find it unusual to meet with people with shared concerns who are not asking them for something.

To protect the objectivity of the university, we will not take on the role of political advocates for particular solutions to problems. But we do expect not only to make options clear but also to state our preferences for solutions. We are told that Vice President Mondale has said that he would like to have as an advisor a one-armed social scientist, one who could not say about everything: "On the other hand." We reject the myth that science is value-free and will accept responsibility for defining the values implicit in policy options and for making explicit the value commitments that inform our analyses and recommendations, in sum, the responsibility for taking a position. Further, we propose to operate an intellectual open-shop, insisting always on the right to independent publication and on the right of access of any responsible party, regardless of political alignment, to our work at any stage of its development.

But in our efforts to contribute to policymaking, our expectations are modest. In a democracy the making of policy is and should be a political process involving trade-offs among competing interests; compromise is its essence and contradiction in purpose inevitable. Knowledge is essential but not commanding; the government warns against smoking but subsidizes tobacco farmers. Academic people may be singularly inept in political business and are wise to leave it to the experts. What the university community can contribute to the process is knowledge generated by the scientific and scholarly enterprise. Such knowledge may never be commanding but it will always be important, and its significance can be enhanced by improving the knowledge-transfer process with service of improved policymaking.

Policy Analysis: A Conservative Process?

A number of people who have studied policy analysis as it is usually done say it is intrinsically a conservative enterprise. One commentator notes: "The thoroughgoing policy analyst who gives due consideration to political feasibility, balancing conflicting group interests, and analyzing implementation strategies will not come up with anything but prescriptions for mild incremental change" (Rein, in Green, 1979, p. 7). We hope that the policy analysis and synthesis plan described earlier will enable us to break with this conservative tradition by allowing—no, requiring—the play of intelligence of representatives of a number of disciplines on all aspects of the knowledge-policy problem in a systematic address to major policy issues, including child abuse.

Public Policy and Child Abuse

Do we want to eliminate child neglect and abuse in America, to the true limits of our ability to achieve that goal, or do we want simply to contain child neglect and abuse below the threshold of public indignation? I think we all know that the procedures we have developed to contain the problem of child abuse will not solve it. Our hotlines and case registers, our shifts of personnel from other urgent problem areas to this currently popular one, our public education campaigns may help some, but not enough.

In fact, these procedures may divert attention from the problem: the abuse of children in America. Do we indeed affirm as the only acceptable outcome that children in our country shall not be abused or neglected? This is probably an achievable goal; other countries have come close to achieving it—Denmark for instance. If elimination of child neglect and abuse is our goal, then we must face the problem squarely, and in all its complexity, as Ed Zigler has wisely instructed us. Child abuse is a swatch from the fabric of a violent and abusing society. We must mitigate, even if only in modest measure, the inequity of access to resources in our society for both parents and children; the Supreme Court must reverse its stand on the permissibility of corporal punishment in the schools—whipping children must be forbidden; if preachers preach a literal interpretation of "spare the rod and spoil the child," as they seem frequently to do in my community, how is one to differentiate child abuse from an excess of Christian zeal? Gun control is a necessary measure; not only must we quit selling soap and cereals by violence on TV shows, but we must have television that honestly poses questions of living, with some grace and with evidence of altruistic impulse; and neighborhoods must be reestablished as sources of mutual assistance and community among families. Above all, we need new knowledge about the wellsprings of violence in general and of child abuse in particular, knowledge that has been analyzed, integrated, and made available in forms useful to policymakers. We must learn how to transfer knowledge to improve the policy process.

As Bacon said, knowledge is power. We need to learn how to put that power to use in the service of families and children today, and of a competent and caring society tomorrow.

18

Child Health Policy
and Child Abuse

Julius B. Richmond and Juel Janis

In examining the problem of child abuse it is easy to be pessimistic. Efforts to deal with the problem are handicapped by significant gaps in our understanding of it. As Edward Zigler (this volume) has noted, we need a better data base, improved research, and a more clearly developed definition and classification of the problem. Yet, while acknowledging these needs, a number of promising developments give cause for optimism.

We are now at a point where we have enough insight into many of the conditions associated with child abuse to allow us to develop effective strategies to deal with this problem. In some cases these strategies are already being implemented; in others, because they represent approaches beneficial for children at risk of child abuse as well as for all children, it is likely that they will be adopted within the next decade.

Before discussing some of these strategies, it will be helpful to review briefly some relevant statistics on the family, the single parent, and the teenage mother since these data point up certain potential problems that are pertinent both to the issue of child abuse as well as to children's health and general well-being.

Certainly the family of 1978 is significantly different from the family of only a generation ago. The following statistics illustrate some of these differences: In 1948, only 26 percent of married women with schoolage children worked outside the home. By 1976 that figure had more than doubled (Keniston et al., 1977). Further, "while the overall number of children in the United States under the age of six has declined since 1960, by about 4.5 million, in 1973 the number of children living with single mothers had increased by 54 percent" (Harman, 1978). Between 1910 and 1960 about 25 percent of all children were in families that suffered the loss of a parent either through death or divorce (President's Commission on Mental Health, 1978c). Today it is estimated that four to five out of ten children born in the 1970s will spend a part of their childhood in a one parent family (Keniston et al., 1977).

Children growing up in families headed by single mothers are far more likely to be poor. That is, while 9 percent of children living in families headed by men were at income levels lower than the officially determined poverty level, 52 percent of those children in single mother families were in that condition (Harman, 1978).

In single-mother-headed families, there is a significant percentage of unmarried adolescent girls who are becoming pregnant at an early age, and are often choosing to keep their babies. While recent trends in overall teenage childbearing indicate a decline in birth rates, with a rise only in birth rates for very young girls, what is of particular concern is the large increase in the percentage of illegitimate births among adolescent women: from 1960 to 1974, the proportion of teenage births occurring out of wedlock jumped from 15 to 36 percent. To put this in a somewhat broader perspective, over half (53%) of the 1974 total of 418,000 illegitimate births in the United States were to teenage mothers (Baldwin, 1976).

The recently passed Adolescent Health, Services and Pregnancy Prevention and Care Act of 1978 reflects an effort on the part of the Congress and the Administration to respond to the many problems posed by teenage pregnancy, and represents an attempt to establish a program to develop networks of community-based services to prevent teenage pregnancy and to provide care for pregnant adolescents (Public Law 95-626).

This Act allows the Secretary of the Department of Health, Education and Welfare to make grants to help communities provide core services to eligible persons;[1] coordinate and provide linkage to other health and social service providers; and provide supplemental services when necessary.[2] In this legislation special attention will be given to agencies or organizations that can bring together a wide range of needed core and supplemental services in a comprehensive single-site project, or that can establish a well-integrated network of such services.

1. Core Services include a variety of services ranging from pregnancy testing, maternity counseling and family planning services to primary and preventive health services. They also include referrals for pediatric care, educational and vocational services, and adoption services.

2. Supplemental services include child care to allow an adolescent parent to continue her education or to work; consumer education and homemaking; and counseling for extended family members of the pregnant adolescent.

To return to some of the statistics just quoted, the question to be raised is: "What do these figures mean for those of us concerned not only with preventing child abuse but also with promoting conditions that will foster the healthy growth and development of children?

First, it seems clear that many children are being born today to young women who are themselves still children and who are too often poorly prepared to raise their new infants. Second, they tell us that there are many children growing up today in families that lack the kind of support that in the past was often provided by two parents or by an extended family. And, it is also apparent that because of family separations and inadequate financial resources, many parents, but especially single mothers, often lack the kind of emotional or financial support that will allow them to be good parents.

With respect to the problem of lack of financial support, although there is some controversy over whether a larger percentage of child abuse occurs in low-income families, or whether that assumption is an artifact of our reporting system, the data on abuse and neglect of children in low-income families is certainly disturbing. According to a recent report from the American Humane Association, almost half of the children who were abused or neglected in 1976 were in homes with an income of less than $5000 per year (American Humane Association, 1978).

It was not really until 1960, with the work of Henry Kempe and his associates in Colorado and the dramatic reference to "the battered child," that a nationwide professional and public awareness of abuse occurred. What followed is well known. The Children's Bureau formulated a model child abuse reporting law; by 1967 all of the States had their own laws, most of which were mandatory; and in 1974 Federal legislation was passed creating the National Center on Child Abuse and Neglect.

The National Center on Child Abuse and Neglect, through its demonstration programs, grants, information dissemination, and coordination efforts of different federal programs represents positive steps to deal with this problem. Yet, there are relatively limited funds available for this work. So the issue today seems to be: "Where do we go from here?" If we can view the problem of child abuse as one that requires a multifaceted approach, we can begin to answer the question.

Despite the fact that we still do not have a sufficient data base on child abuse, it does seem that there are certain things we do know and can agree on: Rearing children is adversely affected by bearing them at too early an age; having a low-birth-weight child or a child whose growth and development is slower than normal; lacking the support of friends and neighbors when the parent is under stress; worrying about being unemployed or not having enough money to meet basic needs; and not knowing what to expect developmentally from a child. These factors point to some strategies that can not only help to reduce child abuse, but promote the health and well-being of all children in this country.

Basically, these strategies involve (1) renewed interest in and attention to the issue of enhancing parenting abilities; (2) recognition of the need for and positive benefits of support systems; (3) awareness of the need to enhance the collaboration between the public and the private sector as a means of maximizing both financial and professional resources to deal with problems associated with child abuse, and (4) acknowledgement of the importance of an integrated service delivery system that can ensure comprehensive continuing care for all children from infancy through adolescence.

The problem of parenting is particularly serious for adolescent parents. A typical description of teenage mothers commonly notes that they often lack adequate social support from other family members or friends; have inadequate financial resources, which places an additional source of strain on them; and that they do not have an adequate understanding of child development.

While there is still some uncertainty about the precise nature of the relationship between adolescent parents and child abuse, one study of child abusers in Georgia in the two-year period from July 1975 to July 1977 reported that natural mothers who abuse their children were more likely than other mothers to have begun childbearing in their teenage years, and that children born out of wedlock were 2.5 times more likely to be abused than children born in wedlock (Morbidity and Mortality Report, 1979, p. 33).

Carolyn Newberger has proposed a conceptual approach, useful in understanding the problems of teenage parenting, which suggests that "parent's understanding of children, the parent-child relationship, and the parental role has an inherent structure or organization that can be figured into a logical system of hierachically organized and qualitatively distinct levels." In particular, she notes that the levels are developmental and that "the levels descriptively discriminate among parents." According to Newberger the developmental level at which a person organizes his or her awareness of people, relationships, and roles, will bear a relationship to behavior such as child abuse. As a test of this hypothesis she conducted a study in which she found that it was possible, on the basis of an assessment of parental awareness, to distinguish between parents who abused a child and their matched counterparts (Newberger, 1978).

Findings such as these appear to point to the potential value of programs that can increase young parents' understanding of their own behavior and provide them with general information regarding child growth and development. Many people are still quite skeptical about the positive effects of parent development programs, but there does seem to be some evidence—albeit tentative—to suggest that parent education can have a significant impact on the welfare of children. The development of curricula (that include direct experience) on child growth and development for schoolage youth and the information and training component of the newly passed legislation of Adolescent Health Services all represent worthwhile attempts to promote parent education.

The Administration of Children, Youth, and Families, in the Department of HEW, is currently sponsoring efforts to promote improved parenting in a number of different programs under its jurisdiction, including child abuse projects, foster care and adoption programs, teenage pregnancy projects, parent-child development centers, and Head Start and Home Start programs. Among some of the larger programs under their jurisdiction is a Teenage Pregnancy and Parenting Program at the Hill Health Center in New Haven, Connecticut, which includes among its aims "the promotion of the maternal-infant bond as well as the enhancement of the emotional and physical well-being of both mother and child." The Child Development Center at Howard University in Washington, D.C., has a Teen Parents Project offering health care to mothers and infants as well as assistance in parenting skills and help in monitoring the developmental progress of the infants. The Mailman Center for Child Development at the University of Miami has been awarded a grant to provide weekly home visits to mothers to provide training in childrearing and infant stimulation.

Within the Department of Health, Education and Welfare, the National Institute of Mental Health in the Public Health Service has as one of its major new initiatives a program to improve parental competency for schoolage parents and single divorced parents. This program includes efforts to promote early affectional ties between parents and their infants and to enhance parents' ability to promote their children's physical and cognitive development.

It is gratifying to see that these programs, as well as others that are not federally funded, are now typically designed to include an acknowledgement that different families have different needs and requirements. It is also encouraging to see programs designed to educate for parenthood before it arrives; provide guidance when the child is growing; and strengthen the family by linking it to other sources of community support throughout the child's development. This leads to a discussion of the need to strengthen social and community support systems.

Twenty years from now social historians will refer to the 1970s as the period when the concept of support systems really took hold. There is almost no psychological or sociological journal today that doesn't contain some article discussing the significance of social and community support systems.

For many of us, the concept of support systems seems to be a revival of the earlier settlement house approach to providing help to individuals and to families. Settlement houses are, however, no longer with us. But we have revived the concept in a somewhat expanded mode.

This new interest in support systems is not accidental. There is a close connection between the changing nature of the family—as described in the statistics quoted—and the attention currently being paid to this concept. For when families are no longer able to provide the kind of emotional support that is expected from them traditionally, or when we don't have a family close by, it seems to be terribly important to be able to make connections with other groups of people.

Jane Howard in her new book *Families* (1978) captured the essence of this need when she wrote:

> The trouble with the families many of us were born to is not that they are meddlesome ogres but that they are too far away. In emergencies we rush across continents and, if need be, oceans to their sides, as they do to ours. Maybe we even make a habit of seeing them, once or twice a year, for the sheer pleasure of it. But blood ties seldom dictate our addresses. Our blood kin are often too remote to ease us from our Tuesdays to our Wednesdays. For this we must rely on our families or friends. If our relatives are not, do not wish to be, or for whatever reasons cannot be our friends, then by some complex alchemy we must transform our friends into our relatives. If blood and roots don't do the job, then we must look to water and branches.

Blood and roots or water and branches—we all need them in one form or another, and they seem to be especially crucial to those of us who are often least likely to have them: the poor, the single parent, and the emotionally disturbed. And this raises the problem of child abuse once again.

As might be expected, one of the recurring observations made about abusing parents is their social isolation and lack of connectedness to supportive neighbors or community groups (Elmer, 1977; Garbarino & Crouter, 1978; Giovannoni, 1971; Newberger & Hyde, 1975). Typically, abusive individuals are described as "isolated," almost devoid of association outside the home, "and without social or emotional support." This point is dramatically illustrated in the study reported by Eli Newberger and his colleagues, which indicated that the single factor distinguishing child abusing families from nonabusing families was the absence of a telephone in the homes of child abusing families (Newberger, Reed, Daniel, Hyde, & Kotelchuck, 1977; Morse, Hyde, Newberger, & Reed, 1977).

Largely in response to these findings, as well as to others that link an inadequate support system to an increased incidence of both physical and mental illness, the President's Commission on Mental Health created a special task force to deal with this issue. The creation of this task force was, incidentally, only one part of a larger programmatic emphasis by the Commission on efforts directed at the prevention of mental illness (President's Commission on Mental Health, 1978b).

The Commission submitted its findings in April 1978. As a follow-up to the Commission's report a group was formed in the Department of Health, Education and Welfare to develop proposals designed to implement the report's recommendations. This group has now prepared a paper that includes a number of recommendations of ways the National Institute of Mental Health can encourage efforts both to enhance our understanding of support systems and to disseminate information that is already known about these systems to social service and health professionals.

The HEW group, in commenting on the Commission's attention to social and community support systems, pointed out that this was the first time that a prestigious nationwide study group in the field of mental health gave such prominence to the role of such nonmental health systems.

The recommendations of the HEW group, still in draft form, are far reaching. They include the development of strategies to encourage deliberate and systematic NIMH research proposals on social support systems, the inclusion of training materials for mental health professionals in this area, and the development of demonstration programs to identify effective ways to establish linkages between community mental health services and local community support systems.

So far this discussion has touched on approaches that are important not only for those of us concerned with child abuse but for the health and well-being of all children. Turning now to the provision of services to those children and families who are particularly at risk for child abuse, it should be noted that although there is some question about whether the problem of child abuse is more likely to occur in low-income families, we do know that when it occurs among these families, they are the ones most likely to receive services from the public sector. This often means that those families with the most serious social and psychological problems are the ones most likely to be dependent upon public agencies. Unfortunately, these public agencies are too often both understaffed and under-trained. As a result, many of the people in these agencies are frequently not well-equipped to deal with the problems that face them with these multiproblem families.

The emotional "burn-out" phenomena of individuals who work directly with child abusing parents is both well known and understandable. In this situation we need to bring together people in public agencies with professionals from academic and medical institutions as well as private agencies, in order to link professionals with the highest levels of sophistication, knowledge, and competence with individuals who are directly responsible for service delivery.

In 1975, the Judge Baker Guidance Center in Boston initiated just such a collaborative effort with the State of Massachusetts (Burd & Richmond, 1979). This public-private partnership involves a contract between the Judge Baker Guidance Center and the Massachusetts Department of Welfare. The contract calls for the professional staff at Judge Baker to provide on-going, in-service training and professional assistance to the staff in the Welfare Department. This collaboration brings the consultants into a close and continuing relationship with the workers and makes the consultants available at the time of crisis and is, therefore, in the best tradition of clinical training. Moreover, it provides for continuity in training and an opportunity for the upgrading of quality. It minimizes the "we" and "they" problems that traditionally beset relationships among public and private agencies, and, most important, it does not exempt the workers with the highest order of skills from dealing with the most difficult problems.

Any approach that can improve child health in general will also lessen the likelihood of child abuse. Efforts to encourage an approach to child health that emphasizes primary prevention are particularly important, as are efforts to ensure services to those children and their families who are most in need. In particular, we refer here to an effort to create a system of health and social services that places families in a system where they aren't lost and don't "fall through the cracks." In the case of multiproblem families this means creating an integrated service system that ensures continuing contact and follow-up by staff from either a health or a social service agency from the prenatal period on through the school years.

HEW is currently sponsoring a particular demonstration project that seems to contain many of the key ingredients for such a system (Olds, 1978). The project includes: the use of home-based nurse-educators; prenatal care and education for the mother; the participation of other family members; training in child growth and development; the provision of transportation to make health care easily accessible; regular contacts with a physician or health clinic; health and developmental screening; and a means of linking the mother and the family to community health and social service support systems.

However, this particular project only includes services for mothers and their infants. Eventually, we would like to create programs that will provide services that extend from the prenatal period and infancy, throughout childhood, and into adolescence.

In talking of new programs and new efforts we must also add that it is essential that any new program as well as the many existing categorical programs for children be brought together in an integrated fashion. In a society such as ours, with its multiplicity of services, we should have the creativity to be able to bring these services together. In the case of child abuse, in particular, the complexity of the problem makes this type of service integration even more imperative.

Child abuse must be seen within a larger context of factors affecting child health in general. Accordingly, we would note that the United States stands on the threshold of achieving the goal of optimal care for all of its children. It has the knowledge base, the technology, and the finest health professionals any society has ever known. Given such resources it is inconceivable that this nation would not succeed in its efforts to eliminate child abuse.

VIII

NEW DIRECTIONS

19

An Agenda for Action

Catherine J. Ross and Edward Zigler

This book provides a basis for further scholarly exploration; it also proposes some sound approaches to policies for preventing child abuse. In establishing our agenda for action, we have tried to set realistic priorities that seemed both possible to implement and economically sound. Our recommendations fall into three broad categories: areas for further investigation or reevaluation; concrete proposals for immediate action; and suggestions for eventual broad social reform.

A wide range of organizations and individuals have roles in solving the problem of child abuse. They include local, state, and federal agencies; the media; and many existing community and national resources organized for other purposes. The proposals below suggest some special roles for specific groups, but do not always spell them out. The recommendations are guidelines for action that need further consideration and refinement by individuals and organizations concerned with children. We hope that they will provide the impetus for widespread reassessment, discussion, and action.

DEFINING CHILD ABUSE

The Overview to this volume suggests that "policymakers find themselves faced with the impossible task of solving a problem whose magnitude,

This chapter draws from Catherine J. Ross, Lawrence Aber, Karen Alexander, Kirby A. Heller, Karen Nelson, and Deborah Phillips-DeMott, "Conference Recommendations on Child Abuse . . . November 20–21, 1978, Philadelphia, Pa.," available from ERIC Clearinghouse. The authors are grateful to all the participants in that conference, whose ideas are reflected here.

roots, and solutions remain undefined" (Zigler, this volume). No single definition of abuse has succeeded in fulfilling all of the functions that social scientists and social service professionals would like. The United States could undoubtedly respond more effectively to the problem of child abuse if Americans could agree on a definition.

A continuum of definitions exists, ranging from the extremely narrow one limited to life-threatening physical violence to the broadest view of abuse, which includes any interference with the optimal development of children. Because it is difficult to develop a single definition of abuse adequate to all of its statistical and social functions, each particular definition of child abuse must acknowledge the values implicit in it, and the purposes for which it will be used. Many discussions would be clarified by the development of separate working definitions of child abuse for legal, clinical, social service, and research purposes. The standardization of a range of definitions already being used informally by members of different professions would facilitate accurate communication about child abuse.

For the purposes of research or the provision of services on a voluntary basis, the definition of child abuse should be broad enough to include neglect and encompass all forms of child maltreatment. This relatively broad definition should be used in efforts to raise public awareness about the needs of children and families. A narrower definition should be used for the purposes of legal action and intervention in families (Solnit; Uviller; this volume). Such a definition would protect family rights and direct scant resources to the neediest families. A legal definition of abuse might well include only the threat of imminent danger of serious physical harm and avoid concepts such as neglect or emotional abuse.

The distinction between a broad definition for research and a narrow legal definition may, however, prove controversial. Some observers may object to narrowing the legal definition of abuse on the grounds that a narrow definition may restrict entitlement to services. The label of "abused child" currently provides a child with immediate access to more state and local programs than any other designation, and child abuse programs have attracted funding to states and localities. On the other hand, the term "child abuse" is so accusatory that it can discourage parents from seeking help. "Child abuse" as a label can be used negatively to identify social deviants and justify inappropriate intervention, or positively to gain executive and legislative support for funding child welfare services and to provide a framework for clinical case management, program development, and evaluation. Clinical case management and program development may well merit their own definitions of child abuse and neglect.

The question of definitions is far from a semantic one alone, since well-conceptualized definitions can lead to constructive strategies for prevention and help. The disease model should cease to dominate the popular understanding of child abuse (Albee, this volume). Yet this model continues to be a popular one among most laypersons. By emphasizing the illness of the abusive adult, a definition tied to personality disorder discourages creative approaches to the problem of abuse and displaces attention from the child to the child's adult abuser.

The arguments surrounding definitions of abuse revolve around differences in beliefs so basic they may prove intractable. Attitudes toward child abuse depend on whether individuals believe that all forms of physical aggression against children are abusive; whether they give primary consideration to adult motivations and behavior regardless of the actual impact on the child, to the potential harm to the child of adult behavior, or to the actual impact of adult behavior on the child's ongoing physical, social, emotional and sexual development; and whether individuals view existing social services as inherently benign or intrusive.

Because of legitimate disagreements among individuals and members of different professions about some of these issues, we recommend that the National Center on Child Abuse and Neglect in the Department of Health, Education and Welfare convene a national commission on definitions. That commission should develop a standard series of definitions, and explore the appropriate range for every type of definition. It should include representatives of diverse viewpoints. Contributions from child advocates and members of the legal, medical, and social service communities will be essential. The commission should coordinate its efforts with those of similar panels such as the Institute of Judicial Administration/American Bar Association, Juvenile Justice Standards Project (1977).

Legal questions also underlie the debate surrounding what to do about the problem of child abuse. The delicate balance among the rights of children, the family, natural parents, and the state merits continued expert scrutiny by representatives of the legal profession, the helping services, scholars, and the communities whose childrearing values should be supported and enhanced by family law. These groups should meet together at the state level (where most laws governing child abuse are enacted) in order to exchange information, monitor statutes and services, and make their views known to lawmakers. The National Center should develop a model for these local meetings that would describe who should be included, sample agendas, and other organizational materials. Definitions, laws, and services demand continued reevaluation as our society makes progress in defining child abuse and learns more about the extent and causes of the problem.

Until the United States develops a social consensus about what behaviors constitute abuse, the state should be cautious about exercising its legal prerogatives. The state's right to intervene in family life should be limited by the countervailing values of family autonomy, privacy, and integrity unless a clear, identifiable threshold of risk is passed. Notwithstanding this limitation, a variety of policies seems to offer the promise of reducing the incidence of maltreatment while respecting the rights of families.

SOCIALLY SANCTIONED ABUSE

The state and its agents must set the highest possible standard for the care of children in its charge, because of the state's symbolic importance in molding the behavior of private citizens toward children. Various forms of socially sanctioned abuse, including corporal punishment in schools; mistreatment of children in protective, therapeutic, and corrective institutions; and abuse in the foster care and juvenile justice systems suggest that widespread reforms in how the state cares for children are overdue (Aber; Blatt; N. Feshbach; Uviller; all this volume). Popular concern over parental violence against children should not distract concerned citizens from correcting these less sensational, but nonetheless injurious, forms of systematic abuse. Only four states presently ban corporal punishment in schools, despite consistent evidence indicating that such punishment fails to deter misbehavior, discriminates against boys and members of minority groups, and teaches the use of physical aggression while militating against a positive environment for learning (N. Feshbach, this volume). Because the many pressures on teachers and school officials stimulate their fear of relinquishing corporal punishment as a means of self-protection against student violence, we recommend that teachers receive training in alternative methods of discipline and classroom management. Skeptics have pointed out that alternative methods of punishment require a greater commitment of time and energy from teachers (New York Times, July 24, 1979); the benefits of that extra effort must be made to seem compelling. State and federal legislation should prohibit corporal punishment; and parents, government agencies, and advocacy groups should lend force to the law by monitoring schools. The United States is unlikely to adopt the Swedish position banning parents from using corporal punishment on their children, but legislation affecting schools will doubtless communicate changing attitudes to parents, since the acceptance of corporal punishment in public settings encourages physical punishment by parents (N. Feshbach; S. Feshbach; this volume).

The mistreatment of children in residential institutions such as reformatories and homes for the dependent and mentally or emotionally handicapped calls for public attention. Citizens should undertake independent reviews of the care provided by residential institutions. Institutionalized youngsters who are beyond a minimum age might benefit from receiving the kinds of rights gained by adult patients, such as the right of voluntary consent to medication or psychiatric treatment. Personnel in noneducational institutions should receive in-service training on children's needs and acceptable disciplinary techniques.

Deep-seated social approval of corporal punishment seems to legitimize institutional abuse of children in the United States. Several immediate steps can be taken that would attack both the underlying attitudes that perpetuate mistreatment of public wards and the abuses themselves. Educational workshops should be established for adults who staff schools and institutions. Policymakers should give further consideration to the problems inherent in attempting to balance the needs and rights of staff, parents, and children. States should establish mechanisms to assist parents and other concerned citizens in monitoring the quality of care and lobbying for necessary statutory changes. Government agencies should be empowered to cut off funds when violations occur and encourage citizens to report malfeasances to them. Although the extreme measure of withholding funds from an entire facility or district should be reserved to repeated or flagrant violations, the threat of that ultimate action would help to effect reforms. The establishment of structures to encourage and support the monitoring of public institutions by citizens' groups is an important practical step that has had precedents in other areas of institutional care.

Young people should serve on community boards and visiting committees monitoring schools and institutions, where they can be effective advocates for the needs of their contemporaries. National organizations of young people such as the Girl and Boy Scouts, Boys and Girls Clubs, and church groups might consider giving priority to the investigation, publicity, and lobbying concerning all forms of child maltreatment.

REDUCING THE INCIDENCE OF CHILD ABUSE

Social services should be available before a family finds itself in serious difficulty. As George Albee has so eloquently stated, "compelling humanitarian and moral arguments can favor one-to-one individual intervention to ease suffering," but that constitutes treatment, not prevention (this volume). We must move away from viewing child abuse as a circumscribed malady so that social service agencies can begin to develop broad supportive family and child programs designed to prevent abuse from occurring. The various stresses of 24-hour parenting, combined with social and structural tensions, lead to situations in which some parents become abusive; support services for parents would help to alleviate those tensions (Albee; Gelles; Richmond & Janis; all this volume).

Citizens concerned about child abuse should enhance and use the many supportive services and institutions that exist in virtually every community (Richmond & Janis, this volume). Child abuse prevention should be integrated not just with the social welfare system but with the network of agencies with which most families interact. Those institutions include schools, churches, and places of employment. An immediate and essential step involves communication, cooperation, and coordination among the groups in each community that serve parents.

Every community needs an inventory and evaluation of general support services, and services for families experiencing difficulties. Examples of this kind of inventory exist in centers that catalogue available day care facilities. Volunteer groups such as the Junior League, Jaycees, or PTA could shoulder responsibility for preparing inventories. Single-door referral services or child care bureaus should be fomed to provide ongoing access to and updating of the information. National organizations should develop models for surveying resources and establishing referral services.

It seems crucial to reeducate the "gatekeeper" figures in each community—clergy, teachers, and child care workers, doctors, and social service personnel—so that they will offer guidance and support instead of negative judgment alone to troubled parents. In seeking to mobilize a variety of professionals and neighbors to help families, we are redefining the very term "gatekeeper," which has previously been applied to those who label child abuse for the purposes of coercive intervention and legal action (Gelles, 1979, p. 150). Widespread education efforts, perhaps through paraprofessional neighborhood child care experts, should aim to develop awareness of the difficult task facing parents. Such experts should aim to encourage self-help, rather than to report suspects. Friends, neighbors, and community leaders should assist families experiencing stress or difficulties to seek help before child abuse joins the list of their problems. Simple means, such as posters in supermarkets to indicate the range of services available to families, might help to reach the isolated families that appear to be at great risk of abuse. These and other preventive measures would cost relatively little compared to the legal fees and long-term intervention required once physical abuse occurs.

Restraint should guide the efforts of experts who offer advice so that they enhance, not undermine, the confidence of parents in their own skills, decisions, and discretion. That principle notwithstanding, demographic and social changes have combined to leave many new parents ill-acquainted with the rudiments of the job they have undertaken (Richmond & Janis, this volume).

Support and education for the difficult task of parenthood should be available to new and expectant parents. Buddy systems could pair two sets of new parents, or new parents with those who have a one-year-old child. These couples could share concerns or frustrations and offer each other reassurance or informal advice. Hospitals and doctors should educate adolescent parents as well as the parents of premature, handicapped, and other children at high risk of abuse about the kinds of problems they will encounter, and the services available to them (Ainsworth; Richmond & Janis; Zigler; all this volume).

Families that perceive themselves to be at high risk of abuse may also need special services. Crisis day care and hot lines should be available on a 24-hour basis in every community. Older citizens could receive training to help deliver crisis day care, along the lines of ACTION's Foster Grandparent program. CETA workers could also be used for day care, or equally important, as home visitors and parent aides (see Adnopoz, 1979). Because families may find the different service agencies they come into contact with confusing, "one-door service" would simplify the call for help. Finally, public officials should not require that families perceived as being "at risk" of abuse comply with unrealistic and/or unavailable services (Solnit, this volume).

Parenting education holds promise as a means of stemming child abuse. Support for parenting education as a preventive strategy rests on several assumptions. Parents' unrealistic expectations about their children contribute to the likelihood of their using methods of discipline or losing their tempers with unanticipated results. Knowledge about child development and skills for handling children would, we suspect, lessen the incidence of unintentional abuse. Until evidence bears out that supposition, parent education remains a relatively inexpensive way to influence many families. By serving everyone, educational programs bypass the need to predict who might be a potential abuser and avoid the labeling that characterizes many prevention programs. When carefully designed to protect cultural diversity, parenting education need not discriminate against any socioeconomic or ethnic group.

Popular support for family life education, which offers useful precedents, has been increasing, despite some public resistance resulting from fear of intrusion into family privacy and hesitancy on the part of professional educators (Scales, 1978). Such problems make the full participation of local teenagers and parents crucial to the success of parenting education. Increased state involvement, including mandates concerning curricula and funding for the development and evaluation of programs, would ease implementation of parenting education. A review of existing parenting educational curriculum plans is an important first step. Some new materials probably need to be developed. Model curricula should be widely disseminated to community organizations as well as school systems, and should receive scrutiny to ensure that programs are as culturally unbiased as possible. Finally, researchers should evaluate the effectiveness of parent education in general and of different approaches to it.

Parenting education should be an integral part of school curricula from kindergarten through high school, perhaps in conjunction with broader family life education. Programs should also be available on a voluntary basis for parents adjusting to new stages in their children's development. Clearly, this wide view of parenting education suggests a community-based approach in which schools would be only one source of education. Parents and young people should be actively involved in planning and refining the curricula. The opportunity to observe and care for children should be integrated into programs for schoolage students and expectant parents.

Teenagers themselves have suggested that, in addition to receiving factual information about child development and child care, students should learn about what kinds of stress on parents may generate abusive behavior, and should be familiar with services that are available to all members of their families. Adolescents, in programs such as Youth-Helping-Youth, have demonstrated greater success than adults in providing victims of abuse with a supportive environment, helping them cope, teaching them parenting skills and, perhaps more important, "defining the kind of treatment and care they have a right to expect" (Garbarino & Jacobson, 1978). Young people have suggested that children of all ages need to know where they can seek help both during childhood and when they later become parents. "If you can't help the parents of today," they have asked, "please help us, the parents of tomorrow" (Ross, Aber, Alexander, Heller, Nelson, & Phillips-DeMott, 1978, p. 19).

THE COMMUNICATIONS INDUSTRIES:
TELEVISION, NEWSPAPERS, AND MAGAZINES

The communications industries can play two major roles in helping to combat the problem of child abuse: first, they can rally support for new policies; and second, they can contribute to the creation of a sophisticated awareness of social problems such as abuse and neglect.

Television, which has joined families and schools as a major agent of socialization, could play a uniquely effective role in helping to change attitudes toward children and childrearing. Specific changes ranging from the increased use of public service announcements to more complex portrayals of family life and problems within standard entertainment series as well as in "specials" aimed at both adults and children are necessary. An emphasis on increasing the appreciation of children and their needs, a reduction in the incidence of violence depicted, a portrayal of alternatives to physical punishment for children, and the expanded use of realistic problems and families in television plots constitute essential first steps (Gerbner; Signorielli; this volume).

Most programs that have been aired on child abuse have focused on where abusive parents can seek help. Parents Anonymous has frequently figured prominently in these programs to the exclusion of other means of prevention and treatment. Although the self-help approach Parents Anonymous uses aids some families, especially those already well-motivated, its prominence on television fosters an exaggerated belief in the efficacy of individual control. The media may focus on organized parents' groups for reasons of convenience that are not clear to viewers. Such groups provide quick, convenient sources of information and interviews. In order to become more realistic and thorough, future programs should begin showing the social sources of child abuse. Producers and censors should strive to be sensitive to the possible impact of sensational coverage on individuals and on public policy (Aber; Osmer; Uviller; all this volume).

More public service announcements on child abuse and family stress should be developed and aired in prime time. Instead of just warning parents that certain behaviors constitute abuse, public service announcements along the lines of the cancer warning signals may be helpful. Such announcements could suggest that if parents experience stress, they should not hesitate to seek assistance in caring for their children. Messages should give concrete information about various kinds of help and where to obtain them. A second series of public service messages could be developed that would help children understand what constitutes abusive behavior and where to seek help for themselves. Such announcements would need to be designed with great caution to avoid any suggestion of hysteria or interference in normal family discipline; the announcements should differentiate between the tensions most families experience and situations in which children are endangered. These television "spots" should be aimed at children of all ages and be aired on Saturday mornings and in cartoon periods as well as with shows that attract teenage viewers. Citizens' groups must initiate public service announcements, but can rely on network personnel for help in designing effective messages (O'Brien, Schneider, & Traviesas, this volume).

The media primarily reports on what exists and what is known. It cannot transform social behavior, or be more advanced than the state of knowledge in any field. Persons concerned with child abuse and other social problems should learn how best to use the media, and how to share information with reporters and producers so that they can develop stories (Wilkinson, this volume). Child advocates should use the resources of local stations as well as networks, and offer their services as consultants on children's issues to advisory boards for networks and magazines. Ongoing committees might help guide media policy on child and family issues. Similarly, regional meetings between local journalists and television station producers and local advocates, scholars, and social service representatives could lead to more sophisticated understanding and coverage of social problems.

Research Issues

"To address public policy related to the problems of people," Nicholas Hobbs has concluded, "requires knowledge from many disciplines . . . integrated across disciplines and then translated into simple and usable forms" (this volume). Nearly all of the authors in this volume stressed the relatively primitive state of research on child abuse and related issues, and suggested questions for future exploration. The authors in this volume concur that further research concerning all aspects of child abuse would provide the knowledge necessary to design effective social policies. Wide ranging research priorities include studies on the etiology, prevention, treatment, and effects of abuse on children and families.

Many questions for basic research remain unanswered. In the areas of prevention and service delivery, for example, it would be important to determine what correlation, if any, exists between the availability of support services in a community and the incidence of abuse. Does the very knowledge that services exist ease family tension and reduce the incidence of violence? How much child abuse really exists, and is it concentrated in particular areas or subpopulations? How well are different models of social service programs succeeding in reducing abuse? Why are infants under the age of two more likely to be victims of abuse than are older children? Do parents from ethnic groups that maintain strong extended family ties, and who live near their relatives, engage in less abusive behavior than more isolated parents?

Federal and state governments could help support needed research by reserving between one and five percent of all funds devoted to children's services or child abuse services for basic research that will ultimately improve services. Federal agencies involved in research about children should coordinate their efforts by pooling resources along the lines of efforts in child development research already coordinated by the federal Administration for Children, Youth and Families.

Child Abuse and Social Realities

Although programs to prevent child abuse cannot await broader social reform, we cannot ignore the relationship between social reform and the quality of life for children and families. We have attempted to develop concrete and manageable policy proposals that realistically appraise the current mood of fiscal austerity regarding social welfare. However, a recurrent theme of this volume is the need of the United States to reform its social environment, confront structural problems, and support policies that enhance family life. In addition to the specific strategies for preventing abuse outlined above, basic reforms are needed to reduce the incidence of child abuse and attack conditions that inhibit the optimal development of children.

A national commitment to the well-being of children would be reflected in policies designed to guarantee every child decent medical care and nutrition; reduce the unemployment often correlated with violence toward children; and guarantee base-line standards of living, adequate housing, day care, and social services (cf. Keniston et al., 1977; National Academy of Sciences, 1974; Silver, 1978). Interested professionals should monitor all proposed legislation to see how it will affect children. Advocacy networks at both the state and federal level, along the lines of experiments now being conducted by the Children's Defense Fund and other groups, should be expanded and strengthened.

The federal government's National Center on Child Abuse and Neglect, important as it may become, should not overshadow either state and local governments, or the private sector. Large companies should expand their efforts to devise employment policies and services that would foster family life. Child care professionals and advocates should offer their services in setting up such programs. Ongoing coalitions at the local level among private and public organizations and corporations to coordinate and facilitate the development of an environment conducive to family life would enlarge the potential impact of each experiment. Sponsors of programs that strengthen families should publicize their model programs along with cost analyses.

None of our suggestions require radical innovations. Models for many of the approaches we propose are readily accessible. They exist in Head Start's Parent and Child Centers, in programs mounted for other pur-

303

poses by the National Institutes of Mental Health, the Office of Education, and even by ACTION. Many localities have already made a start. But popular reconceptualization of the definition and scope of child abuse, and an integration of existing programs and ideas is overdue. The comparative perspective offered in Chapter 7 summed it up well: The real need is not for increased funding for child abuse services, but for an integrated system of services for children and families (Kahn & Kamerman, this volume). Even though specific actions may help to prevent and contain child abuse, it is so closely related to the general problems facing American children and families that in the long run massive social reform and advocacy seem necessary. Child abuse cannot be separated from the range of children's policy issues, but it may serve as a focal point for obtaining needed social reforms.

References

Abt Associates, *Final Report of the National Day Care Study: Children at the Center* (Washington, D.C.: U.S. Government Printing Office, 1979).

Adnopoz, Jean A., "Parent Aides: Effective Supports for Families," available from the Coordinating Committee for Children in Crisis, New Haven, Connecticut, 1979.

Ainsworth, Mary D. S., "The effects of maternal deprivation: A review of findings and controversy in the context of research strategy," *Deprivation of maternal care: A reassessment of its effects*, Public Health Papers, No. 14 (Geneva: World Health Organization, 1962).

Ainsworth, Mary D. S., "The development of infant-mother attachment," in Bettye M. Caldwell and Henry N. Ricciuti, eds., *Review of child development research*, Vol. 3 (Chicago: University of Chicago Press, 1973).

Ainsworth, Mary D. S., "Bowlby-Ainsworth attachment theory: Commentary to Rajeck, D. W., Lamb, M. E., and Obmascher, P., Toward a general theory of infantile attachment: a comparative review of aspects of the social bond," *Behavioral and Brain Sciences*, 1, 1979, pp. 436–439.

Ainsworth, Mary D. S., Blehar, M. C., Waters, E., and Wall, S., *Patterns of attachment: A psychological study of the strange situation* (Hillsdale, N.J.: Lawrence Erlbaum Associates, 1978).

Albee, George W., "A competency model must replace the defect model," in Lynne Bond and James Rosen, eds., *The primary prevention of psychopathology: Promoting social competence and coping in adulthood* (Hanover, N.H.: The University Press of New England, 1979).

Albee, George W. and Joffe, Justin M., eds., *The primary prevention of psychopathology: The issues* (Hanover, N.H.: The University Press of New England, 1975).

Alsager v. District Court 406 F. Supp. 10 (1975).

Alvy, Kerby T., "Preventing child abuse," *American Psychologist*, 30, No. 9, September 1975, pp. 921–928.

American Humane Association, *Highlights of the 1974 National Data*, National Clearinghouse on Child Neglect and Abuse (Denver: American Humane Association, 1974).

American Humane Association, *National Analysis of Official Child Neglect and Abuse Reporting* (Denver: American Humane Association, 1978).

Andrews, S. R., Blumenthal, J. B., Bache, W. L., III and Wiener, G., *Fourth year report: New Orleans Parent Child Development Center*, unpublished document, March 1975.

Annotated Law of Massachusetts 71:376.

Areen, J. Intervention between parent and child: A reappraisal of the State's role in child abuse and neglect cases. *Georgetown Law Journal*, 63, 1975, pp. 887–910.

Arend, R., Gove, F., and Srofe, L. A., "Competence in preschool and kindergarten predicted from infancy," *Child Development*, in press.

Ariès, Philippe, *Centuries of Childhood: A Social History of Family Life* (New York: Knopf, 1962).

Azrin, M. H., Hutchinson, R. R., and Hake, D. F., "Pain-induced fighting in the squirrel monkey," *Journal of the experimental analysis of behavior*, 6, No. 4, October 1963, p. 620.

Azrin, Nathan, "Pain and aggression," *Psychology Today*, 1, No. 1, May 1967, pp. 27–33.

Baker v. Owen, 395 F. Supp. 294, 96 S. Ct. 210 (1975).

Baldwin, J. A. and Oliver, J. E., "Epidemiology and family characteristics of severely abused children," *British Journal of Preventive Social Medicine*, 29, No. 4, 1975, pp. 205–221.

Baldwin, Wendy H., "Adolescent pregnancy and childbearing—Growing concerns for Americans," *Population Bulletin*, 31, No. 2 (Washington, D.C.: Population Reference Bureau, 1976).

Bandura, Albert, "Influence of models' reinforcement contingencies on the acquisition of imitative responses," *Journal of Personality and Social Psychology*, 1, No. 6, June 1965, pp. 589–595.

Bandura, Albert and Walters, Robert H., *Social learning and personality development* (New York: Holt, Rinehart and Winston, 1963).

Becker, Howard S., *Outsiders* (New York: Free Press, 1963).

Beezley, Pat, Martin, Harold, and Alexander, Helen, "Comprehensive family oriented therapy," in Ray E. Helfer and C. Henry Kempe, eds., *Child abuse and neglect: The family and the community* (Cambridge, Mass.: Ballinger, 1976).

Behlmer, George K., "The child protection movement in England, 1860–1914," unpublished Ph.D. dissertation, Stanford University, 1977.

Belsky, J., "Three theoretical models of child abuse," *Child Abuse and Neglect: The International Journal*, 3, 1978, pp. 37–49.

Bell, Silvia M., "Cognitive development and mother-child interaction in the first three years of life," monograph in preparation, 1978.

Bell, Silvia M. and Ainsworth, Mary D. S., "Infant crying and maternal responsiveness," *Child Development*, 43, No. 4, December 1972, pp. 1171–1190.

Bem, Daryl, "Constructing cross-situational consistencies in behavior: Some thoughts on Alker's critique of Mischel," *Journal of Personality*, 40, No. 1, March 1972, pp. 17–26.

Bennie, E. H., and Sclare, A. B., "The battered child syndrome," *American Journal of Psychiatry*, 125, No. 7, January 1969, pp. 975–979.

Berkowitz, Leonard, *The development of motives and values in the child* (New York: Basic Books, 1964).

Billingsley, A., "Family functioning in the low income black community," *Casework*, 50, 1969, pp. 563–572.

Blatt, Burton, *Exodus from pandemonium: Human abuse and a reformation of public policy* (Boston: Allyn and Bacon, 1970).

Blatt, Burton, *Souls in extremis* (Rockleigh, N.J.: Allyn and Bacon, 1974).

Blatt, Burton, "Instruments of change—The executive," in Robert B. Kugel, ed., *Changing patterns in residential services for the mentally retarded*, 2nd ed. (Washington, D.C.: President's Committee on Mental Retardation, 1976).

Blatt, B., Bogdan, R., Biklen, D., and Taylor, S., "From institution to community: A conversion model," in E. Sontag, ed., *Educational programming for the severely and profoundly handicapped* (Reston, Virginia: Council for Exceptional Children, Division of Mental Retardation, 1977).

Blatt, Burton and Kaplan, Fred, *Christmas in Purgatory: A photographic essay on mental retardation*, 2nd ed. (Boston: Allyn and Bacon, 1966).

Blatt, B., Ozolins, A., and McNally, J., *The family papers: A return to purgatory* (New York: Longman, Inc., in press).

Blumberg, M., "When parents hit out," *Twentieth Century*, Winter 1973, pp. 39–44.

Boggs, E. "The making of public policy: What others do with what we say," *Birth defects: original article series*, 12, No. 27, 1976, pp. 149–161.

Bongiovanni, Anthony, "A review of research on the effects of punishment: Implications for corporal punishment in the schools," in J. Wise, ed., *Proceedings: Conference on corporal punishment in the schools: A national debate* (Washington, D.C.: National Institute of Education, 1977). NIE P–77–0079.

Bourne, Richard and Newberger, Eli H., " 'Family autonomy' or 'coercive intervention'? Ambiguity and conflict in the proposed standards for child abuse and neglect," *Boston University Law Review*, 57, No. 4, July 1977, pp. 670–706.

Bourne, Richard and Newberger, Eli H., eds., *Critical perspectives on child abuse* (Lexington, Mass.: D. C. Heath and Co., 1979).

Bowers, Kenneth, "Situationism in psychology: An analysis and a critique," *Psychological Review*, 80, No. 5, September 1973, pp. 307–336.

Bowlby, John, *Attachment and Loss*, Vol. 1, *Attachment* (New York: Basic Books, 1969).

Bowlby, John, *Attachment and Loss*, Vol. 2, *Separation: Anxiety and Anger* (New York: Basic Books, 1973).

Bremner, Robert, ed., *Children and youth in America: A documentary history*, 3 volumes (Cambridge, Mass.: Harvard University Press, 1970–1974).

Bronfenbrenner, Urie, "The origins of alienation," *Scientific American*, 231, No. 2, August 1974, pp. 53–61.

Bullard, Dexter M., Jr., Glaser, Helen H., Heagarty, Margaret C., and Pivchik, Elizabeth C., "Failure to thrive in the neglected child," *American Journal of Orthopsychiatry*, 37, No. 4, July 1967, pp. 680–690.

Burd, Ronald and Richmond, Julius B., "The public and private sector: A developing partnership in human services," *American Journal of Orthopsychiatry*, 49, No. 2, April 1979, pp. 218–229.

Burgess, Robert L., "Child abuse: A behavioral analysis," in Benjamin B. Lahey and Alan E. Kazdin, eds., *Advances in clinical psychology* (New York: Plenum Publishing Corporation, 1978).

Burgess, Robert L. and Conger, Rand P., "Family interaction in abusive, neglected and normal families," *Child Development*, 49, No. 4, December 1978, pp. 1163–1173.

Buss, Arnold H., "Physical aggression in relation to different frustrations," *Journal of Abnormal and Social Psychology*, 67, No. 1, 1963, pp. 1–7.

Caffey, John, "Multiple fractures in the long bones of infants suffering from chronic subdural hematoma," *American Journal of Roentgenology*, 56, No. 2, August 1946, pp. 163–173.

Caffey, John, *Journal of pediatric X-ray diagnosis*, 2nd ed. (Chicago: Year Book Publications, 1950).

Caffey, John, "Some traumatic lesions in growing bones other than fractures and dislocations: Clinical and radiological features," *British Journal of Radiology*, 30, No. 353, May 1957, pp. 225–238.

California state assembly report on corporal punishment (Sacramento, Calif.: State Publishing Office, 1973).

Caplan, Gerald, *Principles of preventive psychiatry* (New York: Basic Books, 1964).

Caplan, G., Mason, E. A., and Kaplan, D. M., "Four studies of crisis in parents of prematures," *Community Mental Health Journal*, 1, 1965, pp. 149–161.

Caplan, G., Nathan, S., Morrison, Andrea, and Stambaugh, Russell J., *The use of social science knowledge in policy decisions at the national level* (Ann Arbor: Institute for Social Research, University of Michigan, 1975).

Carlestam, Gösta and Levi, Lennart, *Urban conglomerates as psychosocial human stressors* (Stockholm: Kringl Boktoyckiret P. A. Norstedt and Söner, 1971).

Carthy, J. D. and Ebling, F. J., eds., *The natural history of aggression* (London: Academic Press, 1964).

Cazenave, Noel A. and Straus, Murray A., "The effect of social network embeddedness on black family violence attitudes and behavior: A search for potent support systems," paper presented at the annual meetings of the National Council on Family Relations, Philadelphia, 1978.

Center for Disease Control, "Child abuse in Georgia, 1975–1977," *Morbidity and Mortality Weekly Report*, 28, No. 3, January 1979.

Chase, Naomi F., *A child is being beaten* (New York: Holt, Rinehart and Winston, 1975).

Chase, Naomi F., "You dare to say we abuse our kids? Abuse! No! We beat them hard because they misbehave!" *New York Times*, January 3, 1976, p. 21.

Chicago Teacher's Union, *Chicago Union Teacher*, March 1978, pp. 1–4.

Children's Defense Fund, *Children without homes: An examination of public responsibility to children in out-of-home care* (Washington, D.C.: Children's Defense Fund, 1979).

Clark, Kenneth B., *Patterns of power* (New York: Harper and Row, 1974).

Cleveland Board of Education v. LaFleur, 414 U.S. 632 (1974).

Cohen, Stephen J. and Sussman, Alan, "The incidence of child abuse in the U.S.," unpublished report submitted to the Office of Child Development, 1975.

Coleman, S. H., *Humane society leaders in America* (Albany: American Humane Association, 1924).

Comer, James P., "Spanking," *New York Times*, December 29, 1975, p. 25.

Commission on Children's Rights, *Barnes ratt: On forbud not aga* (Stockholm: Swedish Department of Justice, 1978).

Commonwealth of Massachusetts and Alliance (AFSCME-SEIU) AFL-CIO, *Agreement, between July 1, 1977–June 30, 1980* (1977).

Connell, D. B., "Individual differences in attachment: An investigation into stability, implications, and relationships to structure of early language development," unpublished doctoral dissertation, Syracuse University, 1976.

Cottle, Thomas J., "Review of Naomi F. Chase, *A child is being beaten* (New York: Holt, Rinehart and Winston, 1975)," *New Republic*, 173, No. 21, November 22, 1975, pp. 28–30.

Curtis, George, "Violence breeds violence," *American Journal of Psychiatry*, 120, October 1963, pp. 386–387.

Daniel, Jessica H. and Hyde, James N., "Working with high-risk families," *Children Today*, 4, No. 6, November–December 1975, pp. 23–25.

DeFrancis, Vincent, "Testimony before the subcommittee on children and youth of the committee on labor and public welfare," U.S. Senate, 93rd

Congress, 1st Session, on S. 1191 Child Abuse Prevention Act (Washington, D.C.: Government Printing Office, 1973).

DeLissovoy, Vladimir, "Child care by adolescent parents," *Children Today*, 2, No. 4, July–August 1973, pp. 22–25.

DeLozier, P., "An application of attachment theory to the study of child abuse," unpublished doctoral dissertation, California School of Professional Psychology, 1979.

DeMause, Lloyd, ed., *The History of Childhood* (New York: The Psychohistory Press, 1974).

DeMause, Lloyd, "Our forebears made childhood a nightmare," *Psychology Today*, 8, No. 11, April 1975, pp. 85–88.

Derdeyn, Andre P., "Child abuse and neglect: The rights of parents and the needs of their children," *American Journal of Orthopsychiatry*, 47, No. 3, July 1977, pp. 377–387. (a)

Derdeyn, Andre P., "A case for permanent foster placement of dependent, neglected and abused children," *American Journal of Orthopsychiatry*, 47, No. 4, October 1977, pp. 604–614. (b)

Divoky, Diane, "Child abuse: Mandate for teacher intervention?" *Learning*, April 1976, pp. 4–22.

Dohrenwend, Barbara S. and Dohrenwend, Bruce P., eds., *Stressful life events: Their nature and effects* (New York: Wiley, 1974).

Dokecki, Paul R., "Toward influencing those who make public policy for families and children: A liaison strategy," paper presented at the meeting of the American Psychological Association, San Francisco, August, 1977.

Dollard, John, Doob, Leonard, Miller, Neal E., Mowrer, O. Hobart, and Sears, Robert, *Frustration and Aggression* (New Haven: Yale University Press, 1939).

Dukette, R., *Structured assessment: A decision-making guide for child welfare* (Washington, D.C.: U.S. Dept. of Health, Education and Welfare, 1978).

Eisenstadt v. Baird 405 U.S. 438 (1972).

Elmer, Elizabeth, *Children in jeopardy* (Pittsburgh: University of Pittsburgh Press, 1967).

Elmer, Elizabeth, *Fragile families, troubled children: The aftermath of infant trauma* (Pittsburgh: University of Pittsburgh Press, 1977).

Ennis, Bruce and Litwack, Thomas, "Psychiatry and the presumption of expertise: Flipping coins in the courtroom," *California Law Review*, 62, No. 3, May 1974, pp. 693–752.

Ennis, Phillip H., *Criminal victimization in the United States: A report of a NORC survey to the President's Commission on Law Enforcement and Administration of Justice* (Washington, D.C.: Government Printing Office, 1967).

Erlanger, Howard S., "Social class and corporal punishment in childrearing: A reassessment," *American Sociological Review*, 39, No. 1, February 1974, pp. 68–85.

Escalona, Sibylle K., "Children in a warring world," *American Journal of Orthopsychiatry*, 45, No. 5, October 1975, pp. 765–772.

Evans, Richard I., *Konrad Lorenz, the man and his ideas* (New York: Harcourt, Brace, Jovanovich, 1975).

Evans, Sue L., et al., "Failure to thrive: A study of 45 children and their families," paper presented at the 22nd Annual Meeting of the American Association of Psychiatric Services for Children, Philadelphia, November 1970.

Fanshel, David, "Status changes of children in foster care: Final results of the Columbia University Longitudinal Study," *Child Welfare*, 55, No. 3, March 1976, pp. 143–171.

Farber, I. E., "Sane and insane: Constructions and misconstructions," *Journal of Abnormal Psychology*, 84, No. 6, December 1975, pp. 589–620.

Farley, A., Kruetter, D., Russell, R., Blackwell, S., Finkelstein, H., and Hyman, I., "The effects of eliminating corporal punishment in the schools: A preliminary survey," *Inequality*, 23, Summer 1978.

Ferguson, Lucy R., "The competence and freedom of children to make choices regarding participation in research: A statement," *Journal of Social Issues*, 34, No. 2, Spring 1978, pp. 114–121.

Feshbach, Norma D., "The effects of violence in childhood," *Journal of Clinical Psychology*, 11, No. 3, Fall 1973, pp. 28–31.

Feshbach, Norma D., "The relationship of child-rearing factors in children's aggression, empathy and related positive and negative social behavior," in Jan DeWit and Willard Hartup, eds., *Determinants and origin of aggressive behavior* (The Hague: Mouton, 1974).

Feshbach, Norma D., "Corporal punishment in the schools, a special case of child abuse," paper presented in the Open Forum on the Use of Corporal Punishment at the American Psychological Association Meetings, Washington, D.C., 1976.

Feshbach, Norma D., *Task force on the rights of children and youth* (Washington, D.C.: American Psychological Association, 1977).

Feshbach, Norma D., "Dimensions of children's rights," keynote address presented at the Conference on Children's Rights: Issues and Viewpoints, Florida State University, Tallahassee, November 3, 1978.

Feshbach, Norma D., "Empathy training: A field study in affective education," in Seymour Feshbach and Adam Freczek, eds., *Biological and social perspectives on aggression: Its roots and its combat* (New York: Praeger, 1979).

Feshbach, N. D. and Campbell, M., "Teacher stress and disciplinary practices in schools: A preliminary report," paper presented at the American Orthopsychiatric Association Meeting, San Francisco, March 27–31, 1978. ERIC ED 162228.

Feshbach, Norma D., and Feshbach, Seymour, "The relationship between empathy and aggression in two age groups," *Development Psychology*, 1, No. 2, 1969, pp. 102–107.

311

Feshbach, Norma D. and Feshbach, Seymour, "Children's aggression," *Young Children*, 26, No. 6, 1971, pp. 364–377.

Feshbach, Norma D. and Feshbach, Seymour, "Punishment: Parents' rites vs. children's rights," in Gerald P. Koocher, ed., *Children's rights and the mental health profession* (New York: Wiley, 1976).

Feshbach, Norma D. and Feshbach, Seymour, eds., "The changing status of children: Rights, roles, and responsibilities," *The Journal of Social Issues*, 34, No. 2, Spring 1978. (a)

Feshbach, Norma D. and Feshbach, Seymour, "Towards a historical, social, and developmental perspective on children's rights," *Journal of Social Issues*, 34, No. 2, Spring 1978, pp. 1–7. (b)

Feshbach, Norma and Hoffman, Martin, "Current literature on corporal punishment: Concerns, commentary, and possible research directions," *American Secondary Education*, 8, No. 1, 1978, pp. 19–27.

Feshbach, Seymour, "The function of aggression and the regulation of aggressive drive," *Psychological Review*, 71, No. 4, July 1964, pp. 257–272.

Feshbach, Seymour, "The development and regulation of aggression: Some research gaps and a proposed cognitive approach," in Jan DeWit and Willard W. Hartup, eds., *Determinants and origin of aggressive behavior* (The Hague: Mouton, 1974).

Feshbach, Seymour and Feshbach, Norma D., "Alternatives to corporal punishment: Implications for training and controls," *Journal of Clinical Psychology*, 11, No. 3, Fall 1973, pp. 46–48.

Fontana, Vincent J., *The maltreated child: The maltreatment syndrome in children*, 2nd ed. (Springfield, Ill.: Charles C Thomas, 1970).

Fontana, Vincent J., *Somewhere a child is crying: Maltreatment—causes and prevention* (New York: Macmillan, 1973).

Forer, Lois G., "No one will listen," in Beatrice Gross and Ronald Gross, eds., *The children's rights movement: Overcoming the oppression of young people* (Garden City, Long Island: Anchor Press/Doubleday, 1977).

Frankel, M., "Social, legal, and political responses to ethical issues in the use of children as experimental subjects," *Journal of Social Issues*, 34, No. 2, Spring 1978, pp. 119–121.

Freud, Sigmund, "A child is being beaten (a contribution to the study of the origin of sexual perversions: 1919)," in Freud, *Collected Papers*, Vol. 2 (New York: Basic Books, Inc., 1959).

Friedman, David, "Corporal punishment in the schools," paper presented at the annual convention of the American Psychological Association, Washington, D.C., September 4, 1976.

Fuller, Frances F., "Concerns of teachers: A developmental conceptualization," *American Educational Research Journal*, 6, No. 2, March 1969, pp. 207–226.

Furrow, David, Gruendel, Janice, and Zigler, Edward, "Protecting America's children from accidental injury and death: An overview of the problem and an agenda for action," in preparation for publication, 1979.

Galston, Richard, "Observations of children who have been physically abused by their parents," *American Journal of Psychiatry*, 122, October 1965, pp. 440–443.

Garbarino, James, "A preliminary study of some ecological correlates of child abuse: The impact of socioeconomic stress on mothers," *Child Development*, 47, No. 1, March 1976, pp. 1780–1785.

Garbarino, James and Crouter, Ann, "Defining the community context for parent-child relations: The correlates of child maltreatment," *Child Development*, 49, No. 3, September 1978, pp. 604–616.

Garbarino, James and Jacobson, Nancy, "Youth helping youth in cases of maltreatment of adolescents," *Child Welfare*, 57, No. 8, September–October 1978.

Garrett, Karen A. and Rossi, Peter H., "Judging the seriousness of child abuse," *Medical Anthropology*, 2, No. 1, Winter 1978, pp. 1–48.

Gastil, Raymond D., "Homicide and a regional culture of violence," *American Sociological Review*, 36, June 1971, pp. 412–427.

Gaylin, William, Glasser, Ira, Marcus, Stephen, and Rothman, David, *Doing Good: The Limits of Benevolence* (New York: Pantheon Books, 1978).

Gelles, Richard J., "Child abuse as psychopathology: A sociological critique and reformulation," *American Journal of Orthopsychiatry*, 43, No. 4, July 1973, pp. 611–621.

Gelles, Richard J., "Community agencies and child abuse: Labeling and gatekeeping," paper presented to the Study Group on Research and the Family, Ann Arbor, Michigan, 1975. (a)

Gelles, Richard J., "The social construction of child abuse," *American Journal of Orthopsychiatry*, 45, No. 3, April 1975, pp. 363–371. (b)

Gelles, Richard J., "Violence towards children in the United States," *American Journal of Orthopsychiatry*, 48, October 1978, pp. 580–592.

Gelles, Richard J., "The Social Construction of Child Abuse," in David G. Gil, ed., *Child Abuse and Violence* (New York: AMS Press, 1979) pp. 145–157.

Gelles, Richard J. and Straus, Murray A., "Determinants of violence in the family: Toward a theoretical integration," in W. Burr, R. Hill, F. I. Nye, and I. Reiss, eds., *Contemporary theories about the family* (New York: Free Press, 1978).

George, Clay E. and Main, Mary, "Social interactions of young abused children: Approach, avoidance, and aggression," *Child Development*, 50, 1979, pp. 306–318.

Gerbner, George, Gross, Larry, Signorielli, Nancy, Morgan, Michael, and Jackson-Beeck, Marilyn, "The demonstration of power: Violence profile no. 10," *Journal of Communication*, Summer 1979.

Gil, David G., "Physical abuse of children: Findings and implications of a nationwide survey," *Pediatrics*, 44, No. 5, Part 2 (Supplement), November 1969, pp. 857–864.

Gil, David G., *Violence against children: Physical child abuse in the United States* (Cambridge, Mass.: Harvard University Press, 1970).

Gil, David G., ed., *Child abuse and violence* (New York: AMS Press, Inc., 1979).

Gil, David G. and Noble, John H., "Public knowledge, attitudes and opinions about physical child abuse in the United States," Brandeis University, papers in Social Welfare, No. 14, 1967.

Ginsburg v. New York 390 U.S. 629 (1968).

Giovannoni, Jeanne M., "Parental mistreatment: Perpetrators and victims," *Journal of Marriage and the Family*, 33, No. 4, November 1971, pp. 649–657.

Giovannoni, Jeanne and Billingsley, Andrew, "Child neglect among the poor: A study of parental adequacy in families of three ethnic groups," *Child Welfare*, 49, No. 4, April 1970, pp. 196–204.

Glackman, T., Martin, R., Hyman, I., McDowell, E., Berv, U., and Spino, D., "Corporal punishment, school suspension, and the civil rights of students: An analysis of Office for Civil Rights School Surveys," *Inequality in Education*, September 1978, pp. 61–65.

Goldstein, Joseph, Freud, Anna, and Solnit, Albert J., *Beyond the best interests of the child* (New York: Free Press, 1973).

Goodman, Paul, *Growing up absurd* (New York: Alfred A. Knopf, 1956).

Graham, Frances K., Charwat, Wanda A., Honig, Alice S., and Weltz, Paula C., "Aggression as a function of the attack and the attacker," *Journal of Abnormal and Social Psychology*, 46, No. 4, October 1951, pp. 512–520.

Green, E., "Policy analysis, knowledge, and power: A proposal for citizens' self-help," unpublished manuscript, Vanderbilt Institute for Public Policy Studies, 1979.

Greven, Phillip, *The Protestant temperament: Patterns of child-rearing, religious experience, and the self in early America* (New York: Alfred A. Knopf, 1977).

Griswold v. Connecticut 381 U.S. 479 (1965).

Gruber, A. R., *Foster home care in Massachusetts, a study of foster children, their biological and foster parents*, Governor's Commission on Adoption and Foster Care, Commonwealth of Massachusetts, 1973.

Haim, Andre, *Adolescent Suicide* (New York: International Universities Press, 1974).

Hansburg, Henry G., *Adolescent separation anxiety* (Springfield, Ill.: Charles C Thomas, 1972).

Hansburg, Henry G., "The use of the Separation Anxiety Test in the detection of self-destructive tendencies," in D. V. Siva Sankar, ed., *Mental health in childhood*, Vol. 3 (New York: P.J.D. Publications, 1976).

Harlow, Harry F., "The development of affectional patterns in infant monkeys," in Brian M. Foss, ed., *Determinants of infant behavior*, Vol. 1 (New York: Wiley, 1961).

Harlow, Harry F., "The maternal affectional system," in Brian M. Foss, ed., *Determinants of infant behavior*, Vol. 3 (New York: Wiley, 1963).

Harlow, H. F. and Harlow, M. K., "Psychopathology in monkeys," in H. D. Kimmel, ed., *Experimental psychopathology: Recent research and theory* (New York: Academic Press, 1971).

Harman, David, *Early childhood: A new look at policy making* (Aspen, Colo.: Aspen Institute for Humanistic Studies, 1978).

Helfer, Ray E. and Kempe, C. Henry, eds., *The Battered Child*, 2nd ed. (Chicago: University of Chicago Press, 1974).

Helfer, Ray E. and Kempe, C. Henry, eds., *Child abuse and neglect: The family and the community* (Cambridge, Mass.: Ballinger, 1976).

Hiner, N. Ray, "Children's rights, corporal punishment, and child abuse," *Bulletin of the Menninger Clinic*, 43, No. 3, May 1979, pp. 233–248.

Hobbs, Nicholas, *Mental health, families and children* (Austin: University of Texas Printing Division, 1976).

Hoffman, Ellen, "Policy and politics: The child abuse prevention and treatment act," *Public Policy*, 26, No. 1, Winter 1978, pp. 71–88.

Hoffman, Martin L., "Moral internalization, parental power, and the nature of the parent-child interaction," *Developmental Psychology*, 11, 1975, pp. 228–239.

Holmes, Thomas H. and Rahe, Richard H., "The social readjustment rating scale," *Journal of Psychosomatic Research*, 11, No. 2, 1967, pp. 213–218.

Holt, John, *Escape from childhood* (New York: E. P. Dutton, 1974).

Howard, Jane, *Families* (New York: Simon and Schuster, 1978).

Howland, T., "Court intervention in behalf of abused children: A descriptive study," unpublished senior thesis, Harvard University, 1974.

Huckabay, Loucine M., "A developmental study of the relationship of negative moral-social behaviors to empathy, to positive social behaviors and to cognitive moral judgment," unpublished doctoral dissertation, University of California at Los Angeles Graduate School of Education, 1971.

Humphreys, Lloyd G., "Corporal punishment," *American Psychologist*, 30, No. 6, June 1975, pp. 708–709.

Hurt, M., Jr., *Child abuse and neglect: A report on the status of the research* (Washington, D.C.: U.S. Government Printing Office, 1975). U.S. Dept. of Health, Education, and Welfare Pub. No. (OHD) 74–20.

Hyman, Irwin, Bongiovanni, Anthony, Friedman, Robert, and McDowell, Eileen, "Paddling, punishing and force," *Children Today*, 6, No. 5, September–October 1977, pp. 17–25.

Hyman, I. and Wise, J., *Corporal punishment in America: Readings in history, practice and alternatives* (Philadelphia: Temple University Press, 1979).

Ingraham v. Wright 430 U.S. 651 (1977).

Institute of Judicial Administration–American Bar Association, Juvenile Justice Standards Project, *Standards relating to abuse and neglect* (Cambridge, Mass.: Ballinger, 1977).

Jarvis, Edward, *Insanity and idiocy in Massachusetts: Report of the commission on lunacy, 1855* (Cambridge, Mass.: Harvard University Press, 1971). (Originally published by William White, Boston, 1855.)

Jeffery, Margaret, "Practical ways to change parent-child interaction in families of children at risk," in Ray E. Helfer and C. Henry Kempe, eds., *Child abuse and neglect: The family and the community* (Cambridge, Mass.: Ballinger, 1976).

Jenkins, E. F., "The New York Society for the Prevention of Cruelty to Children," *Annals of the American Academy of Political and Social Sciences*, 26, November 1905, pp. 774–777.

Jenkins, E. F., "The New York Society for the Prevention of Cruelty to Children," *Annals of the American Academy of Political and Social Sciences*, 31, March 1908, pp. 492–494.

Jenkins, Shirley and Norman, Elaine, *Filial deprivation and foster care* (New York: Columbia University Press, 1972).

Johnson, C. L., *Child abuse in the Southeast: An analysis of 1172 reported cases* (Athens: University of Georgia, Athens Welfare Research, 1974).

Kadushin, Alfred, *Child Welfare Services* (New York: Macmillan, 1967).

Kahn, Alfred J. and Kamerman, Sheila B., *Not for the poor alone* (Philadelphia: Temple University Press, 1975).

Kahn, Alfred J. and Kamerman, Sheila B., *Social Services in International Perspective* (Washington, D.C.: U.S. Government Printing Office, 1976) Stock No. 017–062–00108–1, pp. 66–93.

Kakalik, James S., *Services for handicapped youth: A program overview* (Santa Monica: The Rand Corporation, 1973).

Kamerman, Sheila B., "Cross-national perspectives on child abuse and neglect," *Children Today*, 4, No. 3, May–June 1975, pp. 34–37.

Kamerman, Sheila B. and Kahn, Alfred J., "European family policy currents: The question of families with very young children," preliminary draft of a working paper, Columbia University, 1976.

Kamerman, Sheila B. and Kahn, Alfred J., *Family policy: Government and families in fourteen countries* (New York: Columbia University Press, 1978).

Kamerman, Sheila B. and Kahn, Alfred J., "The day care debate: A wider view," *The Public Interest*, 54, Winter 1979, pp. 76–93. (a)

Kamerman, Sheila B. and Kahn, Alfred J., "Work and family in industrialized societies," *SIGNS, Journal of Women in Culture and Society*, 4, No. 4, Summer 1979. (b)

Kaplan, David M., Smith, Aaron, Grobstein, Rose and Fischman, Stanley E., "Family mediation of stress," *Social Work*, 18, No. 4, July 1973, pp. 60–69.

Kempe, C. Henry, Silverman, Frederick, Steele, Brandt, Droegemueller, William, and Silver, Henry, "The battered child syndrome," *Journal of the American Medical Association*, 181, No. 1, July 7, 1962, pp. 17–24.

Kempe, Ruth S. and Kempe, C. Henry, "Assessing family pathology," in Ray E. Helfer and C. Henry Kempe, eds., *Child abuse and neglect: The family and the community* (Cambridge, Mass.: Ballinger, 1976).

Kempe, Ruth S. and Kempe, C. Henry, *Child abuse* (Cambridge, Mass.: Harvard University Press, 1978).

Keniston, Kenneth and The Carnegie Council on Children, *All our children: The American family under pressure* (New York: Harcourt, Brace, Jovanovich, 1977).

Kessler, Marc and Albee, George W., "Primary prevention," *Annual Review of Psychology* (Palo Alto, Calif.: Annual Reviews Press, 1975).

Keyserling, M. D., *Windows on day care: A report on the findings of members of the National Council of Jewish Women on day care needs and services in their communities* (New York: National Council of Jewish Women, 1972).

Kohlberg, Lawrence, "The development of children's orientations toward a moral order: Sequence in the development of moral thought," *Vita Humana*, 6, Nos. 1–2, 1963, pp. 11–33.

Kohlberg, Lawrence, "Stage and sequence: The cognitive-developmental approach to socialization," in David A. Goslin, ed., *Handbook of socialization theory and research* (Chicago: Rand McNally, 1969).

Kravitz, Harvey, Dreissen, Gerald, Gomberg, Raymond, and Korach, Alvin, "Accidental falls from elevated surfaces in infants from birth to one year of age," *Pediatrics*, 44, No. 5, Part 2 (Supplement), November 1969, pp. 869–876.

Kunitz, Stephen, "Professionalism and social control in the progressive era: The case of the Flexner Report," *Social Problems*, 22, No. 1, October 1974, pp. 16–27.

Lamb, Michael E., "Fathers: Forgotten contributors to child development," *Human Development*, 18, No. 4, 1975, pp. 245–266.

Langer, William, "Infanticide: A historical survey," *History of Childhood Quarterly: The Journal of Psychohistory*, 1, No. 3, Winter 1974, pp. 353–366.

Lauderdale, Michael, Anderson, Rosalie, and Cramer, Stephen, eds., *Proceedings of the second annual conference on child abuse and neglect, April 17–20, 1977*, Vols. 1 and 2, DHEW Pub. No. (OHDS) 78–30147 (Washington, D.C.: U.S. Dept. of Health, Education and Welfare, 1978).

Laurer, Brian, Ten Broeck, Elsa, and Grossman, Moses, "Battered child syndrome: Review of 130 patients with controls," *Pediatrics*, 54, No. 1, July 1974, pp. 67–70.

Leavitt, Jerome E., ed., *The battered child: Selected readings* (Morristown, N.J.: General Learning Press, 1974).

Levine, Murray and Levine, Adeline, *A social history of the helping services:*

Clinic, court, school and community (New York: Appleton-Century-Crofts, 1970).

Levine, Richard S., "Caveat parens: A demystification of the child protection system," *University of Pittsburgh Law Review*, 35, No. 1, Fall 1973, pp. 1–52.

Light, Richard J., "Abused and neglected children in America: A study of alternative policies," *Harvard Educational Review*, 43, November 1973, pp. 556–598.

Lofland, Lyn H., *A world of strangers* (New York: Basic Books, 1973).

Lorenz, Konrad, *On Aggression* (New York: Harcourt, Brace & World, 1966).

Lovaas, O. Ivar and Bucher, Bradley D., *Perspectives in behavior modification with deviant children* (Englewood Cliffs, N.J.: Prentice-Hall, 1974).

Loving v. Virginia 388 U.S. 1 (1967).

Lubove, Roy, *The professional altruist: The emergence of social work as a career, 1880–1930* (Cambridge: Harvard University Press, 1965).

Lynn, Laurence E., Jr., *Knowledge and policy: The uncertain connection* (Washington, D.C.: National Academy of Sciences, 1975).

McCord, William, McCord, Joan, and Howard, Alan, "Familial correlates of aggression in nondelinquent male children," *Journal of Abnormal and Social Psychology*, 62, No. 1, 1961, pp. 72–93.

McKinley, Donald G., *Social class and family life* (New York: Free Press, 1964).

Maden, Marc F. and Wrench, David F., "Significant findings in child abuse research," *Victimology*, 2, Summer 1977, pp. 196–224.

Madsen, Clifford K. and Madsen, Charles H., Jr., *Parents and children, love and discipline: A positive approach to behavior modification* (Northbrook, Ill.: AHM Publishing Corp., 1975).

Main, Mary, "Exploration, play, and level of cognitive functioning as related to child-mother attachment," unpublished Ph.D. dissertation, Johns Hopkins University, 1973.

Main, Mary, "Avoidance in the service of proximity," in K. Immelman, G. Barlow, M. Main, and L. Petrinovich, eds., *Behavioral development: The Bielefeld Interdisciplinary Project* (New York: Cambridge University Press, in press). (a)

Main, Mary, "The 'ultimate' causation for some infant attachment phenomena: Further answers, further phenomena, and further questions," *Behavioral and Brain Sciences*, in press. (b)

Main, M. and Londerville, S. B., "Compliance and aggression in toddlerhood: Precursors and correlates," paper in preparation, 1978.

Maine Laws, 17 AMRSA; 106; sut.; 2.

Mark, Vernon H. and Ervin, Frank R., *Violence and the brain* (New York: Harper and Row, 1970).

Masland, Richard L., Sarason, Seymour B., and Gladwin, Thomas, *Mental subnormality: Biological, psychological, and cultural factors* (New York: Basic Books, 1958).

Matas, Leah, Ahrend, Richard A., and Sroufe, L. Alan, "Continuity of adaptation in the second year: The relationship between quality of attachment and later competence," *Child Development*, 49, No. 3, September 1978, pp. 547–556.

Maurer, Adah, "Corporal Punishment," *American Psychologist*, 29, No. 8, August 1974, pp. 614–626.

Maurer, Adah, *Corporal punishment handbook* (Berkeley, Calif.: Generation Books, 1977).

Maurer, Adah, "Violence must end," *The Last Resort*, 7, No. 1, September–October 1978.

Milowe, I. D. and Lourie, R. S., "The child's role in the battered child syndrome," *Abstracts of the Society for Pediatric Research*, 1964, p. 1079.

Mintzer, Barry and Casaly, John, *Representing the abused and neglected child in Massachusetts* (Boston: Commonwealth of Massachusetts, Office for Children, 1977).

Mischel, Walter, "Continuity and change in personality," *American Psychologist*, 24, No. 11, November 1969, pp. 1012–1018.

Mischel, Walter, "Toward a cognitive social learning reconceptualization of personality," *Psychological Review*, 80, No. 4, July 1973, pp. 252–283.

Mitchell, Robert E., "Some social implications of high density housing," *American Sociological Review*, 36, No. 1, February 1971, pp. 18–29.

Mnookin, Robert H. "Foster care: In whose best interest?" *Harvard Educational Review*, 43, No. 4, November 1973, pp. 599–638.

Moore v. City of East Cleveland 431 U.S. 494 (1977).

Mooris, Desmond, *The naked ape* (New York: McGraw-Hill, 1967).

Morbidity and Mortality Weekly Report, "Child Abuse in Georgia, 1975–77," Vol. 28, No. 3, Center for Disease Control, Public Health Services, U.S. Dept. of HEW, Atlanta, Georgia, January 26, 1979.

Morse, Abraham, Hyde, James, Newberger, Eli H., and Reed, Robert, "Environmental correlates of pediatric social illness: Preventive implications of an advocacy approach," *American Journal of Public Health*, 67, No. 7, July 1977, pp. 612–615.

Murphy, A., "Child abuse increases during Yule season," *Behavior Today*, 7, January 12, 1976, p. 4.

Murray, Ann D., "Maternal employment reconsidered: Effects on infants," *American Journal of Orthopsychiatry*, 45, No. 5, October 1975, pp. 773–790.

Mussen, Paul, H., Conger, John J., and Kagan, Jerome, eds., *Readings in child development and personality*, 2nd ed. (New York: Harper and Row, 1970).

Nagi, Saad, "Child abuse neglect programs: A national overview," *Children Today*, 4, No. 3, May–June 1975, pp. 13–18.

Nagi, Saad Z., *Child maltreatment in the United States* (New York: Columbia University Press, 1977).

The Nation, ed., "More of the Same," 198, No. 15, April 6, 1964.

National Academy of Sciences, *Toward a national policy for children and families, the report of the Advisory Committee on Child Development* (Washington, D.C.: National Academy of Sciences, 1976).

National Center on Child Abuse and Neglect, *Child abuse and neglect: The problem and its management*, 3, Pub. No. 75–300075, U.S. Dept. of Health, Education, and Welfare (Washington, D.C.: U.S. Government Printing Office, 1976).

National Center on Child Abuse and Neglect, *Annual review of child abuse and neglect research*, 1978, Pub. No. (OHDS) 79–30168 (Washington, D.C.: U.S. Dept. of Health, Education and Welfare, 1978). (a)

National Center on Child Abuse and Neglect, *Child abuse and neglect: State reporting laws* (Washington, D.C.: U.S. Dept. of Health, Education and Welfare, 1978). (b)

National Research Council, *Knowledge and policy in manpower. A study of the Manpower Research and Development Program in the Department of Labor* (Washington, D.C.: National Academy of Sciences, 1975).

National Society for Autistic Children, "White Paper on behavior modification with autistic children," revised by Clara and David Park and members of the Professional Advisory Board, NSAC, of a statement drawn up by Creighton Newsome (1975).

Nelson, Richard R., *The moon and the ghetto* (New York: W. W. Norton, 1977).

New Jersey Revised Statutes (1968), 18A: 6–1.

New York State Department of Mental Hygiene, "Governor Carey recommends $924 million DMH budget," *Mental Hygiene News*, January 1976, p. 1.

New York State Legislative Review, *Construction of mental hygiene facilities* (Albany: New York Legislative Commission on Expenditure Review, 1973).

Newberger, Carolyn M., "Parental conceptions of children and child rearing: A structural development analysis," doctoral dissertation, Harvard University, 1978.

Newberger, Eli H., "The myth of the battered child syndrome," in Stella Chess and Alexander Thomas, eds., *Annual progress in child psychiatry and child development*, 1974 (New York: Brunner/Mazel, 1975).

Newberger, Eli H., "Trauma X guidelines," unpublished paper, Children's Hospital Medical Center, undated.

Newberger, Eli H., Hagenbuch, John, Ebeling, Nancy, Colligan, Elizabeth, Sheehan, Jane, and McVeigh, Susan, "Reducing the literal and human cost of child abuse: Impact of a new hospital management system," *Pediatrics*, 51, No. 5, May 1973, pp. 840–848.

Newberger, Eli H. and Hyde, James N., "Child abuse: Principles and implications of current pediatric practice," *Pediatric Clinics of North America*, 22, No. 3, August 1975, pp. 695–715.

Newberger, Eli H., Reed, Robert, Daniel, Jessica, Hyde, James, and Kotelchuck, Milton, "Toward an etiologic classification of pediatric social illness: A descriptive epidemiology of child abuse and neglect, failure to thrive, accidents, and poisonings in children under four years of age," paper presented at the biennial meeting of the Society for Research in Child Development, Denver, April 11, 1975.

Newberger, Eli H., Reed, Robert, Daniel, Jessica, Hyde, James, and Kotelchuck, Milton, "Pediatric social illness: Toward an etiological classification," *Pediatrics*, 60, No. 2, August 1977, pp. 178–185.

Nickel, Ted W., "The attribution of intention as a critical factor in the relationship between frustration and aggression," *Journal of Personality*, 42, No. 3, September 1974, pp. 482–492.

Novaco, Raymond W., *Anger Control* (Lexington, Mass.: Lexington Books, 1975).

Office for Children and Department of Public Welfare, *Child Abuse and Neglect Fact-Finding Commission Final Report* (Office for Children, Commonwealth of Massachusetts, 1978).

Office of Civil Rights, *United States elementary and secondary schools, 1976* (Washington, D.C.: U.S. Government Printing Office, 1979).

Okpaku, Sheila, "Psychology: Impediment or aid in child custody cases?" *Rutgers Law Review*, 29, No. 5, Late Summer 1976, pp. 1117–1153.

Olander, Herbert and Farrell, Mary E., "Professional problems of elementary teachers," *Journal of Teacher Education*, 21, No. 2, Summer 1970, pp. 276–280.

Olds, David, *Prenatal/Early infancy projects* (Elmira, N.Y.: Comprehensive Interdisciplinary Developmental Services, Inc., 1978).

Packard, Vance, *A nation of strangers* (New York: Simon and Schuster, 1974).

Parke, Ross D., "The role of punishment in the socialization process," in Ronald A. Hoppe, G. Alexander Milton, and Edward C. Simmel, eds., *Early experiences and the processes of socialization* (New York: Academic Press, 1970).

Parke, Ross D. and Collmer, Candace W., "Child abuse: An interdisciplinary analysis," in Mavis E. Hetherington, ed., *Child development research*, Vol. 5 (Chicago: University of Chicago Press, 1975).

Pastore, W., "The role of arbitrariness in the frustration-aggression hypothesis," *Journal of Abnormal and Social Psychology*, 47, 1957, pp. 728–731.

Pediatric News, "One child dies daily from abuse: Parent probably was abused," *Pediatric News*, 9, April 1975, p. 3.

Pelton, Leroy H., "Child abuse and neglect: The myth of classlessness," *American Journal of Orthopsychiatry*, 48, No. 4, October 1978, pp. 608–617.

Persons released from state developmental centers (Albany: New York Legislative Commission on Expenditure Review, 1975).

Pfohl, Stephen, "The 'Discovery' of Child Abuse," *Social Problems*, 24, No. 3, February 1977, pp. 310–323.

Phillips, M. H., Shyne, A. W., Sherman, E. A., and Haring, B. L., *Factors associated with placement decisions in child welfare* (New York: Child Welfare League of America, 1971).

Piaget, Jean, *The moral judgement of the child* (New York: Harcourt-Brace, 1932).

Pike, V., Downs, S., Emlen, A., Downs, G., and Case, D., *Permanent planning for children in foster care: A handbook for social workers* (Washington, D.C.: U.S. Dept. of Health, Education and Welfare, 1977).

Prescott, James W., "Deprivation of Physical Affection as a Primary Process in the Development of Physical Violence," in David G. Gil, ed., *Child Abuse and Violence* (New York: AMS Press, 1979) pp. 66–137.

President's Commission on Mental Health, *Report to the President . . . ,* Vol. 1, *Commission's report and recommendations to the President.* (Washington, D.C.: U.S. Government Printing Office, 1978). (a)

President's Commission on Mental Health, *Report to the President . . . ,* Vols. 2–4, *Task panel reports* (Washington, D.C.: U.S. Government Printing Office, 1978). (b)

Prince v. Massachusetts 321 U.S. 158 (1943).

Quilloin v. Walcott 98 S. Ct. 549 (1978).

Radbill, Samuel X., "A history of child abuse and infanticide," in Ray E. Helfer and C. Henry Kempe, ed., *The Battered Child*, 2nd ed. (Chicago: University of Chicago Press, 1974).

Rein, Martin and White, Sheldon H., "Can policy research help policy," *The Public Interest*, 49, Fall 1977, pp. 119–136. (a)

Rein, Martin and White, Sheldon H., "Policy research: Belief and doubt," *Policy Analysis*, 3, 1977, pp. 239–272. (b)

Reitman, Alan, "Corporal punishment in the schools: The civil liberties objections," in J. Wise, ed., *Proceedings: Conference on corporal punishment in the schools: A national debate* (Washington, D.C.: National Institute of Education, 1977). NIE P–77–0079.

Reitman, Alan, Follman, Judith and Ladd, Edward, *Corporal punishment in the public schools: The use of force in controlling behavior* (New York: American Civil Liberties Union, 1972).

Reston, James, "On learning and earning," *New York Times*, December 7, 1975, p. 15E.

Richette, Lisa A., *The throwaway children* (New York: Dell Publishing Company, 1969).

Richmond, Julius and Weinberger, Howard L., "Session II. Program implications of new knowledge regarding the physical, intellectual, and emotional growth and development and the unmet needs of children and youth," *American Journal of Public Health*, 60, No. 4 (Supplement), April 1970, pp. 23–67.

Robinson, Nancy M., and Robinson, Halbert B., *The mentally retarded child: A psychological approach*, 2nd ed. (New York: McGraw-Hill, 1976).

Rodham, Hilary, "Children under the law," *Harvard Educational Review*, 43, No. 4, November 1973, pp. 487–514.

Roe v. Connecticut 417 F. Supp. 769 (1976).

Roe v. Wade 410 U.S. 113 (1973).

Rogers, Carl M. and Wrightsman, L., "Attitudes towards children's rights: Nurturance or self-determination," *Journal of Social Issues*, 34, No. 2, Spring 1978, pp. 59–68.

Rohner, Ronald P. and Rohner, Evelyn C., "A multivariate model for the study of parental acceptance-rejection and child abuse," University of Connecticut at Storrs, published in ERIC/ECE, 1978.

Rosenshein, B. and Furst, N., "Research in teacher performance criteria," in Bunnie O. Smith, ed., *Research in teacher education* (Englewood Cliffs, N.J.: Prentice-Hall, 1971).

Ross, Catherine J., "Society's children: The care of indigent youngsters in New York City, 1875–1903," unpublished Ph.D. dissertation, Yale University, 1977.

Ross, Catherine J., Aber, Lawrence, Alexander, Karen, Heller, Kirby A., Nelson, Karen, and Phillips-DeMott, Deborah, "Conference Recommendations on Child Abuse . . . November 20–21, 1978, Philadelphia, PA." Available from ERIC Clearinghouse.

Rotenberg, Mordechai, *Damnation and Deviance: The Protestant ethic and the spirit of failure* (Riverside, N.J.: Macmillan, 1978).

Rutherford, R. B. and Neil, R. S., "The role of punishment with behaviorally disordered children," in R. B. Rutherford and A. Prieto, eds., *Severe behavior disorders of children and youth* (Lafayette, Penn.: Council for Children with Behavior Disorders, 1978).

Ryan, William, *Blaming the Victim* (New York: Random House, 1971).

Scales, Peter, "Sex Education and the Role of the Federal Government," *Searching for Alternatives to Teenage Pregnancy, A Special Publication of the National Alliance for Optional Parenthood* (Baltimore: Alliance for Optional Parenthood, 1978).

Scheerenberger, R. C., "A study of public residential facilities," *Mental Retardation*, 14, No. 1, 1976, pp. 32–35.

Schneider, Carl W., Hoffmeister, James, and Helfer, Ray E., "A predictive screening questionnaire for potential problems in mother-child interaction," in Ray E. Helfer and C. Henry Kempe, eds., *Child abuse and neglect: The family and the community* (Cambridge, Mass.: Ballinger, 1976).

Schucter, A., *Child abuse intervention*, prescriptive package prepared for the National Institute of Law Enforcement and Criminal Justice, LEAA, U.S. Department of Justice, 1976.

Shantz, David W. and Voydanoff, Douglas A., "Situational effects on retaliatory aggression at three age levels," *Child Development*, 44, No. 1, March 1973, pp. 149–153.

Shapiro, Vivian, Fraiberg, Selma, and Adelson, Edna, "Infant-parent psychotherapy on behalf of a child in a critical nutritional state," *Psychoanalytic Study of the Child*, 31, 1976, pp. 461–491.
Shinn, Eugene, "Is placement necessary? An experimental study of agreement
among caseworkers in making foster care decisions," unpublished dissertation, Columbia University School of Social Work, 1968.
Shorter, Edward, *The making of the modern family* (New York: Basic Books,
1975).
Silver, George A., *Child health, America's future* (Germantown, Md.: Aspen
Systems Corp., 1978).
Silver, Larry B., Dublin, Christina C. and Lourie, Reginald S., "Does violence
breed violence? Contributions from a study of the child abuse syn-
drome," *American Journal of Psychiatry*, 126, No. 3, September 1969,
pp. 404–407.
Silverman, Frederic N., "Radiologic aspects of the battered child syndrome," in
Ray E. Helfer and C. Henry Kempe, eds., *The Battered Child*, 2nd ed.
(Chicago: University of Chicago Press, 1974).
Silverstein, N. and Krate, R., *Children of the dark ghetto: A developmental
psychology* (New York: Praeger, 1975).
Sims v. Texas Department of Welfare 438 F. Supp. 1179 (1977).
Skinner, Angela and Castle, Raymond, *Seventy-eight battered children: A
retrospective study* (London: National Society for the Prevention of
Cruelty to Children, 1969).
Smith v. Organization of Foster Families for Equality and Reform, 97 Sup. Ct.
2094; 431 U.S. 816 (1977).
Social and Rehabilitation Services, *Protective services for abused and neglected
children and their families: A guide for state and local departments of
public social services on the delivery of protective services*, Pub. No.
77–23042, U.S. Dept. of Health, Education, and Welfare, Public Services Administration, 1977.
Spender, Stephen, Preface to Muriel Gardiner, *The deadly innocents* (New
York: Basic Books, 1976).
Spinetta, John J. and Rigler, David, "The child-abusing parent: A psychological review," *Psychological Bulletin*, 77, No. 4, April 1972, pp. 296–304.
Stark, Rodney and McEvoy, James, "Middle class violence," *Psychology Today*,
4, No. 6, November 1970, pp. 52–65.
Steele, Brandt F. and Pollock, Carl B., "A psychiatric study of parents who
abuse infants and small children," in Ray E. Helfer and C. Henry
Kempe, eds., *The Battered Child*, 2nd ed. (Chicago: University of Chicago Press, 1974).
Stern, Leo, "Prematurity as a factor in child abuse," *Hospital Practice*, 8, No.
5, May 1973, pp. 117–123.
Stolz, Stephanie B., Weinckowski, Louis A., and Brown, Bertram S., "Behavior
modification: A perspective on critical issues," *American Psychologist*,
30, No. 11, November 1975, pp. 1027–1048.

Stone, Alan, *Mental health and law: A system in transition*, U.S. Dept. of Health, Education and Welfare, DHEW Pub. No. (ADM) 76–176, 1975.

Straus, Murray A., "Family patterns and child abuse in a nationally representative American sample," paper presented at the 2nd International Congress on Child Abuse, London, 1978.

Straus, Murray A., "Measuring intrafamily conflict and violence: The conflict tactics (CT) scales," *Journal of Marriage and the Family*, 41, No. 1, February 1979, pp. 75–88.

Straus, Murray A., Gelles, Richard J., and Steinmetz, Suzanne K., *Behind closed doors: Violence in the American family* (Garden City, N.Y.: Anchor/Doubleday, 1979).

Strauss, Peter and Strauss, Joanna, "Review of Joseph Goldstein, Anna Freud and Albert Solnit, *Beyond the best interests of the child* (New York: Free Press, 1973)," *Columbia Law Review*, 74, No. 5, June 1974, pp. 996–1015.

Swift, Susan S. and Melby, Robert, "Persons released from state development centers," *New York Legislative Commission on Expenditure Review*, December 18, 1975.

Swift, Susan S. and Melby, Robert, *A report to speaker Stanley Steingut* (Albany: The Assembly Joint Committee to Study the Department of Mental Hygiene, March 1976).

Tardieu, Ambroise A., *Etude medico-legale sur l'infanticide* (Paris: J. B. Bailiere et fils, 1868).

Tinker v. Des Moines School Board, 89 Sup. Ct. 733; 393 U.S. 503 (1969).

Thomson, Ellen M., Paget, Norman W., Bates, Doris W., Mesch, Morris, and Putnam, Theodore I., *Child abuse: A community challenge* (East Aurora, N.Y.: Henry Stewart, Inc., 1971).

United States Department of Health, Education and Welfare, *Juvenile Court Statistics* (Washington, D.C.: U.S. Government Printing Office, 1973).

United States Department of Health, Education and Welfare, "Child Abuse and neglect grant program priorities—Fiscal years 1979 and 1980," *Federal Register*, 44, No. 48, Book 2, March 1979, pp. 13252–13434.

United States Department of Justice, *Uniform crime reports for the United States, 1975* (Washington, D.C.: U.S. Government Printing Office, 1976).

United States House of Representatives, Committee on Education and Labor, House of Representatives, "Proposed Extension of the Child Abuse Prevention and Treatment Act," Hearings, February 25, 1977.

United States Senate, Committee on Labor and Public Welfare, *Child Abuse Prevention and Treatment Act*, July 10, 1973, Senate report 93–308. (a)

United States Senate, *Hearing before the Subcommittee on Children and Youth, of the Committee on Labor and Public Welfare, on S. 1191*

Child Abuse Prevention and Treatment Act, 1973 (Washington, D.C.: U.S. Government Printing Office, 1973). (b)

Wald, Michael, "State intervention on behalf of 'neglected' children: A search for realistic standards," *Stanford Law Review*, 27, No. 4, April 1975, pp. 985–1040.

Wald, Michael, "State intervention on behalf of 'neglected' children: Standards for removal of children from their homes, monitoring the status of children in foster care, and termination of parental rights," *Stanford Law Review*, 28, No. 4, April 1976.

Waters, E., Wippman, J., and Sroufe, L. A., "Attachment, positive effect and competence in the peer group: Two studies in construct validation," *Child Development*, 50, 1979, pp. 821–829.

Weiss, Carol H., "Improving linkage between social research and public policy," in Laurence E. Lynn, Jr. *Knowledge and policy: The uncertain connection* (Washington, D.C.: National Academy of Sciences, 1978).

White House Conference on Children, 1970, *Report to the President* (Washington, D.C.: U.S. Government Printing Office, 1971).

Whiting, Beatrice, ed., *Six cultures: Studies of child rearing* (New York: Wiley, 1963).

Williams, G. J., "Abused children: Legalized child battering in U.S. public schools: An editor's reflections on pain," *Journal of Clinical Child Psychology*, 4, No. 3, 1975, pp. 56–57.

Wolff, Peter H., "The natural history of crying and other vocalizations in early infancy," in Brian M. Foss, ed., *Determinants of infant behaviour*, Vol. 4 (London: Methuen, 1969).

Wood, F. H. and Lakin, K. C., "The legal status of the use of corporal punishment and other aversive procedures in schools," in F. H. Wood, and K. C. Lakin, eds., *Punishment and aversive stimulation in special education* (Minneapolis: Department of Psychoeducational Studies, University of Minnesota, 1978).

Wooden, Kenneth, *Weeping in the playtime of others: America's incarcerated children* (New York: McGraw-Hill, 1976).

Wooley, Paul V. and Evans, William A., Jr., "Significance of skeletal lesions in infants resembling those of traumatic origin," *Journal of the American Medical Association*, 158, No. 7, June, 1955, pp. 539–543.

Young, Leontine R., *Wednesday's children: A study of child neglect and abuse* (New York: McGraw-Hill, 1964).

Zigler, Edward, "Metatheoretical issues in developmental psychology," in Melvin H. Marx, ed., *Psychological Theory*, 2nd ed. (New York: Macmillan, 1963).

Zigler, Edward, "Controlling child abuse in America: An effort doomed to failure?" paper presented at the National Conference on Child Abuse and Neglect, Atlanta, January 6, 1976.

Zigler, Edward, "Vision without a blueprint," rev. of Kenneth Keniston and the Carnegie Council on Children, *All our children: The American family under pressure* (New York: Harcourt Brace Jovanovich, 1977), *Contemporary Psychology*, May 1978, p. 289.

Zigler, Edward, "Controlling child abuse in America: An effort doomed to failure?" in Richard Bourne and Eli H. Newberger, eds., *Critical perspectives on child abuse* (Lexington, Mass.: Lexington Books, 1979).

Zigler, Edward and Child, Irvin L., eds., *Socialization and personality development* (Reading, Mass.: Addison-Wesley Publishing, 1973).

Zigler, Edward and Hunsinger, Susan, "Supreme Court on spanking: Upholding discipline or abuse?" *Young Children*, 32, No. 6, September 1977, pp. 14–15.

Zimbardo, Phillip G. and Ruch, Floyd, *Psychology and life*, 9th ed. (Glenview, Ill.: Scott, Foresman, 1975).

Editors

GEORGE GERBNER is Professor of communications and Dean of the Annenberg School of Communications at the University of Pennsylvania, where he heads the Cultural Indicators research project, a study of trends in television content and its effect. He served as co-chairman of the national conference on child abuse held in Philadelphia on November 20–21, 1978. He is editor of the *Journal of Communications* and *Mass Media Policies in Changing Cultures* (1977).

CATHERINE J. Ross is Assistant Professor of history at the Yale University Child Study Center, and a member of the Yale History Department. She was previously a postdoctoral fellow at Yale's Bush Center in Child Development and Social Policy, and served as program director for the national conference on child abuse held in Philadelphia on November 20–21, 1978. She has written on the history of childhood and social welfare, and is currently completing a social history of child welfare programs in New York City.

EDWARD ZIGLER is Sterling Professor of psychology and Director of the Bush Center in Child Development and Social Policy at Yale University. He served as the first Director of the Office of Child Development and as Chief of the United States Children's Bureau in the Department of Health, Education and Welfare. He was co-chairman of the national conference on child abuse held in Philadelphia on November 20–21, 1978.

Contributors

J. Lawrence Aber is the Assistant Director and co-founder of the Day Care and Families Project, a longitudinal study of child abuse in the Department of Psychology and Social Relations at Harvard University. He is also a Clinical Fellow in Psychology at Beth Israel Hospital, Harvard Medical School. He served as Special Assistant to the Director of the Massachusetts Office for Children, a child advocacy agency within the state government, from 1977–1979.

Mary D. Salter Ainsworth is Commonwealth Professor of psychology at the University of Virginia and past President of the Society for Research in Child Development. She is the author or co-author of six books, including *Infancy in Uganda: Infant Care and the Growth of Love* (1967) and *Patterns of Attachment: A Psychological Study of the Strange Situation* (1978).

George Albee is Professor of psychology at the University of Vermont. He has published widely on primary prevention, and recently served as coordinator of the Task Force on Primary Prevention for the President's Commission on Mental Health. He is a past President of the American Psychological Association.

Peter Almond is a journalist, film writer, and producer. He was formerly the Associate Director of the Carnegie Council on Children, with responsibility for its media and public affairs activity. He also served as a research associate for the Council's study of the impact of television on children and families. His career has also included work as a community planner and as a reporter/producer for public television programs at WNET-New York.

Burton Blatt is Centennial Professor and Dean of the School of Education at Syracuse University. He is the author or co-author of 15 books on the mentally retarded and their care, including *Christmas in Purgatory: A Photographic Essay* (1966), an account of conditions in five state institutions, and *The Family Papers: A Return to Purgatory* (in press) a report of field studies at 14 residential centers. He is past President of the American Association on Mental Deficiency.

John Mack Carter is editor-in-chief of *Good Housekeeping* magazine. He has also served as editor-in-chief for the *Ladies' Home Journal* and *McCall's*, and was president and chairman of Downe Communications, Inc. He is Vice President of the Media Liaison Committee of the National Center for Voluntary Action and a consultant to the National Cancer Institute.

Norma Deitch Feshbach is Professor of education and psychology at UCLA, where she heads the early childhood and development studies program in the

Graduate School of Education and serves as co-director of the Bush Training Program in Child Development and Public Policy. She is past chair of the American Psychological Association's Task Force on the Rights of Children and Youth, and President of the Western Psychological Association.

SEYMOUR FESHBACH chairs the Psychology Department at UCLA, where he is conducting a study of how fantasy and empathy affect aggressive behavior in children. A past President of the Western Psychological Association, he is the co-author/editor of three books, including *Changing Aggression: Biological and Psychological Perspectives*, to be published by Jossey-Bass.

RICHARD J. GELLES is Associate Professor and chairman of the department of sociology and anthropology at the University of Rhode Island. He recently conducted the first national survey of domestic violence and is co-author of *Behind Closed Doors: Violence in the American Family* (1980), a book based on that research.

NICHOLAS HOBBS is Professor of psychology and of preventive medicine, and Director of the Center for the Study of Families and Children at the Institute for Public Policy Studies at Vanderbilt University, where he formerly served as Provost. A past President of the American Psychological Association, and first Director of selection and research for the Peace Corps, he is the author of *The Futures of Children: Categories, Labels, and Their Consequences* (1974).

JUEL JANIS is Special Assistant to the Assistant Secretary for Health, Education and Welfare. Before coming to HEW she was Director of the Behavioral Science Program and the Associate Professor in the Department of Pediatrics, at the University of Massachusetts Medical School in Worcester, Massachusetts.

ALFRED J. KAHN is Professor of social policy and social planning at the Columbia University School of Social Work and co-director of Cross-National Studies of Social Service Systems and Family Policy. He is the author or co-author of 10 books, including *Not for the Poor Alone* (1975) and *Family Policy: Government and Families in Fourteen Countries* (1978), both with Sheila Kamerman.

SHEILA B. KAMERMAN is Associate Professor of social policy and social planning at the Columbia University School of Social Work and co-director of Cross-National Studies of Social Service Systems and Family Policy. She is author or co-author of numerous books, including several with Alfred J. Kahn, and of the forthcoming volume *Parenting in an Unresponsive Society: Managing Work and Family Life*.

DONN H. O'BRIEN is Vice-President, program practices, CBS/Broadcast Group. He joined CBS in 1957 and served in various TV production, news, financial, and administrative capacities before joining the CBS Television network in 1976. He is responsible for the overall acceptability of all programs and commercials that appear on the CBS Television network.

Margaret Osmer is Director of Programs for the Council on Foreign Relations. She was previously an ABC News Network correspondent based in Washington, and a co-anchor person of the morning news on *Good Morning America*. She was co-producer and reporter for an award-winning documentary on divorce, and for a two-part series on wife beating. Before joining ABC in 1973, she was associated for 12 years with CBS, where she produced "A Cry for Help," a special on child abuse for *60 Minutes*.

Julius B. Richmond is Assistant Secretary for Health, in the Department of Health, Education and Welfare, and Surgeon General, United States Public Health Service. Before joining HEW, he served as chairman of the department of preventive and social medicine at Harvard Medical School, psychiatrist-in-chief at Children's Hospital Medical Center, and Director of the Judge Baker Guidance Center in Boston. He had previously been Dean of the medical faculty and Professor of pediatrics at SUNY at Syracuse. He was the first Director of both the national Head Start Program and the Office of Health Affairs in the Office of Economic Opportunity.

Alfred R. Schneider is Vice-President of American Broadcasting Companies, Inc. He has administrative responsibility for the broadcast standards and practices department and for ABC Media Concepts, the nontheatrical educational licensing department of ABC. He is also a senior member of the National Association of Broadcaster's Television Code Review Board.

Nancy Signorielli is research coordinator at the Annenberg School of Communications, University of Pennsylvania, where she is investigating the portrayal of characters such as the elderly and women in network television drama. She has also conducted research for the Civil Rights Commission, the Corporation for Public Broadcasting, and the Foundation for Child Development.

Albert J. Solnit is Sterling Professor of pediatrics and psychiatry at Yale and Director of the Yale University Child Study Center. A co-author, with Joseph Goldstein and Anna Freud, of *Beyond the Best Interests of the Child* (1973), and *Before the Best Interests of the Child* (1979), he is past President of the American Academy of Child Psychiatry, the American Psychoanalytic Association, the Association of Child Psychoanalysis, and the International Association for Child Psychiatry and Allied Professions.

Herminio Traviesas is Vice-President, broadcast standards policy, for the National Broadcasting Company, Inc. He is a past president of the Hollywood Radio and Television Society and a member of the National Academy of Television Arts and Sciences.

Rena K. Uviller is a Civil Court Judge in New York City. She previously served as Director of the Juvenile Rights Project of the American Civil Liberties Union. She is on the board of directors of the New York City Criminal

Justice Agency and a member of the New York State Governor's Task Force on violent juvenile offenders.

Tom Wilkinson is the metro editor of *The Washington Post*. He is a recipient of the Stanford University Journalism Fellowship and the American Political Science Association award for excellence in political reporting.

Name Index

Subject Index

abandonment, 258
abused child
  attitude of the state and, 70, 74–75,
    77–78
  characteristics of, 16–18, 43–45, 102–3,
    141, 168, 175–76, 262–63, 302
  education about abuse of, 300, 301
  identification of, 145
  infant-mother attachment and, 39–41
ACTION, 299, 304
adolescence
  child abuse and, 284
  teenage mothers, 281
  parenting education and, 284–85, 299–
    300
Administration for Children, Youth and
    Families, 255, 302, 303. *See also*
    Office of Child Development
adoption, 123, 146
Advertising Council, 238
age
  abused children and, 18, 90, 95, 169, 175
  of abusive parents, 94–95, 169–70, 173
  of victims of violence on TV, 241–44,
    247
aggression, 13, 48, 108, 138. *See also*
    violence
  classes of antecedent instigations of,
    49–59
  corporal punishment and, 205–6, 296
  disinhibition theory of, 18
  Kohlberg scale, 59

aggressive motivation, 57–59
alcoholism
  child abuse and, 19, 170, 173, 174
American Association on Mental De-
    ficiency, 187
American Bar Association, 7
American Broadcasting Company, 232,
    233, 234, 252, 255
American Civil Liberties Union, 30, 211
American Humane Association, 11, 85,
    283
American Orthopsychiatric Association,
    211
American Psychological Association, 214
anger, 54, 55–56
  in infant-mother attachment, 39–41
Annenberg School of Communications,
    154
attachment
  abusing mothers and, 42
  "anxious-avoidant/resistant," 38–41, 45
  ethological-evolutionary theory of, 35–
    37, 41
  infant-mother, 37–44
    in strange situation, 38, 45
    spiral effects, 44
  as "risk" indicator, 44–45
attorney(s)
  child placement decision and, 176
authoritarianism
  child abuse and, 97, 102
autism, 141–142